JOY
STARTS HERE

the transformation zone

E. James Wilder
Edward M. Khouri
Chris M. Coursey
Shelia D. Sutton

Revised 2021

www.joystartshere.com

Also published in Korean and Dutch

Joy Starts Here: the transformation zone

By: E. James Wilder Ph.D.
    Edward M. Khouri Jr.
    Chris M. Coursey
    Shelia D. Sutton M.A.

Copyright 2013, 2014, 2021

ISBN 9798735702931

Published by:
        Joy Starts Here
        P.O. Box 1711
        Holland, MI 49422

        www.joystartshere.com

Printed 2021 by Life Model Works under special license

Scripture quotations from:

THE HOLY BIBLE, NEW INTERNATIONAL VERSION®, NIV® Copyright © 1973, 1978, 1984, 2011 by Biblica, Inc.™ Used by permission. All rights reserved worldwide.

Scripture taken from The Expanded Bible. Copyright © 2011 by Thomas Nelson, Inc. Used by permission. All rights reserved.

Scripture taken from the New King James Version®. Copyright © 1982 by Thomas Nelson, Inc. Used by permission. All rights reserved.

Cover design by The Brandvertisers, Inc.

Back cover photo by Christopher Kamman.

Dedicated to

Jane Lakes Willard

Gentle Protector

The multigenerational flow of life of all four authors has been shaped and deepened by Jane and Dallas, her beloved late husband.

May joy continually return to all who start joy.

For Group Study

- You will receive the greatest benefit from this book if you use all the nine weekly Bible studies, exercises, joy actions and assessments in a small group.
    * The small group can be one that is already established or it can be as simple as inviting a few friends out for coffee.
    * In an adult education setting, break into small groups during each session.
- During each session point the group to the next week's exercises and assessment. Ask them to do that first, and then if they have time to read the text.
- Don't allow your group to spend a lot of time debating the text. The benefit comes from learning the right-brain skills in the exercises not from using your left-brain to debate the text.
- Encourage your group to "sneak" many of these exercises into various family, school, church and work interactions.

The secret of joy is falling in love with the Lover of your soul and being able to connect and communicate with those of your own family, friends, church, and community is a glorious reality! This book will enable you to experience joy in a very practical and helpful way, with study guides and notes that provide an incredible model for you to experience this process. The credible contribution of gifted authors and teachers make this an ideal volume for personal, small group, and community study. *Joy Starts Here* will be an invaluable aid.

I heartily commend this book to all who wish to experience this marvelous gift of the Spirit. His ability alone develops and brings forth fruit. With my 90 years of life and many amazing opportunities of sharing the love and joy of Christ, I have found that He alone is the source of unspeakable joy for the journey. May this be your portion as well as you share the secret of His true joy and peace.

> Cliff Barrows
> Billy Graham Evangelistic Association, billygraham.org

So many approaches to recovery, healing, and therapy - Christian and otherwise - focus on what's wrong or sick and needs to be fixed. Too seldom do they focus on the goal of health toward which recovery aims. That's one of many strengths that stand out in *Joy Starts Here* - the authors constantly keep before us the vision of thriving, joy, and shalom for which we all hunger and thirst in our deepest soul. I learned a lot from this helpful, practical, positive resource.

> Brian D. McLaren
> Author/speaker/activist, brianmclaren.net

Joy Starts Here is a wonderful addition to the growing body of literature on this vital topic. The authors are skilled messengers of joy, who are competent healers and tacticians. Enter the starting gate, and pursue joy with this valuable tool at your side. You will not be disappointed.

> Father John Catoir
> President St. Jude Media, Former Director of the Christophers
> messengerofjoy.com

I highly recommend *Joy Starts Here* to every person and group of persons who desire to discover, live and share Godly designed and intended joy – joy in the Lord, joy in ourselves and joy in each other. I am a member of Madonna House Apostolate, an international, multigenerational adult community of Roman Catholic women and men, lay and ordained priests. Each of us has made a lifetime commitment to form together a family of love in Jesus Christ and to live and share the Gospel without compromise across the world. I was first introduced to the Life Model in 1995 and have been benefiting in personal healing and strengthening ever since.

> Patrick Stewart
> Director of Training at Madonna House, madonnahouse.org

Get this book, read it to your family, do the exercises and watch as God does something wonderful in your life. My husband and I cannot thank you enough for all the truths--both logical and experiential--that we have learned from the Life Model. Joy does indeed start here! I used to think that fixing all of us would make my family safe, but I am learning to surrender my predatory ways, own my weaknesses, and live in transparency and authenticity. Connecting to God has brought healing to my own life, restored my sense of who I am as God's beloved daughter, and powerfully affected my ministry. In the last five months we have taken more than 100 people through the *Thriving Community* series (including a group at our local jail) and stand in awe as we see people recover, heal and mature. Thank you Shepherd's House!

Betsy Stalcup Ph.D.
Executive Director of Healing Center International
Church of the Apostles Anglican
healingcenterinternational.sharepoint.com

This book offers a shortcut to transformation by showing us ways to cooperate with how the brain is wired to run best on joy. Emotional maturity is at our doorstep through skills practiced in everyday life.

Jan Johnson D.Min.
Speaker and author of 20 books including *Renovation of the Heart in Daily Practice: Experiments in Spiritual Transformation* with Dallas Willard.
JanJohnson.org

What a powerful reality unfolds in these chapters for Spiritual Formation to Christlikeness! One can only hope every pastor in America gets this book in their hands and applies it forthright.

George Ackron
Director for Renovator Ministries
renovatorministries.org

Another great Life Model™ book that not only challenges me personally to grow more joy, but also lays a foundation for whole communities to be transformed by joy as the strong learn to care for the weak through interactions with "the God who is always with us." Every leader, everywhere will benefit from this book, but especially pastors and leaders in the church that want to be making disciples.

Kenneth D. Smith
Ministry and Discipleship Coach, CityNet Ministries.

Dr. Wilder and colleagues have created a densely packed, multi-disciplinary wealth of information built from their own experiences in counseling, teaching and addiction. Their premise that joy is primarily experienced through relationships and essential to healthy life is backed by scientific research. This book sheds light on how and why joy is lost, the variety of things we try and substitute for it, and how best to get joy back. This is a valuable resource.

> David I. Levy MD
> Neurosurgeon and author of *Gray Matter*
> drdlevy.com

Rarely do writers create such a practical, transparent look into what it means to build and live in a joyful environment. And it's for everyone - from the average Christian sitting in church to the shattered person recovering from being part of the dark world of sex trafficking. A must read for all who understand the Lord's emphasis in John 15:11 -- *"These things I have spoken to you so that My joy may be in you, and that your joy may be made full."*

> Dr. Alaine Pakkala Ph.D. - Psychoneuroimmunology
> Author, advocate and
> ldm.homestead.com, lydiapress.com

Never before have we more urgently needed to hear the message of this important work. In a world that continues its search for meaning and depth, we seem only able to expand our manufacture of mere artificial substitutes. In this volume, our guides provide thorough, concrete, and desperately needed help on the way to renewing our minds, regenerating our relationships, and embodying the kingdom of God on earth.

> Curt Thompson MD
> Psychiatrist, author of *Anatomy of the Soul*
> beingknown.com

A profound truth that we have discovered in developing the Immanuel process (also known as the Immanuel approach) is that God has designed our brains to work best in community. The authors of *Joy Starts Here* expand on this truth in their teaching that the Immanuel process spreads best when the weak and the strong are growing together in the context of multi-generational community, and in their teaching that character transformation requires joyful interactions with both God and other people. This book is full of nuggets, and a strategic resource for any church or individual wanting to experience character transformation and build healthy community.

> Karl Lehman, MD
> Psychiatrist, international speaker, author of *Outsmarting Yourself*, over 30 training DVDs and the term *Immanuel approach*
> kclehman.com, www.immanuelapproach.com

Joy Starts Here is a book of immense value. I appreciate the wisdom with which it speaks to the huge problem of the immaturity that undermines and destroys the effectiveness of our leaders and those they lead, both inside and outside the church. Whether or not you are familiar with the Life Model, you will benefit greatly from this excellent collection of the insights God has given the authors into fresh and important truths that are vital to cultivating personal and corporate maturity.

Dan Rumberger, Psy.D.
Psychologist and Deeper Walk International Board of Directors

Joy Starts Here is a potentially revolutionary book for those who will invest the time to absorb its message and apply its teaching. I know of few resources in the Christian community with the potential to change lives as this book.

Marcus Warner Ph.D.
President Deeper Walk International, speaker and author
deeperwalkinternational.com

Joy Starts Here finds the common ground between diverse disciplines - medicine, theology, psychology, among many others - and explains the human heart in a clear, simple, non-technical way, so that God's people can learn about themselves, others, and even God Himself. *Joy Starts Here* gives us a way to propagate God's own joy and transform homes, churches, communities, and even cultures. Let Joy start with you and spread like Pentecost. To God be the glory!

Mr. Kim Campbell, PA-C, M. Div.
Former medical director for The Voice of the Martyrs, USA

"Joy is the daughter of calm." This simple yet profound quote from the Christian classic, *God Calling* by A J Russell captures much of the essence of this book. My friend Ed Khouri and his colleagues will help you deeply explore the connections between God's sustaining joy and His shalom. May you be blessed as you embark on this journey.

Christopher McCluskey, PCC, CMCC, BCC
Best-selling author and president of the Professional Christian Coaching Institute
professionalchristiancoaching.com

Please note - you have no idea what this book is talking about, you think you do, but you don't.

Sharon J. MacKinnon

This is recovery at its very best. Anyone can grow mentally, physically and spiritually from reading this text.

> Robert R. Perkinson Ph.D.
> Clinical director of Keystone Treatment Center, author of the best-selling book in the world on chemical dependency counseling.
> robertperkinson.com

Being an addiction counselor and author for over 35 years I have found that finding joy is one of the most important and difficult tasks in the process of restoration. The authors of Joy Starts Here have blended biblical principles with the latest research on the brain to provide both understanding and a practical guide.

> Michael Dye CADC , NCAC II
> Founder of the Genesis Process and Programs
> genesisprocess.org

Joy Starts Here is a deeply significant book for individuals, churches and communities around the world. The three building blocks of multigenerational community, Immanuel Lifestyle – awareness of God's interactive presence with us, and practicing relational brain skills are a challenge to the ways that we lead our lives, organize our communities and act as church. I read the book while traveling through some low-joy communities in the Balkans. The truth, challenging perspectives and applicable tools contained within the book helped me to make sense of some of the things that I saw, and influenced the way that I interacted with the people that I met on that trip. *Joy Starts Here* is an authentic antidote to the shallow "positive thinking" ideology that has so strongly influenced society and the church.

> Treflyn Lloyd-Roberts
> General Secretary of ISAAC (International Substance Abuse and
> Addiction Coalition). ISAAC serves in approximately 70 nations.

Discovering JOY is like remembering the essence of a wonderful dream lost with the demands of the day. God IS glad to be with us. Indeed, our JOY starts here!

> Dr. Jean LaCour President ISAAC
> President, NET Training Institute, international trainer/speaker
> netinstitute.org

This book is a must read for all who seek to be transformed people who will transform people (Fr. Richard Rohr). The lack of joy in many Christ-followers has a reason. This book not only explains well why that is but also offers real remedies for change.

> Valerie E. Hess M.M.
> Speaker, musician and author of books such as *The Life of the Body: Physical Well-Being and Spiritual Formation* with Lane M. Arnold.

God is my strength and portion, God my exceeding joy.
These words by Sir Robert Anderson enforce the message of *Joy Starts Here*. The stories move the reader; the exercises provoke the reader, call the reader to action. Parents need to bring joy into the household; teachers need to bring joy into the classroom; employers need to bring joy into the workplace. However, we all need to find our resting place, our "exceeding joy," in God, in Jesus Christ.

        Jane Hancock
        Co-director, UCLA Writing Project
        Retired Teacher with over 40 years experience
        centerx.gseis.ucla.edu/writing-project

As a classroom educator and principal for over thirty years, I am convinced *Joy Starts Here* is crucial for teachers and principals. Students spend 14,000 plus hours in classrooms from kindergarten through twelfth grade. These growing up years should be times of joy and transformation, rather than dread and mere passing of time as it has been for so many. Wilder and co-authors give clarity to this fundamental building block in relationships through descriptions and explanations with which every reader can identify. The all-important questions are answered, "How does one establish well being?" and "How does one maintain joy in varied circumstances?" The writers speak for themselves as they share examples from their lives in a fashion that is intimate but brief. In a time when neuroscience speaks of the importance of mindfulness, every person would benefit from the knowledge of human behavior as presented from a theological, philosophical, and psychological perspective.

        Maryellen St. Cyr
        Founder of Ambleside Schools International and author
        amblesideschools.com

A book like this (and possibly other books in your series) should be required reading in college for students studying psychology and sociology, especially teacher training. These books would certainly open eyes to the parts of real life that people are embarrassed to share. Who knows? Maybe, students will see themselves and serve others better.

        Myrna Perry
        Retired teacher

A real breath of fresh air-- deliciously full of rare insights and reasons to hope.

        Karen Struble, Ph.D, Clinical psychology
        Child development, college instructor, author, parent educator

Contents

Part Two — Joyful Immanuel Lifestyle　　121

Author Biographies
E. James Wilder Ph.D.

Dr. Jim Wilder is a coauthor and leading developer of the *Life Model*. Since 1988, he has given over 100 conferences and professional presentations in nine countries. His teachings on trauma and addiction recovery are highly regarded by seasoned professionals. Dr. Wilder has helped write ten books (translated into nine different languages), sixteen teaching sets and numerous articles. He developed *The THRIVE Training* program with Chris and Jen Coursey and the *Connexus* program with Ed Khouri. He has been a professor and visiting guest speaker at numerous universities. He has served as a consultant or board member for various missions and been active in training and service in North America, South America, Asia, Africa, Europe and India.

Dr. Wilder received an M.A. in Theology from Fuller Theological Seminary in 1981, and in 1982, his Ph.D. in Clinical Psychology from the Fuller Graduate School of Psychology. Wilder was ordained in the Church of the Brethren in 1984 and became an elder in the Church of the Nazarene in 1994. He is currently developing the highly specified field of study known as *Neurotheology*.

His training includes such areas as family, child, adolescent, sexual, vocational, bilingual, behavioral and neuropsychological assessment and treatment, along with experience in groups; inpatient, outpatient, Vietnam veterans, biofeedback and alcoholism units. Wilder worked in Christian counseling centers providing pastoral care from 1977 until 2011 and has served as director, assistant director, clinical director and director of training.

lifemodelworks.org

Author Biographies
Edward M. Khouri Jr.

Ed Khouri is a pastoral counselor who has been working with hurting people since 1980. He has a B.A. from the University of Maryland, and was ordained in 1988. He is the co-founder and director of *Equipping Hearts for the Harvest*, a non-profit ministry that seeks to empower leaders, churches, ministries, missionaries, and workers to skillfully serve individuals and communities locally and globally.

Ed has worked extensively as a counselor, trainer and writer. He has worked with substance abusers and their families in diverse settings, including churches, jails, transitional housing for homeless addicts, and in all phases of residential treatment. He also provided daily supervision for all therapeutic services and staff in a 96-bed state licensed substance abuse treatment program. As a trainer, he leads workshops in churches and ministries to help equip workers to serve hurting men and women in their community. He has helped develop curriculum used in Christ-centered and state-licensed treatment programs. Ed was the lead author of *I Was in Prison and You Visited Me*, which is a manual for ministry in residential programs, prisons and jails.

Ed and Dr. Jim Wilder are the co-creators of the *Connexus* program. Of the program's books, Ed has authored *Restarting* and co-authored *Belonging*. Ed has served extensively as an instructor at a variety of international training schools, and specializes in teaching students new, effective and innovative approaches to addiction and trauma recovery.

Ed and his wife, Maritza, are members of the Secretariat of the International Substance Abuse and Addiction Coalition, which has members in over 70 nations. They frequently teach addiction and trauma recovery with *Youth With A Mission's* Addictive Behavior Counseling Schools around the world. In addition to teaching in the US, Ed has taught in Europe, Asia, S. America and Africa. He has worked with students from over 60 nations.

www.equippinghearts.com Equipping Hearts for the Harvest

Author Biographies
Chris M. Coursey

Chris Coursey has spent most of his ministry career applying and developing strategies for *Life Model* training. Chris is a pastoral counselor, leadership consultant, published author, and conference speaker. He speaks nationally and internationally, frequently visiting schools, ministries and churches throughout the United States and Canada in particular on growing and propagating relational joy.

He has been a guest speaker at YWAM schools in Kona, Vancouver, New Jersey, South Korea, Switzerland, Canada and more. He has also been an interview guest on several Christian radio shows in the US, speaking about the role that *Gentle Protector Skills* have for couples, leaders and pastors. Chris is the author of *The Joy Switch* and the coauthor of *The 4 Habits of Joy-Filled Marriages* as well as *The 4 Habits of Raising Joy-Filled Kids* with Dr. Marcus Warner.

Along with Dr. Jim Wilder, Chris co-authored *Share Immanuel and The Healing Lifestyle*. Dr. Wilder and Coursey also developed *THRIVE Training*, which are three interactive training tracks strategically designed for leaders to learn and spread the nineteen gentle protector skills. Along with his wife Jen, Chris now actively leads *THRIVE Training* events along with weekend retreats, and seminars designed to equip leaders and pastors in the *Nineteen Gentle Protector Skills* with the *Share Immanuel Lifestyle*.

Chris earned his Associates Degree from Illinois Central College in 1995. In 1998, he transferred to Eastern Illinois State University to earn his B.A. in Sociology, with a minor in Psychology. Chris earned his M.T. from M.B.I. Yeshiva in Hampton, Virginia in 2007. Chris is an ordained minister with Experience Ministries.

Chris and his wife Jen run the THRIVEtoday organization which focuses on training the Nineteen Gentle Protector Skills.

thrivetoday.org

Author Biographies

Shelia D. Sutton M.A. and M.A.

Shelia Sutton is a Licensed Marriage, Family Therapist, National Board Certified Teacher, UCLA Writing Project Fellow, and an adjunct professor. Shelia's three decades plus years of teaching and consulting interests focus on the relational aspect of education and form the basis of her work preparing teachers for National Board Certification.

Shelia has conducted a wide range of professional development workshops throughout the Los Angeles area since 1996. Her workshops include topics such as, *Thinking Maps, Writers Workshop, Socratic Seminars, Literature Circles,* and *Thriving in the Classroom*. Shelia also serves as an adjunct professor at National University and instructs teachers throughout the United States. At the heart of Shelia's work is her dedication to inspire teachers to create classrooms and instructional practices that promote and foster overall student wellbeing, learning, and success.

Shelia earned her bachelor's degree in English Education from the University of Texas at Austin. Additionally, Shelia holds two master's degrees, one in English with an emphasis in Rhetoric, Composition and Language from California State University at Los Angeles and one in Counseling Psychology from Pacifica Graduate Institute. Shelia also studied *Spiritual Direction* at Pecos Benedictine Monastery in Pecos, New Mexico; *Spiritual Formation* at the Stillpoint Center for Spiritual Direction; "The Converging Religions of the Area" at Tantur University in Jerusalem; and *Thriving* and *The Life Model* at Shepherd's House, Inc. Dr. Jim Wilder has mentored Shelia since 2003.

Shelia's interests include propagating joy through mutual bonding and attachment; brain functioning and its impact on relationship to self and others; maturity and individuation; trauma resolution through Immanuel prayer practices; empathic attunement as an artistic life skill; and writing and story-telling as paths to deeper healing and connection to others. Shelia is licensed as a Marriage Family Therapist in the state of California where she is certified in EMDR and is also a Certified Daring Way Facilitator in the work of Brené Brown..

www.sheliasutton.com R.A.R.E. Living

Appreciation Memories

As joy theorists, we have come to understand the importance of appreciation. We have found a wonderful stream of appreciation experiences flowing into our lives while writing this book together. With heartfelt thanks, we would like to express our gratitude to the people who have made extraordinary contributions of their time, energy and resources.

Suzan Boyd graciously allowed us to spend a week editing in her beautiful, peaceful Montana cabin. Suzan and Maritza Khouri prepared delicious meals. We grew joy bonds eating and singing together around the table. Thank you!

Jen Coursey unselfishly stayed home with Mathew and Andrew so that Chris could travel to Montana and participate fully in our editing trip. We greatly appreciate her dedication to Chris and to this project. Chris greatly enjoyed being able to ride a snowmobile without a spouse on board!

Maritza Khouri supported Ed throughout the project, and helped him overcome significant physical challenges so that they could travel to Montana for editing. Her gentle protector skills and playful sense of humor were a blessing to us all. She also makes amazing snowmen!

Kitty Wilder hosted the writing team for a second round of editing. Her kind, gracious hospitality and delicious smoothies helped create a joyful environment that made the editing much easier. Kitty also served as a proofreader.

Beverly Jordan led a *Joy Starts Here* group to test the beta versions of this book. Bev provided ongoing, timely feedback that helped us make the book better.

Dr. Wanda Morgan provided detailed proofing of the original beta text and shared valuable feedback for the final version of the book. She also worked diligently to corral unruly commas.

Deni Huttula moderated the *Joy Starts Here* forum, and helped launch our online community. Her help was also invaluable when Ed's back surgery prevented his sitting at the computer. Deni typed while Ed dictated portions of the original manuscript.

We really desired our community to help us write this book. *Joy Starts Here* forum members shared their questions, comments and feedback. They helped launch the community, and their input helped us create a much better book. We enjoy working with those whose passion for joy matches ours.

Reviewers who endorsed the book often provided valuable feedback about the flow and content of the original beta version. Thanks to all of you!

Finally, we are extraordinarily grateful for each other. This is a project that was conceived, born and nurtured in the joy we share together.

Preface

Joy is a banquet table to which we are all invited. The places are set, and the table is filled with the delightful aroma that satisfies our deepest longing for life-giving connections with God and with others. There is room at this table for followers of Jesus and those who are not. Churched and unchurched, inside and on the margins, weak and strong, we all are invited to discover joy. We all desire a life of joy.

We hope that many of you will share the joy of this table by forming your own *Joy Starts Here* groups. The only way these groups will succeed is if all of us make a commitment to respond tenderly to the weaknesses we discover in ourselves and in others. Our conversations in *Joy Starts Here* groups around this table should always reflect this tenderness. It is impossible for anyone to share the delicacies of the table if we insist upon criticizing each other, stealing from each other's plates, driving those with weaknesses away, excluding others or even pouncing on each other to find a snack. Tender responses to weakness make the banquet open and enjoyable to all. Those who prefer pouncing on others instead of enjoying the feast exclude themselves from the table.

This book includes many stories of those who shared the table along our journey. Their stories serve as valuable illustrations that help make essential components of *Joy Starts Here* clear. We have changed their names to protect their privacy and make the table safe.

Finally, we have been blessed to have *Joy Starts Here* reviewed and endorsed by a diverse group of honored guests from different backgrounds and perspectives. It is entirely likely that they will not see eye-to-eye about every issue of life and would enjoy quite lively and interesting discussions about those differences if all were sitting together in the same part of the banquet table. We respect their differences, honor their journeys as Christ-followers and recognize that they don't necessarily agree with each other or with us about all issues related to theology. We all agree that the joyful table spread before us is important.

a Simple Way
to Start
JOY

There are things in life that are simple joy starters, a joy that can be passed on from generation to generation and shared by young and old alike.

We believe that something simple can go a long way in starting joy in a community. We believe in the simple joy of flying a kite!

A kite goes beyond cultural barriers, beyond religion, socio-economic status, and gender. Kite flying is teachable, communal, and inter-generational. A kite can capture the imagination of even the most low-joy community. Kites require some effort, but when they finally take flight, joy is inevitable... and people around you will notice!

Flying a kite provides a sense of freedom, a sense of being one with God. The upward draft that sends your kite soaring as you hold on to the line is sure to bring a smile, every time.

You can be a part of this joy movement by simply flying a kite of your own. Experience the joys of flying a kite with those around you. Share the experience with your immediate community members. Teach the younger generation how to fly one. Go to a low-joy community and distribute kites as you watch smiles grow bigger and bigger.

And take pictures! Lots and lots of pictures! Share the joys of the kite flying experience through our social networks. Text it to your friends. Make it your profile picture. Share your story. Share the joy…Simple joy.

So, go fly a kite. We mean it!

Introduction
Joyful Transformation

Do not be afraid, for behold,
I bring you good tidings of great joy
which will be to all people.
Luke 2:10b NKJV

We all want to be part of real change and not simply take a shopping trip to fit ourselves with rose-colored glasses. We cannot make this a "feel good book" by ignoring the severe damage caused by low joy, a damage that spreads from one generation to the next. Yet, we can live fearlessly. We will find that transforming joy requires sharing life tenderly in both our weak and strong moments. Like the "canary in the mine" that signals the presence of poisonous gas, we will find joyful daughters are the best indication that our environment has breathable levels of joy. High joy is the best answer to "global warring." Sustainable joy helps us reduce our toxic predator "footprint" and leave a trail of life instead.

You may be surprised that it takes four chapters to introduce joy-starting. We take an honest look at the realistic demands of a working solution. In our introduction you will discover the joy movement in chapter one, joy in chapter two, the problem with joy substitutes in chapter three and the how to transform low joy places in chapter four.

The Life Model for sustainable joy is based on three things that are not usually found together: multigenerational community, an Immanuel lifestyle and relational brain skills. Take any of these three away and joy levels start to fall quickly. Joy is transforming, but only when it is real joy and when it is combined with the necessary factors for enduring change.

Joy starts here.

Chapter One

Invitation to Joy

Hello! We are so glad you are here! We'd like to briefly introduce ourselves and invite you to join us in a movement to become joy starters. What you hold in your hands is a book, but what we are inviting you to is much bigger and grander than participating in the exercise of reading words on a page. We want you to join us in spreading joy because we wholeheartedly believe now is the time for Christians everywhere to become joy starters!

We can start joy today wherever we are. When one of us starts joy we brighten one low-joy spot in the world. How often do we notice that low-joy places breed problems? If we all started joy today we would produce some healthy global warming. In fact, one group exists for the purpose of bringing joy to the world, and one in three people on earth claim to be a member. This book is a call to Christians everywhere to become joy starters. Wouldn't we all like it if Christians everywhere were known for their joy? Jesus was joy to the world.

Jesus gave joy as the reason for His teaching. "I have told you these things so that you can have the same joy I have and so that your joy will be the fullest possible joy" John 15:11 (EXB).

We acknowledge, and it has been our individual and collective experience, that finding joyful Christians in our midst is not nearly as common as we would like it to be! This may be an experience you share with us. In fact, we suspect it is. We are on a "Christian Titanic," and the relational skills necessary to build and sustain joy are sinking fast into an ocean of darkness. If you are feeling the icy, low-joy waters you will understand why we have included an urgent, blunt description of the iceberg in a book about joy. We realize it may feel like we are yelling in your ear, but some people are still rearranging deck chairs! It's important that we understand why we are sinking (the problem) and why we need to join together around the world to intentionally propagate JOY (the solution).

Joy is relational. Joy is contagious. Joy is transforming. Joy starts with a smile. Joy helps our brain grow better than any health food. Joy reduces stress. Joy has more social impact than looking sexy. Joy improves our immune system more than exercise. Joy protects marriages. Joy raises brighter, more resilient children. Joy improves resiliency after disasters. Joy spreads to transform lives.

Jim, Ed, Chris and Shelia are a multigenerational group of authors whose ages span four decades. Jim is a neuroscientist who mentors us in the field of neurotheology. All four of us are counselors and teachers. Three of us are ordained pastors. We share a love of Jesus and a common interest in neuroscience, theology, recovery, education and transforming church life.

In these pages, we use our stories to illustrate strengths and weaknesses. We've opted to highlight parts of our respective life stories from home, school and church that appropriately illustrate the theory. Our stories are not all-inclusive accounts of our personal experiences but are rather purposefully selected to describe both the pervasive problem of low-joy as well as the solution of growing high-joy in these three distinctive environments.

We've selected home, church and school because these are commonly shared experiences. More importantly, joy is best propagated to the next generation in these settings. The need for joy at work is quickly obvious, and the principles in this book are easily applicable. In order to focus on the places where joy must be started and spread to the next generation, we will limit the discussion in this book to the largest workplace in America — the education system.

For over a decade, advancements in neurotheology have attracted a wave of joy-starters drawn to the transforming power of joy. Both the Bible and neuroscience understand joy as a relational experience in which "someone is glad to be with me." In our lives, this begins at home. If we grow up in low-joy families then school and church provide us with other opportunities. This book will help you become a part of the joy-starting movement.

Because joy is a relational experience, we intend for you to study *Joy Starts Here* as a part of a group. A community context where the weak and the strong can come together is surprisingly important for spreading joy. While we can gather all the concepts by reading in solitude, we cannot practice the essential processes necessary to become joy starters. Reading a book about joy when we are alone tends to lower our joy level.

Many popular books about change promote a single "magic bullet" that will change your life. This is not that book! With something as important as our joy, none of us want to leave out important factors. Flying in an airplane full of holes takes us to the same place as building an identity with holes in our joy. If we want to soar, it is worth thinking a little harder about the factors that sustain our lives.

Sustainable transformation requires thinking about several factors at once. For instance, for joy to transform our lives and our communities, the following three conditions must be in place.

1. The weak and strong are together and interacting.
2. Tender responses to weakness are the rule.
3. The interactive presence of God (Immanuel) maintains shalom.

Perhaps a story will help us see these complex issues as one simple picture. Jim's story illustrates how the face-to-face interactions that create a sense of "being glad to be together" can restore joy to communities where joy has been lost.

Jim's Story

I come from a family tracing back to Adam and Eve. The apple did not fall far from the tree. I am an anachronism, a throwback to a former time. My father was born before World War I. Dad's city was powered by horses. His family had no phone or television, radio was limited, and he chose the theaters with the best piano player because movies did not have sound. My father witnessed the arrival of electric power and he lived in a neighborhood. When he bought an ice cream cone at the store he offered every neighbor a lick on the way home. Everyone sat on the front porch and talked to those who walked down the street as neighbors do.

Because I was born and lived in a high valley in the Andes mountains, I also remember the arrival of electricity. I was sixteen before our first phone was installed and I remember seeing a television for the first time. We walked or rode horses for much of our travels. Carts drawn by people or horse-drawn carriages passed the house all day. Children played together and all the neighbors knew each other. Even without phones, my parents heard about any trouble I got into before I arrived home. It is hard to think of any waking minute from my childhood where I was not in the presence of people actively interacting. Usually there were two or three generations together.

Ten years ago my mother died of dementia and my father moved in with us. He was 90 at the time and almost deaf and blind. We live in the Los Angeles area where people pull into their garages and go directly into their houses. Most people on our street have never spoken to their neighbors.

My father had not been here three months before he knew people for blocks around. A walk around the neighborhood with my father produced stories about nearly every house we passed. One lady was having problems with her family in Iran. Another man planned to do his own roofing. He chatted with Muslims, the drummer with dreadlocks, the Catholic restaurant owner, the Colombian whose avocado tree would not grow, three people with hip replacements, the biker, the African-American army vet, the old bar tender, several Armenian families, dog owners, the gay couple, the parole officer, the home schoolers, the Protestant seminary professor and their children and grandchildren. About one in five cars driving down the street slowed or stopped to greet him. Almost 100% of the drivers waved. He greeted them all with a smile and shared a moment. Many of them came to his 99th birthday party and met each other for the first time. He still thinks that neighborhood exists and, while he is alive, Dad has the skills to make neighborhood happen even in Southern California.

We live in an age where technological advances such as electricity, TV, the internet and smart phones make communication instantaneous and our lives much easier. At the same time, we are rapidly losing our ability to sustain meaningful, face-to-face interactions that grow authentic joy. We are embarking on a journey of discovery, reclaiming relational joy as the fabric that knits together our lives, families, churches and schools.

Chapter Two

Finding My Joyful Identity

What is a joyful identity?
Joy means someone is glad to be with me. The signature of real joy is the sparkle in someone's eyes when they see us that makes their face light up. Joy is children jumping up and down when their dad or mom comes home from work or when they see their grandmother. Joy is a woman running to her husband returning from war. Joy is children playing, tumbling and giggling together. Joy is the smile we cannot help but share. Joy is so special that God offers joy as His reward rather than candy, jewelry, good looks, popularity, whiter smiles or faster internet access. There is a good reason why God promises joy more often than He promises eternal life! Jesus lists joy as the reason for His teaching in John 17:13, "I am coming to you now, but I say these things while I am still in the world, so that they may have the full measure of my joy within them" (NIV).

Jesus also says joy is the reward for a godly life in Luke 6:23a, "Rejoice in that day and leap for joy, because great is your reward in heaven" (NIV).

A quick look at how our brain develops gives us a hint of why God rewards us with joy. Joyful interactions with our mothers, fathers, those who feed us and other primary caregivers shape the structure, chemistry and function of the brain. The foundation of joy that is built in our first year of life profoundly influences our identity and relationships throughout our lifespan. Without joy as a foundation, many of the God-given capacities we receive at birth will not develop, not become strong and will not be retained. The capacities and chemistry that we use as infants become the dominant systems for our brains. If we start our life in fear we will feel anxious about almost everything. But the brain is biased toward joy. Joy is our most powerful desire, and we are designed to seek joyful interactions automatically from birth. If we cannot find joy we may try hard to bury our desire, but we can never escape joy's power. God built us this way.

Joy makes us grow strong, loving relationships with other people. We love as a response to joy. Joy stimulates the growth of the identity region of our brains. We grow the strongest and most stable identity from those who show us joy.

Joy is a high-energy state for the brain. The practice of joy builds brain strength and the capacity to engage life with energy, creativity and endurance. In fact, the capacity for the brain to engage every intense or difficult aspect of life develops out of joy. High-joy people are very resilient. High-joy communities are energetic and productive even in hard times. When we are empowered by joy, we are able to suffer, withstand pain and still maintain intact relationships. Without joy, we view problems as "win or lose" situations, view others as enemies, and solve problems with the option that causes us the least pain, usually at the expense of others. With joy, we are empowered to find creative, mutually satisfying solutions for problems and love to create simply because we can. Dancing, gardening, feasting, celebrating, playing and other endless good things bubble up from joy.

Joy is the excitement around the exchange of everything that is good for life. A short description of the biology of joy will find that infants respond with joy to being fed, held and stroked. Pleasant smells, being kept at just the right temperature, smiles and warm voice tone bring joy. Babies respond with joy to being fed good things. This joy at being fed is designed to bond the baby and the feeder together. We will see later that when anything goes amiss we will become bonded to the food instead of the feeder. Food then becomes a joy substitute, but we are getting ahead of ourselves.

Joy is essential for healing and growing strong identities. Joyful relationships have the power to transform broken lives, families, churches, ministries and ministry teams, schools, neighborhoods and cultures. Ed has seen joy heal lives and relationships while teaching in 20 nations on five continents with leaders, workers and missionaries from 70 nations. Closer to home, he has seen joy transform relationships with his wife and family.

Ed's Story

The leader of the addiction school for missionaries in Brazil picked us up at the airport. My wife and I were in Brazil to help students and ministry teams experience the healing power of joy in their own lives. The scenery changed as we neared the base. I was definitely hoping that the car did not break down! I remembered the warnings I'd heard about this city. Just then, the school leader said, "Ed, our city is the most violent in all of Brazil and our school is located in the worst neighborhood in the entire city." He turned to look at me, smiled and said, "But where else should missionaries be?" I knew we were in exactly the right place to begin growing joy.

My life didn't begin with a lot of joy. I spent my first six months in a foster home. My birth mother and her fiancé put me up for adoption after she became pregnant by another man. I was adopted by two very loving and compassionate parents and my early memories with them were good. Mom was a great source of joy. Her smile and the sparkle in her eyes let me know that she was glad to be with me. She is one of my favorite joy connections. Dad liked to wrestle with me on the floor until the day we discovered we were both older than we thought. I jumped on him and two broken ribs ended our wrestling days. Sometimes we need to learn when to stop.

Church and school went together for me. We attended church as a family every week and I attended Catholic School. The older nuns who taught classes were pretty scary while the younger nuns were approachable, human, compassionate, understanding and many had a great sense of humor. I witnessed a serious commitment to God and making a difference in the lives of others. I saw it was possible to be strongly committed to God and actively care for others.

As an altar boy I served mass for years. I played guitar with nuns and adults in a "folk group" at Saturday night mass. In high school, I had a part-time job as an evening receptionist at the parish rectory where the priests lived. I was profoundly affected by Monsignor Lewis, who was the pastor of our parish. The receptionist's office was next to his, and he was always kind, compassionate and friendly. He was a person I could talk to when I was struggling. At church and at school, I was increasingly developing a sense of compassion and the belief that I could, and would, make a difference in the world by caring for people who were weak, struggling and marginalized.

One night while I was working at the rectory something changed my life forever. While all the priests were out, a woman called the rectory in tears. She told me that she was Catholic, planned to have an abortion the next day and desperately wanted to talk to someone. Her distressing situation touched me deeply. I kept giving her phone numbers to other parishes. Each time, after phoning the number I gave her, she would call me back in tears. One priest was unwilling to talk with her because she refused to give her name. Another would not see her unless she agreed to postpone the abortion. After the fourth call, the nun in charge of the choir arrived for music practice. I hurried to her and explained the situation and looked at her in disbelief when she told me that choir practice was more important. She refused to pick up the phone.

I trudged back up the stairs to talk to the woman nobody wanted to help. Compassion, service and joy, it seemed to me, were reserved for the strong who behaved and not for the weak. I was angry and only got angrier when I returned home and dad became angry at me for being angry. How could people who professed to care deeply about God and loving others refuse to respond tenderly to a woman in this much need?

I began to rebel against people who claimed to care but could not take the time. I rebelled against messages of contempt, humiliation and shame that seemed to accompany failure in families, churches and culture. I became very difficult to live with. My rebellion found an outlet by protesting with some pretty radical groups. I also dove headfirst into the use of alcohol, other drugs and other types of addictions.

I now call addictions BEEPS. BEEPS is an acronym for Behaviors, Events, Experiences, People or Substances that take the place of joyful, life-giving connections with God and with others. BEEPS trigger the release of dopamine and stimulate the pleasure center of the brain much like joyful interactions with other people. BEEPS are joy substitutes to our brains. The way I was living at that time, I was not bringing joy to many people, nor were many people particularly glad to be with me.

An encounter with Jesus and His joy radically changed my life as we will see in chapter seven. I finally found a reason to quit drinking and drugging. Up until then, quitting was something I knew I "should" do, but I really could not find a good reason. Those joyful connections with God and others began to provide what I really needed, and those relationships began to displace the BEEPS in my life. Joy began to awaken my compassion and desire to serve other people. Within a few years I began volunteering at a Christ-centered support group for addicts and their families that met in a local church. I realized that although I was very glad to be with the alcoholics, I was very weak in practical skills. Training at church and secular classes for addiction counselors helped. My wife and I both felt called to full-time ministry with hurting families. We left our jobs and completed a ministry training program. I was ordained a year later.

Despite my training, what I did not realize was that I was still missing a very important joyful foundation for my identity, family and ministry. First, while joyful, "we're glad to be together" experiences seem to happen spontaneously, I had no idea how to build joyful bonds with my wife and daughter. Second, I was missing significant "return to joy skills." For all my compassion, I had no idea how to stay connected when failure or intense negative emotions were involved. The old voices of contempt, humiliation and shame followed me and made it hard for me to be gentle with myself when I made mistakes. Third, I was still strongly motivated by the need to avoid shame. Performing, excelling and avoiding failure made me forget completely about joy. Finally, my training helped me learn to help hurting people spot their wounds, problems and denial. This meant that I was more skilled at helping them discover the negative than I was at helping them build resiliency. I was unable to give others what I did not have personally.

My performance-driven mentality became increasingly draining. My problem-centered focus was not life-giving to me, my family or others. Fortunately, I was blessed to interact with strong, mature mentors who responded tenderly to my weakness. They helped me learn about grace in relationships and identity. By watching one of my mentors, I finally saw an example of a strong person who could be angry but stay connected with other people. We will call this "returning to joy from anger" when we begin to discuss relational brain skills later in this book. It helped me immensely when he was glad to be with me when I was angry, and this connection helped me learn to feel and express anger in ways that were relational and tender.

In spite of my progress, my compassion, service and responsibility became a death trap because I lacked enough joy to be resilient. I finally came to a point at which I was desperate for something new. I realized that most of the work I did in churches and in secular environments with addicts and trauma was not producing the kind of results I hoped to see. Broken relationships, divorce, loneliness, jail, prison, AIDS and death were the fruit of relapse for too many precious lives for which I cared deeply. I knew the training, programs, techniques and strategies most of us used were not as effective as we wanted. I was also desperate for something that would bring joy to my own life and allow me to fully and deeply express the compassionate heart for the hurting that Jesus had given me.

I experienced a significant disability as the result of a chronic, painful and incurable disease, and I lost my marriage. For years I was barely able to care for myself until, on a missionary trip to Spain, God healed me enough so that I no longer needed to use a wheelchair. It was then that I met Maritza and soon after I heard Jim Wilder teach the Life Model explaining joy and describing the effects of both joy and trauma on the brain. I knew I had finally found the piece that had been missing from my life and from addiction and trauma recovery. Joy was powerful and could be learned, practiced and applied relationally to help hurting people heal from the devastation of broken relationships, addictions and trauma. My mind felt like it was exploding with new possibilities, ideas and designs for support groups and treatment.

More importantly, when Maritza and I were married, we committed to build strong joy bonds together as a foundation for our lives and relationships. We attended all three tracks of Chris and Jen Coursey's *THRIVE Training* and practiced exercises to help us grow joyful identities as individuals and as a couple. We became intentional about practicing joy together. I was delighted to finally learn the "return to joy together" skills I had been missing. I discovered that as my identity was rooted in joy, my compassion and ministry stopped killing me. Joyful skills entered our lives and family as we shared the message of joyful recovery with others. With our own transformed lives as inspiration, Maritza and I continue training workers, leaders and missionaries around the world to propagate joy. Joy changed everything about me, my family, relationships and ministry. I intentionally start joy each day. It was exactly this joyful recovery that had brought me to the worst neighborhood in Brazil.

Jim and I created the *Connexus™ for a thriving community* program together so churches and ministries could start joy wherever joy levels were low. *Connexus™* was designed around the principles we will explore in this book.

Our "herd"

By delighting in relationships we create belonging around ourselves. "Creating belonging" means that we continually create a joyful place for others to belong with us. This is exactly what Ed felt when his mom looked at him with a smile and a twinkle in her eye. Joy is what he felt when he wrestled with his dad. When we create belonging, our joy extends an invitation for others to grow joy together with us. Joyful belonging grows relationships, seeks others and builds when others smile back. Creating belonging is the best indicator of maturity at any age. When we create belonging around us, we are growing a network of joyful relationships. Our "herd" is connected and empowered by joy and seeks to invite others to share joy with us.

There are three response styles that distinguish people in our herd. Any one of us can have all three. *Protectors* are the first type of herd members. Untraumatized people who grow up in high-joy homes tend to become protectors. Protectors have strong joyful identities that welcome others and have tender hearts toward weakness. Protectors do not exploit weaknesses but instead help vulnerable herd members grow in joy. Protectors do not enable dysfunctional behavior but quickly protect the weak. When our herd has high-joy, the members tend to develop strong protector skills. Ed's story illustrates that anyone can learn protector skills at any stage in life.

Predators are the primary fear-based response style in the herd. The brain is pre-wired for predator responses. Without training, predator responses are all we have. We need training by gentle protectors who respond tenderly to weakness or we will respond like predators and prey. Predators discover the weaknesses and vulnerabilities of others and exploit them. Predators use weaknesses to obtain or retain dominance in the food chain. Predators fiercely guard their positions and will hurt others in the herd if threatened. Predators also do their best to hide their weaknesses and appear strong to assure their positions. Predators are the most common product of low-joy herds.

Possums are the other fear and anxiety-based response style found in low-joy herds. Possums do not occupy positions of dominance in the herd, and their style is based primarily on avoiding being exploited by predators. Possums have usually been hurt in relationships and will do most anything to avoid being hurt again. Possums hide, avoid, minimize, withdraw and conceal their weaknesses as much as possible. Unfortunately for possums, their low-joy environment creates weaknesses and vulnerabilities that are impossible to conceal. Predators on the prowl are likely to spot and exploit these vulnerabilities, leaving possums feeling ashamed, used and even more fearful.

In high-joy environments, protectors welcome others to their herd with joyful belonging. When protectors are rare it is a sign that our herd has low joy levels. When predators are plentiful and the possums are hiding, we can be sure that joy is low and headed lower.

Understanding joy, grace and shalom

It is important to notice that joy, grace and shalom are all members of one family. Joy is not the same thing as her sister Grace or her sister Shalom. Because the members of this family are so closely related, it is easy to be confused about who they are. Understanding this little biblical family helps us make sense of Bible teaching about joy, grace and shalom (peace).

In the Greek language of the New Testament, Joy and Grace are two forms of the same word. Grace is the third declension form and Joy is the first declension form. Joy is the response to Grace. Since most of us have not heard the word Grace except in the definition "unmerited favor," we can miss the connection. The best translation of Grace into English these days is not the old word "favor" but the word "special." Grace is therefore being really, really special to someone. "Unmerited" means "without having to work for it" so we are very, very special to someone without having to work for it. This is exactly what a baby receives from a loving family, total delight that the baby is very special just the way she or he is. No work by baby is required for smiles, coos, giggles, feeding and Joy. Joy is the response to being the really special one. These two go together, being very special without earning it and total Joy. God cares deeply about Joy. Joy is our response to God's Grace. In the Psalms we find that God expects our response to God's Grace to be high-energy Joy!

While Joy is high energy, Joy's sister Shalom is quiet and low energy. We are all rather weak and cannot sustain a high-energy state for long. God has so wired the brain that every experience of Joy calls for a time of rest to follow. It is an endless cycle: high-energy Joy followed by low-energy Shalom. One cannot live without the other. Remember how it feels to have wound up children in the room? We soon want a bit of quiet and rest. Shalom is that powerful rest that comes when we know everything is right. There is nothing to worry about. We are in the arms of one who loves us and he or she is in our arms. God offers Shalom as a reward for faithfulness almost every time Joy is mentioned. We find Shalom and Joy together in scripture as often as they are in the brain. We will become much better acquainted with Joy in the first part of this book while Shalom will be featured in the second part. For now, we need to know that while they are always together, they are not the same.

Huge errors in reading the scriptures come from mistaking one for the other, as we will see in this chapter.

How does weakness become essential to my joyful identity?

The best way to build my joyful identity comes by developing a tender heart toward weakness. This tender and joyful response comes from seeing weakness as an opportunity to care.

Ed says, One of the greatest gifts I received from my parents was seeing their compassion. I watched my Mom care for her aunt who was paralyzed and mentally impaired from a stroke. Mom was the only family member who visited her weekly, brought her presents and cared for her. Mom happily included me in these visits. My grandmother came to live with us while convalescing so my mom could help her. I remember the pain and compassion in my dad's voice at dinner when he talked about the poor in Haiti. Having come to the US from Haiti in the 1940's, Dad knew how hard life could be. My dad could also fix just about anything. I remember him going out in the evening to help our neighbors or the parish priests by fixing a broken washing machine or television. Mom also volunteered at church and the rectory. I saw compassion in action as my parents took practical responsibility to help others. I learned to see people, lives and culture through eyes of compassion. I learned that I had a personal responsibility and the power to make a difference.

Tenderness is not just an attitude toward weakness in others but a response to our own weakness as well. Why should we have a tender response toward weakness? Think about what we will find next to weakness. Future generations always arise out of young, weak and vulnerable babies. Babies are weak but consider the joy they bring! Heavy loads of fruit weaken branches so they need support. Every area of growth first appears in weakness and vulnerability! Beauty is delicate and fragile. When we pick parts of plants for our vases we choose flowers, some of the weakest parts, thinking they are delicate and beautiful. Healthy cultures treasure wonderful, old people.

Pat is approaching 80 years old and accomplishes more than men half his age. His tenderness toward weakness was an incredible blessing after Ed's major back surgery. Noticing that Ed was not around, Pat asked Maritza, "Is there anything practical I can do to help you?" Maritza realized that she and Ed were running low on firewood. Pat smiled and immediately said, "I have some firewood. What size do you need it?" Maritza told him and he said he would deliver it soon.

A few days later, Pat arrived, wearing a huge smile, and asked where to put the wood. To make things easier for Pat, Maritza and Ed just told him to drop the load in the driveway and they would stack it. Instead, Pat said that he would stack the entire load by himself, and pretty soon, there was a stack of firewood ready for the stove. Pat's joy, smile and tender heart toward Ed's weakness were joyful blessings.

Joy levels build around people who respond warmly to weakness. Anticipating a comforting response to our weakness lets us find help quickly. Problems do not get out of hand when we feel safe to seek help. This anticipation of joy creates adaptability. Without the joyful response we are anticipating, we will experience shame. When we fear being shamed for our weakness we hide our problems.

Being vulnerable with shame helped Debbie stop a predatory pattern in her family. In her pastoral counseling with Ed, Debbie confided that her husband physically abused her. His physical and verbal abuse often occurred in front of their children. She felt fearful, overwhelmed and very ashamed. Ed and Debbie discussed different options available to her, but because her husband was not abusing the children, she chose the possum response of doing nothing.

One day Debbie came to Ed with tears in her eyes when, for the first time, her teenage son hit and pushed her, just like his father did. Her face was downcast, full of shame and sorrow. Debbie's worst nightmare had come true. She had tried to protect her children from the effects of the abuse, but the predatory pattern had now passed on to her son. Now, she did not know what to do.

As Ed felt her distress, he shared her sorrow and shame. Ed told Debbie how glad he was that she had shown her weakness. Slowly, Debbie was able to start asking Ed about her options, and as they brainstormed together, she became determined to take action. The next time Ed saw her, Debbie was smiling. She had followed up with a local domestic violence program. After her work at the women's program, Debbie told both her husband and son that she would never again tolerate abuse in any form. She would call the police, pursue legal action and leave. She also invited them to join her in recovery. Debbie pursued her own recovery and never again reported a single incident of abuse. By risking shame and exposing her weakness, Debbie received a tender response and with the help of many strong people, she was able to stop her predators. Change happens quickly where the weak and strong are together. The response to a weakness will determine if that change is for the better or for the worse.

Caring for others when they are weak allows them to develop a protector identity. When joy levels drop, protectors become scarce and culture decays, producing large herds of predators. In the absence of the transmission of joyful protector skills, everyone comes out a predator or a possum.

If we see weakness as bad, we will hide our weaknesses and punish those who show their weakness. Worse yet, we hide from God. The weak and the strong become enemies. The strong exploit the weak to keep them weak, and the weak try to make the strong weaker when they can. Revenge becomes popular. Much violence is fueled by revenge.

Responses to weakness separate the predators from the protectors. Both predators and protectors watch for weakness in others. For predators it is time to pounce; for protectors it is time to let the weak rest. For predators, weakness in others is time to "get something," and for protectors it is time to give. As predator patterns begin to define our identities, corporate culture and national norms, we are socialized to despise weakness. Joy drops around the powerful. Taking advantage of weaknesses will make the powerful feared and despised, as well as admired and glorified. The new "hope" becomes looking sexy so predators will propagate with us or help us become the top predator. The thrill of the hunt replaces joy.

What protectors do with weakness to build joy

Protectors respond to weakness and create joy in at least three ways. First, protectors amplify every little bit of joy they find instead of amplifying the problems and upsets. In this way, low-joy starts to become high-joy. Second, protectors notice when people are tired and let them rest. Weakness shows up as fatigue, overwhelm and getting tired. Protectors encourage the weak to go a bit farther and then let them rest until joy returns. This cycle of effort and rest builds trust and peace, which we call "shalom." Shalom respects the weakness in others and matches the work to what they can do. The third way protectors respond to weakness is by sharing the distress caused by weakness, even when the protector induced the distress. The result is a bond that pain cannot break, and the relationship stays stronger than the problem. We call this ability "returning to joy" after something has gone wrong. Even when weakness results in failure or pain, it will not keep the weak and the strong apart.

These three factors — building joy, creating shalom and returning to joy — will be explored throughout this entire book, but another simple list might help us picture protectors responding to weakness.

Protectors will:
* Promote play
* Join in joy
* Keep an expectancy and curiosity about what will grow from weakness
* Let everyone rest (even the strong)
* Amplify joy more than distress
* Share all distress including the distress they produce
* Keep problems smaller than relationships
* Keep the focus on the weak while taking good care of themselves
* Maintain their own stability while they stabilize the weak
* Keep predators away
* Encourage the weak to point out weakness in the strong, including the protector
* Encourage the weak to become protectors of the weaknesses around them

The story of Abigail in I Samuel is a great illustration of a protector who worked with weakness to build joy. Abigail was married to a foolish man named Nabal who owned thousands of sheep. David and his men lived nearby and carefully protected Nabal's sheep and servants.

One day when Nabal was celebrating, David sent men to ask for a few provisions. Instead of responding with gratitude that David had been a protector, Nabal was mocking, rude and insulting. When Nabal's response reached David, he and his men turned predatory and went to kill Nabal and everyone in his household.

Abigail heard of Nabal's foolishness and David's anger. She quickly put her protector skills to good use. She sent enough food to provide generously for David and his men. She also got on her own donkey and traveled to meet David.

Abigail found David and quickly tuned in to his distress. She agreed with David that her husband had acted foolishly and without regard for David and his men. She reminded David of his protector identity as the future King of Israel and the destiny God had promised. She asked David to consider if killing Nabal would be consistent with his identity. When David heard her, he said, "Praise be to the Lord, the God of Israel who has sent you today to meet me. May you be blessed for your good judgment and for keeping me from bloodshed this day, and from avenging myself with my own hands" I Samuel 25:32-33 (NIV). Abigail's gentle protector skills allowed her to synchronize with David's distress, help him return to joy, and remember his identity thereby saving everyone in her household. Abigail kept her relationships more important than the problems.

We keep problems smaller than our relationships by finding creative solutions that let us be proud of who we are in hard times. We find and maintain shalom while helping others regulate their feelings and calm down. This response requires developing enough spiritual maturity to stay connected to God's love while someone around us is upset, perhaps even upset with us. Such responses require enough human maturity to be able to care for two or more people at the same time. It takes some maturity to maintain a curious, open eagerness about how this current weakness can help us find God's presence and what God wants to do right here and now.

Growing in three capacities: joy, shalom and return to joy

Joy, shalom and return to joy are not only characteristics of a spiritually and emotionally mature person, but they also help determine the kind of identity our family, school, church and community share. We not only want to grow in joy, shalom and return to joy, but we want all three to spread to groups around us. We will die and kill for the lack of these three capacities. Let us review: Joy is relational; joy is the twinkle in someone's eyes when they see us; joy is the sense we are special before we have to do anything to prove it; joy grows when the weak and the strong are together showing tenderness toward weakness. Our brains are wired to seek joy. Joy is God's gift to us. Joy might remind us of our home, schools and church but perhaps not.

Shalom is a cozy sense that everything is right. Relationships are right. Who we are makes sense. Our reactions to the world please us and God. Shalom is a major part of each joyful identity and community. We call this peace, but "harmony" would be a better word. Our brains are wired to prefer harmony. Harmony is God's gift to us. When we have lost our way and our connection to God, our shalom is gone.

Return to joy is that assurance that even when things go wrong, we will not be abandoned and left in our upset. Without return to joy we find anger, fear and narcissism growing in communities instead of joy. Returning to joy comes from strong attachments to others and a deep sense of who we are that will not get lost when we are in pain. Our brains are wired to desire the way back to joy. Leading us back to joy is God's gift to us. We will take a deeper look into returning to joy in the third part of the book where we consider relational brain skills. Find ways to keep your joy in Chris' book *The Joy Switch*.

Low-joy turns into pseudo-joy cravings

Our life, brain and relationships work best when our relationships are deeply rooted in high-joy connections with God and with others. With a

high-joy foundation, our brain tends to regulate dopamine and other neu-
rotransmitters well, and we manage pleasure, pain and emotions effectively.
This foundation of joy also helps us learn to stay connected with others when
we, or they, are distressed.

Sadly, many of us experience life with low-joy. We grew up in families
where joy was missing, weak or limited. In these low-joy environments,
our brain is organized around anxiety, fear and the avoidance of pain. The
absence of joy and presence of anxiety just seemed normal. We were easily
overwhelmed when things went wrong, and found it hard to recover from
disappointments and distress. We felt trapped in negative emotions. Pleasure
was momentary.

Chronic low-joy creates at least four common problems that keep us from
relational joy. First, we find ourselves without the kind of strong joy bonds we
need with God and others when we are in trouble. Second, we may lack some
relational skills needed to form and maintain joyful relationships. Third, we
are likely to view relationships with a good deal of suspicion and doubt. This
makes it much more difficult for us to engage with other people. Some of us
back off from engaging in relationships entirely, while others are so desperate
for relationships that we overwhelm others when we try to get close. Finally,
we are strongly motivated by anxiety, fear and the drive to avoid shame, failure, disappointment and rejection.

A bland, low-joy life or one of relational pain sets us up to crave "joy
substitutes." Joy substitutes generate temporary feelings of pleasure that help
us regulate internal distress, reduce pain, increase pleasure and escape from
negative emotions. Joy substitutes stimulate the release of dopamine in the
pleasure center of the brain in the same way as genuine joyful relationships,
but only for a moment. While joy gives a lasting "flavor" of satisfaction and
rest, the substitutes are hardly swallowed when we start craving more. The
cravings left behind by joy substitutes are very demanding. Some might say
we cannot eat just one!

What do we substitute for joy?

Joy substitutes create a sensation of "pseudo-joy." Pseudo-joy is a counterfeit
for real joy created when dopamine generated by non-relational things stimulates the pleasure center of the brain. Pseudo-joy can come from Behaviors,
Events, Experiences, People or Substances (BEEPS). BEEPS can include things
like comfort foods, chocolate, sex, work, performance, approval, codependent
relationships, excitement, gambling, entertainment, alcohol, other drugs or
anything that triggers a surge of pleasure. Food and sex are two of the most

common sources of pseudo-joy. BEEPS have the strong potential to turn otherwise harmless things like chocolate, other food or sex into harmful emotional, relational, mental and physical dependence. A high-joy brain is more resistant to the development of harmful attachments to BEEPS. The low-joy brain can be easily hijacked by BEEPS as we will see in greater detail in chapter three.

Happiness or excitement often substitute for joy. While happiness and excitement feel pleasurable, they are not the same as relational joy. For example, if we are football fans and our team wins the Super Bowl or the World Cup, we are likely to be extremely happy. If we see our favorite actor in a great new movie, we will be happy. If we like computers, and our computer is repaired, it's natural to feel happy. None of these things are bad or wrong. But, because they are based on non-relational external circumstances, they should not be confused with relational joy. Because happiness and excitement are based on external circumstances that change continuously, they are not even a reliable source of pseudo-joy!

Joy starts at home, school and church

Joy, shalom and returning to joy keep the weak and strong together. In this section we focus on joy. By now we all want to be joy starters. Let us build joy in our homes, schools and churches. It is time for the 2.2 billion Christians in the world to transform earth's low-joy places with a joy that can be sustained and propagated. We will start by examining how to tell real joy from pseudo-joy. The key to knowing the difference is the way we treat weakness. Let us consider how joy and pseudo-joy look at home, school and church.

Joy starts at home for Nancy

Nancy loved her children. There was joy in the house as Nancy and George painted the childrens' rooms before they were even born. Nancy held, nursed, giggled and cooed with her babies. George took the children out to play and they always sat with the children when anything questionable was on television. Most days there were smiles and laughter in the house although, like all homes, it was not every day. Home was a safe place to be weak because the parents were strong protectors. Joy was easy to find. Regrettably, Nancy could get quite stressed when the children were fussy. When Nancy felt drained, moody and irritated with George, she would eat a little chocolate from her "stash." When the children fussed in the car or in late afternoons, she appeased them and comforted herself with treats. She gave them sugary foods for special occasions. She also discovered the treats for the children were a great way she could talk on the phone in peace. In this rather normal house, the children learned relationships create joy but when relationships turn sour sugar becomes an excellent source of pseudo-joy.

Joy starts at school for Shelia

Shelia is a teacher who uses the power of joy to bring positive changes to her students. She is convinced that joy grows out of relationships, so she begins the school year by initiating relationships with her students. She also provides space and time for students to develop meaningful connections with each other. Shelia learns the name of each student. She discovers the interests of each student by asking about their families, their dreams, even their troubles. She quickly fosters an environment where students are free to laugh and cry together. Students tell funny stories about their days; they also talk about their disappointments. Everyone responds with care and concern. Shelia helps her students grow joy and share belonging with each other. Her classroom is filled with nametags, which the students decorate with symbols and pictures that are important to them. They sit in small groups where they begin to know each other. For the students, these groups become much more than a random group of individuals sitting together in a classroom! They become a place of joyful connection where the students think of other group members as "my people." After a little while, Shelia does not need to call roll. She simply asks, "Are any of your people missing today?"

Students turn to pseudo-joy many times a day by checking the mirror, eating junk food and showing off the coolest technology. Overachievers take too many courses and try for impressive colleges, while the underachievers head for video games instead of joy.

The growth of joy, relationships and belonging help Shelia's students grow academically. Her students often work in teams on project-based assignments. As students collaborate, their energy and creativity bloom because they are genuinely glad to be together. As their capacity for joy grows, their empathy increases and they are happy to be together even when one of them is experiencing difficult emotions or showing weakness. Shelia responds as a joyful protector by tuning in and expressing tender care for anyone struggling with weakness. She shares warmth and comfort, and students know that it is safe to ask for help if they are struggling. Shelia's care, empathy and understanding help her students grow.

Joy starts at church for Susan and Ty

Susan and Ty moved to a new area and tried a church close to their house. They were quickly welcomed at the door by warm, grandparent-aged greeters whose faces lit up upon meeting them. The response surprised Susan and Ty, putting them at ease. The greeters showed Susan and Ty around which helped the young couple feel at home. The lobby was full of diversity and life. People from all age groups were interacting. While Susan inquired about the children's programs Ty noticed coffee and snacks on one of the lobby tables. He wandered over to grab a cup of coffee. Ty was thrilled to discover the church served his favorite brand of a high-end coffee along with the brand of donuts he especially enjoyed, known for their taste, texture and freshness. After eating several donuts and pouring his second cup of coffee, Ty returned to Susan and they found a seat for the service. On their drive home Susan commented how much she enjoyed the atmosphere, the people and the sermon, while Ty was struck by the coffee and donuts. Susan and Ty would return to the church the following Sunday though Ty was much more excited about the coffee and donuts than the people. Even though the church was full of joy and rich in relationships, Ty preferred to gravitate to the snack table for pseudo-joy.

Growing joy

As we go through this chapter, readers may ask, "Joy sounds good, but how can I learn to grow it?" We might identify with possums or predators that fear any signs of weakness will be exploited and used against them. This can be especially difficult if we do not have strong bonds at home or with family members.

The really good news is that no matter where we start, we can acquire new joyful skills and bonds, as well as strengthen joy bonds that we already have. We can expand our capacity for joy and spread our joy to others. Now we will take a look at the kinds of bonds and relationships that help us grow joy safely.

Growing joy with God: One of the places some of us start growing joy is in our relationship with Jesus, who loves to share His joy, shalom, delight and life with us. Jesus has excellent joyful and gentle protector skills, and He is always glad to be with us. Because Jesus was fully human when He walked in low-joy Galilee 2,000 years ago, He completely understands the kinds of struggles each one of us has with joy. He knows what it feels like to be alone, deserted and rejected. He fully understands our failures and weaknesses and is ready to interact with us.

God actually thinks our relationship with Him is bigger and more important than our shortcomings, rebellion and deformities. He places a higher value on relationship, and restoring relationship with us, than He does on the problems we have. God knows that relationship with Him is the basis for overcoming our sins, transgressions and iniquities.

Jesus asks us to enter into relationship with Him by admitting our failures and malfunctions to Him. This way, we agree with Jesus that we have fallen short of His design for our lives. Sin means that we are not fully living the reality of God's design and purpose. In other words, sin is a malfunction. Jesus promises that if we agree with Him about our malfunctions, He will restore us. We bond together in joy. He is faithful and just to forgive, cleanse and restore our joyful connection with Him. The cross makes all of this possible. Jesus did for us what we could never do for ourselves and moved the problem of our malfunctions out of the way so that we could know His love, joy and delight! This is great news because it means we can grow joy in our relationship with God. We will explore connecting with Jesus to grow joy in part two of this book, "The Joyful Immanuel Lifestyle."

Two-way joy bonds: People who are married or have a strong bond with a family member or a close friend are uniquely positioned to begin growing joy. Two-way bonds are the relationships where we can look deeply into someone's eyes, sense what they are thinking and know, "you are mine and I am yours." Two-way bond relationships are so exclusive they are fertile ground for powerful joy bonds. Unfortunately, the powerful nature of two-way bonds also makes them very susceptible to exploitation by predators.

What kinds of relationships are appropriate for two-way joy bonds? We grow joy in a two-way bond with someone with whom we already have a life-long commitment. Joy grows when we strengthen the relationships God has given us. The most obvious relationships in which we can grow an exclusive joy bond are with our children and spouse. Because couples already have a two-way bond, the entire dynamics of the relationship can be transformed when spouses acquire and practice joy skills together. Joy can improve strong marriages and revolutionize marriages that are struggling. Rebekkah and Steve are a good example.

When Rebekkah first heard about the power of joy, she responded with skepticism. While the thought of joy and peace defining her life and marriage was appealing, she questioned if such a thing was possible. Fear and anxiety directed most of her life, including her relationship with her husband. Rebekkah spent much money and time reading self-help books and attending popular seminars that left her disillusioned. Despite her best attempts, the distance between her and Steve only grew.

With their marriage on the line, Rebekkah and Steve decided to try to grow their joy together. They were excited and surprised to see how fifteen minutes of daily "joy practice" began to change them. Rebekkah noticed a growing sense of hope as joy and peace softened her anxiety. Steve began to lower his guard and share his thoughts, fears and struggles with Rebekkah. Their tendency to react and argue diminished as their joy bonds grew stronger. Both Steve and Rebekkah were amazed to discover that joyful interactions with each other were more fun than television, reading and conferences. To their delight, family and friends began to comment about the changes. Rebekkah and Steve found that the small steps they took to grow joy changed the dynamics of their relationship.

Growth and change are fairly simple if we have a strong relationship with a family member. This is not hard for strong people to help strong people. It is not unusual for parents and children to have a strong bond that can produce joyful growth. Siblings can also practice joy skills together. Many of us have strong relationships with friends but have no strong family bonds. Friends can be a place to build two-way joy bonds.

Finally, we never, ever start practicing joy skills in a two-way joy bond with people we do not know very well. The powerful nature of two-way joy bonds creates an extremely high potential for inappropriately sexual and highly codependent relationships. Sexualized, inappropriate and exclusive two-way bonds are a major reason for some of the very public "crash and burn" incidents. Pastors and leaders often leave their spouse and church after these moral failures. Finding "love" is also a major relapse trigger for those in recovery.

Three-way bonds: Three-way bonds are the safest relationships in which we can grow and practice our joy skills. Three-way bonds are different from two-way bonds because they include three people. Three-way bonds provide an excellent relational context in which all three partners can acquire and strengthen joyful protector skills. Because three people are involved, these bonds do not have the same intensity as two-way bonds, which make them less likely to become sexual or codependent.

Three-way bonds are a preferred training environment for use in churches, ministries, schools and communities. Three-way bonds are appropriate for individuals who lack bonded partners or people who do not feel safe in relationship with existing bonded partners. It is not unusual for couples to have problems feeling safe growing joy together. Most Life Model joy-building exercises are done in groups of three to form safe and joyful family bonds. We will look at three-way bonds and multigenerational community in chapter four.

Three-way bonds are more useful for building a joyful identity than two-way bonds. Developmentally, children need strong joy bonds with two people in order to form a strong identity. The stronger the joy bonds with these two figures, the more their identity will be consistent over time, even when things go wrong. While secure two-way bonds are an excellent way to grow joy, they do not solidify our identity in the same way as three-way bonds. We need to develop both two-way and three-way bonds.

Naturally, joy grows best in three-way bonds when all three members are intentional about practicing joy skills together. There is nothing inherently joyful about three predators, three possums, or a mix of both being together in a group. Exercises specifically designed to acquire, practice and grow joyful, gentle protector skills are crucial for success. This is what Life Model Works exercises are engineered to do in families, churches, ministries, schools and communities.

Finally, it may come as a surprise to find that it is possible to grow a three-way bond in which God is the third member of our triad. God absolutely loves to be invited to share joy as the third member in our three-way bond. It is amazing to see how joy is amplified when we invite Jesus to join with us. With practice, we can help each other interact with Jesus. These Immanuel moments help us grow a much stronger identity.

Beware of predators who claim God as the third member of a triad in order to exploit weakness and vulnerability. The relationship will become abusive, inappropriate or sexualized. Building joy with predators will not work.

How am I doing?
- When do I favor true joy or substitutes?
- Do I create joy around me? How do I know?
- Does my joy with others lead to rest? How do I know?
- With whom do I share both joy and upset?

Joy or pseudo-joy: With a quick taste test most of us can tell if a soft drink is diet or regular. We can also learn to distinguish genuine joy from artificial substitutes. Genuine joy must be relational and lead to shalom and rest. Genuine joy draws people together, strengthens relationships and forms lasting connections. We smile with our eyes and faces in a way that makes others feel seen and special. Genuine joy is a warm, inviting expression that uses the face, voice and body. We know we are joyful when interacting and delighting over others feels natural. Substitutes for joy leave us feeling empty, alone, cold and discontent. Some joy substitutes are nothing more than danger mixed with pleasure. When pseudo-joy enters relationships, unrest and anxiety start to propagate.

Creating joy around me: Another sign of being a joyful person is how other people respond. We learn a great deal about our joy levels from the people in our lives. Joy draws people closer. Joyful people convey, "You are important to me because of who you are!" Friends and family help us gauge the level of our joy or fear. Low-joy leaves others anxious, overwhelmed, run-over and drained. In low-joy, a cloud of computers, video games, television, texting and tweeting outnumber face-to-face interactions. We notice low-joy when we need to pretend to be happy so that others will want to be with us.

Allowing rest: Joyful people synchronize joy and rest cycles to create trust in families and communities. Rest leads to growing more joy. As we grow a strong joyful identity, we invite the weak to set the pace. Strength that overwhelms leaves others feeling defensive rather than protected. The strong use their presence and example to guard the weak and guide relationships back to joy and shalom.

Sharing the distress of others: When we are joyful, others gravitate toward us because they feel the freedom to be themselves in pain, problems and all. True joy attunes, refreshes and energizes. Substitutes mask feelings and drain energy. Joy counterfeits are non-relational strategies that may look good but in the end solve the problem at a cost to relationships. True joy reciprocates as we delight in each other and see some of what God sees.

Correcting what we might have heard about joy

Many a Christian child was first introduced to joy with the acrostic:

Jesus first

Others second

Yourself last

This might be a good way to teach about service but joy is not service. The effect on most children is to stop thinking about joy. Not only does this acrostic fail to make sense of joy, it is the formula for misery. What we have done is distance children from the delightful way Jesus welcomed the children and embraced them. Furthermore, as in Ed's story, a commitment to service in the absence of strong empowerment by joy is a recipe for disillusionment, burnout and BEEPS.

Christians have long realized that joy is not happiness, excitement, passion or pleasure. Joy cannot be reduced to a feeling that comes and goes because that emotion would abandon us in our times of need. However, knowing what joy is not still leaves people wondering what joy might be. The dominant philosophy of our age expects "make a choice" as the alternative to "living by emotions." A quick review of the Christian books on joy reveals writers trying to make joy a choice. Let us consider three such books that sadly miss joy.

Choose Joy by Kay Warren (Ravell, 2012) does a reasonable job of telling us what joy is not. Joy does not come from having possessions, having people meet our expectations or having the right personality style. Warren points to God as the true source of joy but adds that people are a "false source of joy" (p. 82). We disagree. To understand Warren's conclusion we must visit her definition of joy. "Joy is the settled assurance that God is in control of all the details of my life, the quiet confidence that ultimately everything is going to be all right. ... Joy is a settled conviction ABOUT God. It's a quiet confidence IN God" (p. 32). We would certainly agree with Warren that to make people the source of our "settled conviction" that everything is going to be all right would be a major mistake, but is that joy? What Warren is calling joy is actually describing the biblical word shalom. Shalom is the quiet experience and conviction that all is in right relationship. If Warren had understood joy and shalom, she could have called this book *Choose Shalom*. Shalom would have given the right name to her teaching that otherwise has much to commend it. However, shalom is not joy and in some ways joy and shalom are remarkably different. We will not understand the Bible or human experience if we stay confused. We are wired for joy and the joy in our brain is a high energy state that builds our strength and stimulates much of the brain to grow. Shalom is a low energy state that quiets us when everything is just right and we can rest. Joy gets things done. Shalom lets us be still.

Warren correctly says that joy and happiness are not the same, but due to her confusion about what joy actually is, her book tends to say that happiness is something we get from people and joy is something we get from God. We agree that happiness is not the same as joy, although they often are found together. Imagine four-year old Julie by a campfire with her parents eating a toasted marshmallow. She is happy. The sugar from the marshmallow would be enough to make her happy. Around the fire there are smiling faces and caring eyes and these bring love, joy and happiness. Suddenly Julie stumbles and starts to fall backwards into the fire. Happiness is gone. Her father rushes to grab her before she can fall in, and Julie wraps her arms around his neck in fear and starts crying. Was Dad eager to be with her and keep her from the fire? Yes! Are they deeply glad to hold each other? Yes! This is joy, characterized by genuine and real gladness to be together in good times and bad. Is this "false joy" as Warren tells us because it is between people? No! We know this father-daughter moment is both real and important. Had Dad sat disinterested while texting on his phone, we would all want him arrested. Joy between people is both real and very important. The difference with God is that while people are intermittent sources of joy, God is a constant. Both sources of joy are real and needed.

Choosing Joy by Angela Thomas (Howard Books, 2011) brings us a mix of sometimes contradictory statements about joy. Thomas has missed the relational nature of joy so sometimes she sees joy as a feeling, and other times joy becomes an action regardless of what we feel. She says, "Joy is a feeling and an action. But learning to live in everyday joy means that we choose the action of joy regardless of how we feel" (p. 13). But joy is about an attachment relationship where we respond with joy to the ones we love. Certainly we can have joy in the presence of pain and make choices to be with those we love even when it hurts. Who has not trembled before entering a hospital room both eager to be with the one we love and dreading the sight we will find there? Yet, joy is not in the action but rather in the motive.

Thomas believes that people are incapable of producing or growing joy. She says, "I cannot produce joy or build a bigger, better version of joy" (p. 36), and "We cannot buy joy at the store or manufacture it with our minds" (p. 47). While she is right about the store, people can produce joy. People can grow larger joy and it is precisely with our minds that we manufacture joy. God has designed our brain to grow with joy, respond to joy, to produce joy in others and to amplify joy. Paul says, "Rejoice with those who rejoice" Romans 12:15a (NIV) and in doing so, we will always find that the joy is amplified. As we begin smiling at a baby, we will watch this happen with our own eyes. Joy is something we can and must produce together.

Thomas continues, "The pursuit of joy is an act of obedience. Choosing joy is a mark of spiritual maturity" (p. 286). Choosing joy is a bit like choosing to nurse a baby. We might choose the method but we do not choose to make the milk. We can ask any father to choose to nurse when mommy does not want to get up and see where that gets us. Joy itself is never a choice. Joy is a response placed in us that can be killed or grown through the choices we make, but when John the Baptist jumped for joy in his mother's womb at the approach of Jesus, it was not some choice on his part but a response to recognition of love and relationship. Evidence of maturity is not found in the "choosing of joy," as Thomas argued. Instead, joy is the evidence of maturity.

Choosing Joy by Dan Lord (Our Sunday Visitor, 2012) is another example of how difficult it is to write about joy without understanding joy as relational. Lord understands right from the start that both God and people are capable of joy. However, he has his own problems dealing with how joy and choice would fit together because he treats joy like a flavor. God has the strong flavor, but other things have flavor in lesser amounts. Lord tells us, "A man smokes an expensive cigar - a small, simple good - and experiences a small, simple peace and satisfaction, a bantamweight joy" (p. 19). Here Lord mistakes peace and satisfaction (shalom) with joy but then goes on to say, "the joy of each Christian comes from Jesus Himself" (p. 19). In this Lord correctly attributes to Jesus the strongest source of joy.

Lord continues by mistaking shalom for joy. He says, "It [joy] is the peace and satisfaction that comes from possessing God" (p. 80). This would be an excellent definition of shalom but it is not the same as joy. Then Lord seems to forget that there are lesser joys and says, "The way to acquire joy, the only way - and there is no other way - is to completely abandon yourself to God's will" (p. 85). Who could argue that we should not completely abandon ourselves to God's will? Lord's mistake is contending that God's will is the only way to acquire joy. As we have seen throughout this chapter, joy is a relational experience with God and other people.

Furthermore, we can grow joy that is completely outside of God's will for us. Good people whose joy levels have dropped often begin to find some real joy in their neighbor's wife. Remember David and Bathsheba? When our joy is low, we notice people who light up when they see us. How many relational train wrecks were started by joy that was not ours to keep? The tragic outcome is not because this is false joy, but because we have taken joy that is not ours and God will not allow us to keep it. Predators constantly try to steal joy, although every time they pounce, the joy seems to flit away. Were God the only one who could give joy, we would all be in a lot less trouble.

The first error we have reviewed taught that choice is what determines joy. Choice is what strong people do. Weak people struggle with why they cannot just choose to be joyful. The second error we have studied is spiritualized joy and making it a private event with God. We have shown that there is every reason for high-joy people to share joy with others and for low-joy people to start practicing joy with others God has placed in their lives. Finally, by believing that only God can give joy, we leave a huge area of weakness undefended. Everyone will, one day or another, find themselves a pint low on joy and be vulnerable to taking joy that is not theirs. Believing there is nothing we can do to build our joy can be dangerous indeed.

Joy Actions

Home: Go fly a kite with your family.

School: Greet someone you do not usually greet.

Church: Smile as you introduce yourself to someone.

Assessment Of Joy

1. I regularly make myself smile remembering things and people I like.

    Never   0 1 2 3 4 5 6 7 8 9 10   *Constantly*

2. I really look forward to seeing the people I see each day.

    I avoid them   0 1 2 3 4 5 6 7 8 9 10   *I really like everyone*

3. I express my appreciation frequently.

    Never   0 1 2 3 4 5 6 7 8 9 10   *Constantly*

4. After people talk with me about problems they feel hopeful and creative.

    We get depressed   0 1 2 3 4 5 6 7 8 9 10   *Everyone thanks me*

5. How joyful am I?

    I never feel joy   0 1 2 3 4 5 6 7 8 9 10   *I constantly feel joy*

6. How joyful is my family?

    Never joyful   0 1 2 3 4 5 6 7 8 9 10   *Always joyful*

7. I find it easy to be content.

    Impossible   0 1 2 3 4 5 6 7 8 9 10   *No effort at all*

8. How many enjoyable meals do you share with others each week?

    0 1 2 3 4 5 6 7 8 9 10⁺

9. Children usually like me.

    I make children cry   0 1 2 3 4 5 6 7 8 9 10   *Children flock to me*

10. My family believes in me.

    Not at all   0 1 2 3 4 5 6 7 8 9 10   *Every one of them*

0   10   20   30   40   50   60   70   80   90   100

Total your scores here. _____
Mark the matching spot on the scale.

For a more complete assessment try the JoyQ at joystartshere.com.

My Joyful Identity Bible Study

Think back on something you appreciate and spend two minutes enjoying appreciation. Next, ask God to make this study interesting for you. Now read the following passage from the gospels.

Scripture John 15:9-20 Read then review the passage for each question.

Chapter Two Question: According to this passage what is the relationship between God's love and our joy?

Joy and Shalom Questions:
1. Is joy part of being glad to be together in this passage?
2. How does joy relate to God? (See also John 16:22-24 and 17:11-16)
3. How does joy shape our identity in this passage?
4. What do we learn about joy and shalom (everything works together) from this passage?

Personal Story Question: When, in your life, did you sense God giving joy to you?

Whole Bible Question: What Bible stories and verses tell us about joy?

Wrap-Up Minute: What do you now know that you didn't know before this week's study?

Bible Study Options:
1. If you or your group would like to study these passages using learning methods that help your brain engage more fully, we offer additional resources at lifemodelworks.org/bonus-resources/ in cooperation with Dr. Bill St Cyr and the Ambleside Schools International.
2. Pastors looking for a deeper study and group resources can find Scripture reflections in *Becoming the Face of Grace* by Ed through equippinghearts.com.

My Life Model Exercises

At the end of each of the following exercises notice how your body feels and what changed both during and after you practiced appreciation. (If your answer is, "It felt good," then ask yourself how you know it felt good. For example, "I felt a lightness in my chest, or my breathing is deeper and I can breathe better." Be specific.) When you meet as a group, discuss the results of your individual exercises for Chapter Two. Pick one of the home, school or church exercises below for this week's practice.

Individual: Family
1. Tell each one of your family members three qualities you appreciate about their character and presence. Be specific with each person about the things for which you are thankful.
2. What did you notice in your family members? (Did their facial expressions change? If so, how? For example, "I noticed my mom's face seemed so serious and strained at the beginning of the exercise, and now the lines in her face are more relaxed and there is a hint of a smile coming on." This is more specific than she did not look happy and now she does. Try to hone into the subtleties you notice.)

Individual: School
1. Students, express at least two qualities you appreciate to three of your classmates and one of your teachers. Teachers and staff, express appreciation to three of your students and one of your colleagues. Parents, express two qualities you appreciate to at least one of your child's teachers.
2. What did you notice as you shared appreciation with your classmates, teachers and colleagues?

Individual: Church
1. Express appreciation specifically to a pastor and secretary in your church by sending a note.
2. As part of your note, include two things you appreciate about their presence and ministry, a scripture verse and a blessing.
3. What do you notice as you share appreciation with your church leadership?

Chapter Three

My Strong Mask

When we are the sparkle in someone's eyes, their face lights up with a smile when they see us. We feel joy. From the moment we are born, joy shapes the chemistry, structure and growth of our brain. Joy lays the foundation for how well we will handle relationships, emotions, pain and pleasure throughout our lifetime. Joy creates an identity that is stable and consistent over time. Joy gives us the freedom to share our hearts with God and others. Expressing our joyful identity creates space for others to belong. Joy gives us the freedom to live without masks because, in spite of our weaknesses, we know we are loved. We are not afraid of our vulnerabilities or exposure. Joy gives us the freedom from fear to live from the heart Jesus gave us. We discover increasing delight in becoming the people God knew we could be.

Even in the best homes, we discover that being open about what we feel does not get the results we want. By eighteen months of age, most children begin hiding some feelings. We learn when to keep our thoughts to ourselves. By junior high we are cultivating a social image to win friends and influence people. Our image management has a hidden side effect. Over time we become uncertain if people like us or our image. Somehow our image always requires us to look stronger than we are. Eventually pastors, teachers, leaders and adults experience difficulty finding close friends or places that do not require image maintenance.

Even deeper, many of us grew up without consistent and strong "glad to be with you" joy experiences. When joy is inconsistent, weak or missing, our fear, anxiety and stress systems shape our brain's structure, chemistry and growth. The lack of joy leaves gaps in our relational style, identity and ability to respond to upsetting emotions. Before long, these malfunctions become such a part of us that we tend to see them as totally normal. We are the last to know we even have a weakness. Some of us wear masks of performance, success and competency. Others wear the spiritual mask. Those of us who greatly fear our own weaknesses may wear many masks to hide our vulnerabilities and avoid further pain. No matter what kind of masks we wear, we want to avoid being pounced upon for our weakness. We fear embarrassment, shame, blame, upsetting emotions and difficult people.

Once we use our image to get results, dates, work, friends or avoid trouble and attack, the mask begins to develop a strength of its own. Masks that work make us dependent on the masks themselves. Since most masks make us look stronger than we are, we grow tired keeping up appearances. All masks slowly kill joy even when they work. Our lack of joy, and the fear we mask, leave our brain craving something. Pseudo-joy is the term we use to describe the things the brain craves in the absence of genuine joy. Pseudo-joy is what we feel when something stimulates the pleasure center of the brain in a way that mimics the joy feeling. Pseudo-joy is artificial and temporary and can never replace the genuine joyful relationships that our brain needs. In this chapter, we are going to take a look at pseudo-joy, pain from a lack of joy and BEEPS.

Shelia's story

My mom and dad married just two weeks after their high school graduation. In between the births of my two brothers Sean and Luke, Grace entered the world with a defective heart. Grace lived nineteen months. My dad was distraught after losing his sweet princess daughter. My mom never recovered.

Five years after Grace died, my mother discovered she was pregnant with twins. Dad, overjoyed at the arrival of his fraternal twin girls, exclaimed, "The Lord took one and gave me two!" However, I looked like Grace and reminded my mom of her grave loss. I believe she took one look at me, and had a difficult, if not impossible, experience bonding with me. My tow-head, blonde wisps of hair and light eyes made me the epitome of Grace, while Ella's chocolate hair and big brown eyes set her apart from Grace, at least in appearance. I think it was my mom's lack of resiliency and low-joy that made it hard for her to attach to me.

Grandma, in her thick, Southern accent, often recounted the story of the day Ella and I arrived home from the hospital.

"You girls couldn't have looked more different. Shelia, you had a head so bald everybody thought you were a little boy. Ella, you had a head full of hair, and you were the spittin' image of my own baby pictures. Honey, you still look just like your ole grandma. On the day Luke saw you for the first time, he announced in his five-year old voice, 'I want this one,' pointing at Ella. 'Sean, you get that one!'"

Everyone laughed and said to Luke, "Oh, how cute you are!" Grandma got a kick out of the story, but each time she recounted the events of that day, I felt lost and lonely. I now believe Luke had picked up on my mother's feelings about me and mimicked them. Ella was embraced. And with no one to see my value, I've struggled with bonding all my life.

Luke's action on that first day he met us set the tone for how he would treat me for the rest of our growing up years. He called me Fatso in place of my real name. He taunted me and offered to stop calling me Fatso if I would get him a glass of iced tea. I succumbed to his demands, desperate for him to stop. Each time I caved and brought him the iced tea, he replied, "Thanks, Fatso." Ella often sided with him in his taunts, and together they pronounced, "You're too sensitive." I never felt good enough. This belief caused me to be fearful and anxious all the time. In spite of this, I knew that Luke and Ella loved me, but none of us were equipped with the capacity to demonstrate our love and affection for each other. Without learning protector skills, our predator and possum reactions seemed normal.

Ella was tiny, and Mom nicknamed her Peanut. She called me Popcorn. In contrast to Ella, I looked chubby, so Luke pounced on what he perceived as my weakness. Because he called me Fatso I believed I was fat. Until I was an adult, I believed our nicknames had to do with our size. In retrospect, it's clear that I was a normal-sized little girl, but my reaction to Luke's name-calling developed into a food addiction. My mom didn't cook for us very often, but when she did, the food was yummy. I loved it when she made chicken and rice in the Crock-pot, but I have few memories of eating home-cooked meals except at Grandma's house. My mom's preference for feeding us involved loading us into the green Grand Prix and heading for the fast food drive-through window. I'd order a certain cheeseburger with fries and a soda. I'd scarf it down, usually before we exited the parking lot. At the chicken franchise, I'd yank the skin off of a chicken breast, inhale it, and give the white meat to Ella. This meant I filled up on the fatty part and missed out on much needed protein. I experienced great comfort and pseudo-joy from eating, and I became "Fatso."

As a young adult, I moved from Texas to the Los Angeles area. I needed to escape a relational entanglement. My addiction to food escalated and I was now using food to protect myself from intimacy, especially with men. My attachment to food was much stronger than my attachment to people. I was living 1500 miles from my family, and soon I realized I spent most of my time alone, except when I was working. I continued our childhood pattern of running out for fast food and still ate most of my meals in my car. If I went to a restaurant, I went alone. I'd bring a book or work to do, so no one seemed to notice I was dining by myself. I also went to movies alone and pigged out on chocolate and diet soda. The darkness of the theater provided the perfect atmosphere for me to nurture and hide my food addiction.

I preferred life this way. I did whatever I wanted; I ate whatever I wanted. This lifestyle I created provided me with a type of pseudo-joy. I believed I was free. But I was lonely, depressed and clinically obese. Each of these factors fostered more loneliness, more depression, and more weight gain.

I devoted my life and resources to teaching instead of creating my own family. In my classroom, I felt successful and safe and experienced much pseudo-joy on a daily basis. I was in control. I knew what was expected. The daily routine helped me deal with the overwhelming depression that flooded me each day as soon as I'd get into my car to drive home. My addictions to food and to work consumed me. My depression kept me isolated and lonely. It was many years before I discovered I had no idea what real joy was.

Growing joy and belonging started for me in my classroom. I focused on propagating joy into the next generation of students. I even spent significant time and energy exploring ways to build joy amongst teachers at my school site. Working with Jim, Ed and Chris on the development of *Joy Starts Here*, however, jolted me awake to aspects of my life I'd been ignoring. I'd done little to confront my food BEEPS. I met with my doctor and a nutritionist and made some radical changes. I learned how to properly feed my body, and I began practicing a new way of eating. I listened to Jim's talks on "Attachment to God," in which he explores how we are meant to attach to the feeder and not to the food. I recognized that my attachment to food needed to be shifted back to an attachment to God. I invited Immanuel to help me with the shift and I got to work.

The process of releasing food as my main source of comfort and self-soothing has been challenging but rewarding. It has meant that I've had to lean into God when I feel any type of upset rather than resort to my usual strategy of stuffing my face. While my body has changed, and that is definitely a plus, the real redemption has occurred in my growing attachment to God as my feeder, as well as my increasing ability to be tender toward my own weakness.

Masks and pseudo-joy

As Shelia's story illustrates, it is very difficult to grow a joyful identity when attachments are not firmly rooted in joy, leaving loneliness, anxiety and fear as the relational norm. In response to the shame and relational pain, Shelia learned to wear a mask to hide her pain and stop the constant criticisms and painful comparisons. She attached to food and work instead of people for comfort and relief. As Shelia's story also illustrates, those of us from low-joy families can learn a tender response to our own weaknesses. We can glue ourselves to the God who feeds us.

Shelia is definitely not the only one who learned to wear a mask to hide her shame, weaknesses and vulnerabilities in an attempt to avoid future pain. Without high-joy interactions, many of us missed the relational and emotional foundation we needed for a strong, consistent identity. Instead, our identities developed in response to fear, anxiety and pain. Our masks evolved to hide our weaknesses. Masks may all look a bit different, but they all attempt to make us feel stronger around people. We remain stuck because no matter how hard we try to mask our weaknesses, masks can never bring us joy. As a result, we all crave pseudo-joy to help manage our pain, emotions, relationships and fears.

Masks make pseudo-identity likely

A foundation of joy from high-joy environments is necessary for our brain to develop healthy emotional and relational skills and a strong, stable identity. We grow to become the people we are created and designed to be! The lack of joy causes us to develop emotional and relational skills that are partially formed or weak. Our identity and self-image tend to be inconsistent, incomplete and less relational than God's design for our lives. Instead of learning to live from the heart Jesus gave us, we develop a false identity based on our lack of joy. We call this false identity a pseudo-identity.

A false sense of self is rarely something we consciously choose. Our lack of joy simply causes the chemistry, structure and organization of the brain to be malformed. The lack of joy also damages the development of our relational attachment center (which helps us bond with others), as well as our fear and anxiety center (which helps us evaluate life, relationships and the world around us). Because all of these exist completely below our level of consciousness, we cannot directly control or access any of these essential areas of the brain, which are foundational for the development and formation of our identity. Regrettably, when our identity rests upon a faulty foundation, it will be malformed and we become far less than God designed for our lives. Our pseudo-identity grows in place of our true, God-given identity. How do pseudo-identities and pseudo-joy grow?

Low joy environments, fear and anxiety

Our brain needs a high-joy environment with mom, dad and caregivers to help us learn to regulate pain, pleasure and emotions internally. Low-joy environments prevent the brain from learning to regulate internally. Joy brings appropriate value to relationships with other people and God. Joyful interactions help our brain develop relational capacity and learn to recover from difficult emotions. In contrast, low-joy environments prevent us from learning to value relationships appropriately. Low-joy prevents us from developing relational skills.

The inability to regulate emotions is common in low-joy families where fear or anxiety is common. While parents and caregivers who are empowered by joy attach to us securely, low-joy families connect from fear and anxiety. While fear may be harder for some of us to identify, feelings of anxiety are easier to notice.

In every low-joy environment, fear and anxiety, rather than joy, propagate. Fear and anxiety shape the structure, function, organization and chemistry of our brain, as well as our identity. The brain is unable to find a stable foundation of joy to regulate primary emotions, pain and pleasure appropriately. Our brain becomes wired so that it is difficult to connect without overwhelming or scaring people. We are left guessing how to fit in. We quickly learn to wear masks in an attempt to appear stronger. In the absence of joy to help regulate pain, pleasure and emotions internally, the brain craves an external source of artificial joy to do what it is unable to do for itself. Strong cravings for pseudo-joy are inevitable.

Attachment pain

Attachment pain is a lonely, isolated feeling that follows insecure attachments, fear bonds, loss of someone and broken relationships. Attachment pain is excruciatingly painful and is the deepest level of distress we can experience. The attachment pain in Shelia's family left her feeling as if she "was never good enough to fit in."

One of the most difficult characteristics of attachment pain is that it adds intensity to everything. When attachment pain is unrecognized, it causes us to overreact. Since attachment pain starts below our level of conscious awareness, we must learn to spot it.

Attachment pain is inevitable. We live in a world in which things fall apart, relationships rupture, people move away and all of us die. Everyone from protectors to predators to possums will experience attachment pain at some point in life. Even those of us with strong joy skills and a solid joyful identity will still experience attachment pain.

Attachment pain can be overwhelming, especially when our brain lacks training in joy. Attachment pain is difficult to regulate internally and, because it adds intensity to everything, it causes even the strongest masks to slip. Attachment pain drives some predators to drop the pretense of being nice. Possums who are experiencing intense attachment pain lose their ability to mask vulnerability. Attachment pain drives possums to hidebecause isolation seems better than becoming food for predators. Possums that stay exposed will express increasing anxiety with emotionally intense outbursts.

Attachment pain almost always leads to intense cravings because it is so difficult to regulate internally. When attachment pain is present and our capacity for joy is low, our brain involuntarily craves relief. The brain begins an automatic search for a source of external pseudo-joy to help regulate internal distress. Because attachment pain exists at such a deep level of the brain, we may not even be aware of our cravings for counterfeit joy. The presence of intense cravings causes predators and possums to mask their cravings and hide sources of pseudo-joy. They do not want their weaknesses exposed.

Ed learned that when he starts craving junk food, especially carbs, chips or sugar, he is experiencing attachment pain. It is easy for him to notice his pseudo-joy cravings at the grocery store when the sweets, chips and empty carbs seem to jump into his cart. These cravings are sometimes subtle, sometimes powerful and usually become highly problematic attachments. Ed has also discovered that by keeping his appreciation levels high, his attachment pain, physical pain and pseudo-joy cravings are much more manageable.

Type A and B trauma

The experience of unresolved trauma, especially early in life, leaves us with chronic joy deficits and high levels of fear and anxiety. Our foundations for life and identity are malformed. Trauma also strongly impacts our ability to regulate upsetting emotions, especially if the trauma memory is unrecognized. Any form of trauma damages our ability to connect with others. Trauma is a joy killer and leads to wearing masks to hide our hurts.

There are two types of trauma, Type A and Type B. Type B traumas are the bad things that overwhelm our existing capacity. Type B traumas include everything we typically consider traumatic such as verbal, emotional, physical or sexual abuse. The list also includes assault, bullying, untimely death and natural disasters. When we grow up in a low-joy environment we will lack the ability to resolve Type B traumas. We are easily triggered into distressing emotional states and find it difficult to form life-giving relationships. Fear and anxiety grow and we wear masks to hide our pain. Type B traumas leave our brain overwhelmed and craving pseudo-joy.

Type A trauma is the absence of the good and necessary things that we need to grow a healthy identity and body. Type A traumas include growing up in a chronic low-joy environment, abandonment, neglect, malnutrition or the lack of appropriate physical touch. Type A trauma is powerful but often unrecognized. Type A trauma produces low joy capacity, unregulated emotions and unsatisfying relationships with others. The relational effects of Type A trauma leave the brain craving pseudo-joy. People with Type A trauma wear masks that hide the lack of relational skills so they appear normal. Possums guess at what "normal" might be to mask their lack of skills. Predators wear a strong mask to make sure that nobody discovers their lack of relational skills.

The presence of predators

The lack of relational skills inevitably reduces us to predators. We must then disguise ourselves in sheep's clothing or display open aggression. We must dominate others and remain at the top of the food chain. As predators we wear masks to look like sheep. Our masks make us appear friendly, approachable and trustworthy and allow us to secretly discover the weaknesses of others for our own purposes. We will use weaknesses for intimidating, threatening, shaming, manipulating and controlling to maintain our position. Before long, we are back behind our mask hunting for fresh prey.

John was a predatory leader in sheep's clothing. At first glance John appeared warm and caring. He performed well outwardly and was able to convince others that he was quite spiritual and highly trustworthy. His appearance of empathy encouraged those who were vulnerable to confide in him. John seemed to be the ideal leader. Those who mistakenly trusted John found another person entirely. John demanded that people only say nice things about him and his leadership. He directed his fury at those who did not praise him. Whenever friends or coworkers tried to correct John, he would attack, punish and break off relationships. Those who trusted John ended up fearing his anger, dreading his outbursts and doing their best to avoid rejection. John was a master at using guilt and weakness to get what he wanted. He set himself up as the king of his castle by standing on the backs of weaker members who were too fearful to tell John the truth about his damaging leadership style. Possum responses kept John in power.

While John had to hide his predatory nature, other predators have so much power they do not need a mask. Every herd member knows and fears these predators for their ruthless aggression and lack of compassion. Without empathy they actively persecute protectors, weaker predators or possums and enjoy making examples of the weak. Open contempt, scorn, humiliation and shame intimidate any challengers.

Pharaoh in the book of Exodus exemplified a ruthless and openly predatory individual at the top of his food chain. He kept Israel in cruel slavery. When challenged by Moses to free the slaves, Pharaoh responded with open scorn and violence. He told the people they were lazy and beat the Israelite foremen. To show the people he was in full control he punished the entire workforce and increased their workload. He was determined to use every means at his disposal to keep the weak in their place. After God intervened Pharaoh falsely promised Moses that he would free the slaves if the plagues stopped. As soon as the plague stopped, Pharaoh reasserted his control and broke his promise. Right up until his defeat at the Red Sea, Pharaoh was preoccupied with remaining in control through intimidation and violence.

Clearly, the predator-possum dynamics bring joy to no one. Predators in all forms kill joy, life and relationships. Predators believe they are always right and everyone else is wrong. Those who challenge the opinion of a predator are likely to be eaten or driven out of the herd. Possums feel better if they conceal weaknesses and avoid being noticed. Nobody is glad to be together, and each herd member seeks his or her own individual preservation. Attachments to pseudo-joy on the part of both predators and prey will result.

The lack of return to joy skills

The last factor that we want to consider that leads to pseudo-joy is the inability to return to joy when we experience upsetting emotions. We will learn much more about returning to joy in part three. For now, it is important to recognize that the inability to stay relationally connected with others when we experience emotions is a strong incentive to find pseudo-joy.

There are six basic unpleasant emotions that we must learn to handle relationally. These emotions are anger, fear, sadness, shame, disgust and hopeless despair. We must learn to handle the emotion we are feeling and stay connected relationally with people we love.

In high-joy environments, parents and caregivers help us when we experience these emotions and remain relationally connected with us. From these interactions we learn that we do not have to disconnect from others when we are upset, and that distressing emotions are an opportunity to grow stronger joy bonds with others. When we learn to handle emotions relationally, our brain learns to regulate them internally and is much less likely to crave pseudo-joy.

However, when we lack return to joy skills we are likely to become stuck. When we are stuck in negative emotions, our relational brain disconnects from other people even if we desire to stay connected. Our brain has to learn to stay relational when negative emotions arise. The combination of staying stuck in negative emotions and relational disconnection leaves our brain in acute distress. Unable to return to joy, our brain craves relief from pain.

Pseudo-joy and BEEPS

BEEPS is the term we use to describe all kinds of pseudo-joy. As we have seen, BEEPS are the Behaviors, Events, Experiences, People or Substances that the brain uses to regulate pain, pleasure and emotion when it is unable to regulate internal distress. While BEEPS come in an infinite variety, in this chapter we will only cover performance for approval, codependency, food, sex and drugs including alcohol. Ed's book *Becoming the Face of Grace* describes BEEPS in the context of leadership while the *Connexus*™ progam helps recovery.

Performance and approval

BEEPS related to work, performance, approval and perfection can be intoxicating sources of pseudo-joy. These BEEPS allow us to wear a "strong" mask by appearing to be successful, competent and respected. Because these BEEPS give both predators and possums the appearance of being strong, we are able to conceal weaknesses. It is hard to seem vulnerable when we look like perfect parents, teachers, pastors, ministry leaders, employers or employees. We may also work hard to gain the approval of "all the right people" in order to feel more secure. Performance and approval allow us to avoid rejection and attract positive attention instead of joy.

Working long hours, avoiding mistakes and doing a good job are not harmful! The damage comes when results become more important than relationships. The pseudo-joy we experience from these BEEPS derives from our mask. While temporarily stopping the cravings, performance and approval can never bring us the kind of genuine joy our brain needs.

Codependency

Codependency is a common form of pseudo-joy based upon the attempt to manipulate others to get what we want. We justify this as being "helpful." Codependency is a form of manipulation and not a characteristic of relationships filled with authentic joy. Without genuine relationships we do not grow joy. Codependency is common in both predators and possums but codependent patterns only create pseudo-joy. For predators they create the illusion of dominance, for possums the illusion of acceptance and safety.

Codependent predators actively seek to manipulate the behavior of others. The position of power allows us to dictate behaviors in families, churches, ministries and schools. When we want to be considered benevolent, we justify our codependent behavior by telling ourselves that we are "doing it for their own good" and that we alone "know what's best." We mistakenly believe that we can maintain order and avoid chaos by being the one with absolute control. By rewarding those who "behave," and using toxic shame and contempt for those that do not, we create a low-joy life that promotes BEEPS.

As possums, we engage in codependency to avoid the loss of a valued relationship. To hold on to our relational partners, we will grow a pseudo-identity to please them and avoid conflict. We do almost anything to avoid rejection. We rescue others from pain and make excuses for inappropriate behavior or abuse to avoid "rocking the boat." Even though we become progressively more damaged our codependent behaviors keeps us stuck.

Attachments to food

Food is an excellent gift from God that can easily become a source of pseudo-joy to both predators and possums. An entire discussion of the dynamics of food as an attachment to BEEPS is beyond the scope of this chapter. However, food as a source of pseudo-joy is what we want to discuss.

God has designed us to attach to the people who feed us. Through the use of senses such as taste, smell and later sight, our developing brain begins bonding with others when they feed us. Our mother is biologically equipped to feed us. Our bond with her and other primary feeders can be exceptionally strong. When joyful feeders are attentive to our needs, we develop secure bonds with them.

When the person who feeds us is not emotionally available, we automatically bond to the strongest remaining source of pleasure, which is the food. We bond with the food that comforts us rather than the one who feeds us. Our attachment to food for pseudo-joy begins early, because food with fat, sugars and salt is a much more reliable source of pleasure and comfort than relationships. Food becomes a non-relational attachment to BEEPS.

Attachments to sex

Sex easily becomes pseudo-joy. Though it makes us uncomfortable to talk about it, the powerful rush of chemicals experienced at orgasm strongly stimulates the pleasure and reward centers of the brain. Orgasm can effectively, but temporarily, mute attachment pain and relational distress. When orgasm repeatedly occurs apart from joyful relationship with our spouse, it can become a BEEPS.

Sex is increasingly becoming an issue for predators and possums in families, churches, ministries and schools. The rise of internet pornography has created highly addictive forms of pseudo-joy that many pursue secretly. Pornography helps temporarily relieve distress and increases pleasure for both men and women. Because it is so easy to access privately, predators and possums are both able to keep this weakness concealed.

Attachments to alcohol or other drugs

Alcohol or other drugs are especially problematic when the brain lacks a foundation of joy. These forms of pseudo-joy release powerful pleasure-causing chemicals in the brain that mimic the effects of joy. Our brains experience euphoria, a false sense of well-being and impaired judgment that causes us to use more alcohol or other drugs. In this state, the pain of weakness and vulnerability may be numbed and temporarily forgotten. Furthermore, because they stimulate the brain so powerfully, ongoing use of these BEEPS can create a pseudo-identity centered on alcohol or other drugs.

While alcohol and illegal drugs are common BEEPS, the abuse of prescription medications has grown tremendously. We are watching the number of pseudo-joy related deaths rise. Whenever pseudo-joy connections exceed the strength of our joyful connections with God and with others, we develop serious attachments to BEEPS.

How am I doing?

By now, we should be asking questions like:

- Where does my joy come from?
- Is it important for me to appear strong, even when I feel weak?
- Do I feel like I am the same person on the inside, as I appear to be on the outside?
- Do I amplify my distress and displeasure when I am upset?
- How strong are my attachments to pseudo-joy or any of the BEEPS discussed in this chapter?

Deep down, what we want most is to grow a joyful identity that can replace our masks, pseudo-identity and pseudo-joy! In order for this material to transform your life reflect on the sources of joy or pseudo-joy that shaped your identity. As long as it is safe, get some feedback from other people. Discuss your tendency to wear a strong mask. Ask a friend, "Do you think I wear a mask to make me look strong?"

Joy Actions

Home: Thank the person in your family that you feel understands you best.

School: Take a picture of something you appreciate to school and tell someone.

Church: Think of someone at church who was willing to express their weakness or vulnerability and thank them.

Assessment Of Pseudo-Joy

1. I try to keep my mistakes a secret.

    No secrets 0 1 2 3 4 5 6 7 8 9 10 *Always*

2. Our diet is too high in comfort foods.

    Great diet 0 1 2 3 4 5 6 7 8 9 10 *We eat for comfort*

3. I often keep doing things in secret that make me feel ashamed.

    Never 0 1 2 3 4 5 6 7 8 9 10 *Constantly*

4. We spend/shop too much.

    No debts 0 1 2 3 4 5 6 7 8 9 10 *Huge problem*

5. I can't let go of a past relationship.

    I can move on 0 1 2 3 4 5 6 7 8 9 10 *I keep holding on*

6. I think that someone at home is trying to keep certain behaviors secret.

    We are all angels 0 1 2 3 4 5 6 7 8 9 10 *Huge problem*

7. This past week, I craved things that are not good for me _____ times.

    0 1 2 3 4 5 6 7 8 9 10$^+$

8. I think that someone at home has binges or abuses power.

    No one 0 1 2 3 4 5 6 7 8 9 10 *Huge problem*

9. Relationships feel very confusing to me.

    Not at all 0 1 2 3 4 5 6 7 8 9 10 *Constantly*

10. I am close to ____ people who abuse prescriptions, drugs or alcohol.

    0 1 2 3 4 5 6 7 8 9 10$^+$

Total your scores here. _____
Mark the matching spot on the scale.

0   10   20   30   40   50   60   70   80   90   100

My Strong Mask Bible Study

Think back on something you appreciate and spend two minutes enjoying appreciation. Next, ask God to make this study interesting for you. Now read the following passage from the epistles.

Scripture Ephesians 6:1-20 Read then review for each question.

Chapter Three Question: According to verse 10 we are to "be strengthened" (present, passive, imperative). The tense of the verb "be strengthened" means that we are to receive strength from God like a boy would be hit by a baseball. How does being strengthened in the Lord compare to our being strong on our own in this passage?

Weakness and Strength Questions:
1. Who are the weak or strong in this passage?
2. What kind of interaction does God desire between weak and strong?
3. What do we learn about joy and shalom (everything works together) from this passage?

Personal Story Question: When have you seen compassion toward weakness that helped you understand God better?

Whole Bible Question: What Bible stories and verses have you heard someone use to argue that we should be strong and tough?

Wrap-Up Minute: What do you now know that you didn't know before this week's study?

My Life Model Exercises

At the end of each of the following exercises, notice how your body feels and what changed both during and after you practiced appreciation. (If your answer is, "It felt good," then ask yourself how you know it felt good. For example, "I felt a lightness in my chest, or my breathing is deeper and I can breathe better." Be specific.)

Complete these exercises before coming to group.

Individual: Family
1. Over a one-week time frame, tell each of your family members three of your favorite shared memories. Include aspects of their personality that you appreciate from the shared memories.
2. Express how much each family member means to you.
3. How did your family members respond?

Individual: School
1. As faculty, staff, or administration at your school, express appreciation to as many of your coworkers (and students) as you can this week. It helps to mention aspects of their personality that you appreciate.
2. What did you notice when you shared the appreciation?

Individual: Church
1. Express appreciation to as many church staff and volunteers as you can this week. It helps to mention aspects of their personality that you appreciate.
2. What did you notice when you shared the appreciation?

When you meet as a group, share your results.

Chapter Four

The Transformation Zone

It is time for Christians everywhere to become joy starters. We have our private joys: our baby is born, our daughter graduates or a vacation brings us together, but joy that spreads starts in the transformation zone. Transformation is a change of identity, something we often desire but just as often find elusive. Yet, we have all experienced moments of transformation, some that last, some for the better, some for the worse, and some we wish we could experience again. Wanting and choosing to change is not enough. Transformation into the identity God has for us requires our engagement with God, ourselves and others.

In this chapter, we are introduced to the transformation zone through telling Immanuel stories and reviewing theory that demonstrate how joy starts and is propagated. Immanuel stories are stories where we are aware of God being with us. Sharing our Immanuel stories helps us know where we have been, who we are and where we want to go. Theory is also essential to finding the conditions necessary for transformation. We introduce how the application of Life Model theory leads to transformation in our homes, schools and churches.

We call the active cluster of conditions necessary for transformation the transformation zone. In order to live in the transformation zone, we need to be able to share our Immanuel stories and know and understand the theoretical basis for creating, sustaining, and propagating joy. For joy to transform our community or group, the following three conditions must be in place.

1) The weak and strong are together and interacting
2) Tender responses to weakness are the rule
3) The interactive presence of God (Immanuel) maintains shalom

Come with us and discover the transformation zone that leads to joy.

Chris' Story

Three hours earlier, I had been sitting in a bar surrounded by laughter and smiling faces. A gal named Becky approached and invited me to a party at her place, knowing that I was the life of any party. Everyone in college seemed to like me, good grades came easily, and I played several sports competitively. But on my way to Becky's party, I was arrested for driving under the influence (DUI). Sitting in jail and waiting to be bailed out, I knew something was not right. I felt depleted and defeated. I would not have thought to call it "low joy" at the time, but if someone had asked, I would have nodded yes. "Something is wrong with my life," I thought to myself, "but what?"

I grew up in an average Christian mid-western family. My parents, Rick and Sandy, worked hard and hoped to raise above-average children. Our public schools were good. My grandparents lived nearby. Mom made sure that my siblings and I attended church most Sundays. I seemed to thrive. I was the middle child and played baseball, basketball and other sports quite well. I had lots of friends and family support. I was attentive in school, didn't get in trouble, went to church, and even prayed. During the summers, I attended Bible classes and church camp when I was not busy with sports and friends. I had many strengths, and the opportunities to develop them. My life was good. It was the kind of life all parents want for their children.

Here I was about to graduate from college, but I sat in a jail thinking, "My life is over," and wishing I were dead. However, I was a strong young man, so after a few days I determined to make the best of the situation. I found a job where I did not need a driver's license. My work involved counseling in a shelter for traumatized people. I figured I could get my life together while helping some people whose joy was lower than mine. I was about to discover what happens when the weak and the strong come together.

Chris has to interact with weaker people: It is safe to say that I had never known people who had been used for sex traffic as children. What I discovered in my first three days at the center made me want to crawl out of my skin. Emotions and problems reverberated throughout the shelter. Unhappy feelings seemed contagious and were often amplified in seconds. While the staff seemed to take this in stride, I knew that whatever it took to stay there was something I did not have. It was not like I didn't care. I found myself drawn to the people and distressed at the horrors they had suffered. I wished they would all get better, but even as staff prayed for those in need, I was planning to pack and leave.

Without being able to express it in words, I was recognizing that being able to party is not the same as bringing joy to people in pain. My friends and I had always used much of our social energy keeping each other out of pain and away from weakness. When people lacked the skills to look good and their pain flooded in, I always felt weaker than they did. I did not like this feeling. It was time to go home to my comfort zone and leave this nightmare behind.

Chris has an Immanuel experience: In my room that night, I decided to be a Christian about my situation, and I prayed before I packed. As I prayed, a thought went through my mind. It was an odd thought that meant little to me at the moment and made no sense. The strange thought sounded like a Bible sort of thing because it was a word and a number, "Isaiah 61." I pulled out a Bible and scanned the table of contents. There was an Isaiah. "What is the chance there are 61 chapters?" I wondered. There were! I was so surprised I checked a second Bible. Isaiah 61 was there too.

What I read next spoke about profound changes and the restoration of joy to all the low-joy places on earth. Even more amazing at the moment was that I knew God was with me. As I read and thought about the content, my viewpoint and feelings seemed to shift. I felt more peaceful and, strangely enough, felt that I should stay. Little could I imagine the transformation that would come into my life over the next few years of living with the weak.

What I was discovering is the heart of this book. Transformations of character only happen when the weak and the strong continue interacting with each other. If we stop and think of the times when our character made remarkable changes or, for that matter, the character of anyone we know, we will find this exact pattern. The weak and the strong must engage in life together for either one to make a lasting change.

Not all interactions between the weak and strong result in positive changes. After all, the abused people I met had interacted with stronger people before and that is when they were hurt. Strong people who hurt the weak respond like predators instead of protectors when they spot weakness. All of us have these predator responses wired into our minds, making predator responses possible for everyone, but some people have a tender response to weakness that brings out a protector response instead. Joy always grows in the presence of protectors. Predators create a low-joy environment. I would soon discover that to live with the weak, I would need to face my own predator responses but this is also where joy starts.

Without ongoing interaction, the strong do not change and the weak do not maintain their gains. I, however, was way outside my comfort zone and prepared to use my strength to get back. One difference between the weak and strong is that the weak cannot find or stay in a comfort zone. Even with a tender response toward weakness, I would have disengaged without something else. When I experienced God's active presence and shalom (peace), I was able to leave my comfort zone and stay in the transformation zone. Staying in the transformation zone requires an awareness of God's presence. With God's help I could see people differently. With God's presence I was not alone. Perhaps most importantly, with God's help, I could learn I did not have to try to be strong. I began developing the Christian character growth that we call maturity.

Chris meets Jim and learns how multigenerational community develops maturity: While I was able to stay in the shelter and learn to seek God's presence, I found that I was becoming very effective at helping. I was not even sure what I should be doing, but I was eager to learn. About that time, I began to learn the Life Model through the teachings of Dr. Jim Wilder, a neurotheologian who visited and spoke on the importance of joy. Jim, the director of Shepherd's House, played a central role in developing the Life Model. He provided me with both a theoretical model to understand the question that I had asked myself in jail, "What is wrong with me?" and a practical model of how it looks to be more mature. Now I had someone stronger to help me with my own weakness. One generation was helping the next. Since the Life Model is based on this principle that the weak and the strong must help each other across the generations in the interactive presence of the Immanuel God who is with us, my relationship with Jim served as the model for how to start living a more joy-filled life. The Life Model taught me that joy is relational as when two or more people are delighted to be together. Joy grows out of love bonds and tender responses to others. Joy helps people discover who they really are, build strong bonds, develop character, resolve traumas, overcome problems and develop the relational joy skills we call maturity.

What Jim taught Chris about joy, an introduction to the theory

Each one of us enters life wired for joy. Joy means someone is glad to be with me. We take joy very personally; we also take the lack of joy personally. Joy grows when people see my weakness and needs, yet still take care of me. Joy disappears when people ignore me or exploit my weaknesses.

How much joy we experience with others establishes our emotional capacity to deal with life. Shaping my brain's abilities, chemistry and strength is more a matter of practicing joy with gentle protectors than it is genetics. In the early years, our joy capacity is at the mercy of our families. Families that are gentle with their young and protective of each other's weaknesses will create high-joy homes. Families who pick at each other's faults, take advantage of being stronger and use weaknesses in ways that create pain will become low-joy homes.

Children who grow up in low-joy homes get a second chance when they go to grade school. Many a child who did not know about joy at home has found joy in a classroom with a new realization of hope. Many children have discovered in friends or in a special teacher the joy they never found before. Here is someone who is really glad to be with me. Here is someone who sees my weakness as an opportunity to help me grow instead of something to despise or exploit. Quite a few of these children go on to become teachers themselves, giving other children a second start in life.

The third start in life often comes at church. Strangely, if a low-joy family already attends church, their children may not find joy there. However, people from low-joy homes who are new to church often discover a God of love and the welcome of a church family. For them, church provides the joy their souls have been seeking all their lives.

When low-joy families attend church regularly but stay low joy, something is not working. The most common causes are that the church does not adequately engage the weak and strong members together in ways that are life-changing. The church becomes separated into comfort zones where people keep their weaknesses hidden by interacting with people who are similar to them. Children from low-joy homes decide eventually that the church has no solution, and perhaps everyone else there is in the same trouble.

Being joy starters is our intended nature. Every three-month old baby is a natural joy starter. We might expect joy to grow all our lives. Other people would create joy for us when they were glad to be with us and we would generate joy being glad to be with them. The three most likely sources of joy in our lives — families, schools and churches — would reliably teach joy since joy is the most powerful factor in determining the ultimate success of all three institutions. If only we were undamaged human beings, we would grow and propagate joy all our lives. However, many of us find ourselves wounded and disconnected struggling to exist in a low-joy lifestyle. What can we do about it? Let us examine our lives a moment and see how we can make joy start here with us.

Chris reviews his life

As I think back on the start of my transformation, I can still remember the deep desire to protect the precious souls I met. I was learning that being a Christian meant interacting with the weak as well as the strong. Somehow I do not think that was taught much in my family, church or school. I did have a tender heart toward weakness but, in spite of my tender response to the weak, I quickly noticed it was hard to be consistent.

I liked being a protector as long as I felt strong. When I felt hurt, I would fight my predator urges to snap, pounce, or use others to make me feel better. When I felt attacked, I played a possum role, hoping to be left alone. Sometimes it was very hard to stay engaged, and that created a tension in my relationships with people whose joy levels were lower than mine. I wanted to do more, but I felt severely limited in my capacity to connect, comfort, and join my friends when they were upset. My performance was only as good as my ability to manage my own pain. I prayed that I would not drown and pleaded with God for some kind of change.

Immanuel faithfully met me and pleasantly surprised me by reiterating, "Jesus is glad to be with me." These Immanuel moments kept me going but something was still wrong. As I learned more about my weakness, I would also interact with stronger people who demonstrated Immanuel's joy and strength in action. And something did change. My strength started to increase. I could love, lead and serve with much more creativity, availability and capacity. The combination of serving the weak and interacting with the strong bolstered my hope and added much needed resilience. My maturity increased. I was living the transformation I had been searching for. All the busyness, partying and happy facade of my college years had covered my need for genuine, relational joy.

As my joy grew I started to evaluate a familiar, internal radar I had tried to hide. Like a magnet, I was always drawn to pursue relationships with girls I perceived as vulnerable or insecure. I felt compelled to develop a relationship with them. I knew the words that would make them feel special. By trying to "fix" these girls, I hoped they would want to stay with me. Rather than safeguard their weaknesses, like a true protector would, I pounced on their need in order to make me feel special. Fear motivated this predatory pattern. Admitting my predatory responses to mature men and women resulted in the appropriate training on how to use my personal power to protect rather than pounce. Protecting brought the joy I really wanted.

With my protector skills growing, another response surfaced. I realized that when interactions or relationships did not go my way, I could not get back to joy. When that happened a possum response came out, and I would roll over and play dead. Shame feelings seemed to be the worst. When I encountered shame, a record started in my mind. "Chris, you are no good. You will never amount to anything. Give up. You are a failure." I felt like road kill. The possum response also followed any correction, criticism or failure. This time, I needed to grow protector skills that would help me return to joy in this stunted part of my identity. As I shared this weakness with Jim and other mature people, I started to learn that failure is not death. Joy gave me strength to feel big feelings. I learned that being upset would not be the end of me.

Until this point in 2002, the Life Model remained a powerful explanatory theory based on the best of theology and neuroscience, but no one had attempted to see if low-joy people could become high-joy by learning joy skills. People were encouraged by my growth, but as my joy began to climb, I was curious to see if joy could spread enough to help the hurting people I saw each day. When Jim proposed an experiment in propagating joy, I was more than ready to help.

Putting the Life Model theory to work

Together, Jim and Chris began developing and testing a series of exercises to help people acquire and then strengthen joy skills. These exercises were named *THRIVE Training*. The results of using these exercises were immediate for most people who had a partner with whom to learn and practice. Progress was much slower and more complicated for people who had no one in their life who was regularly available and glad to be with them. Regrettably, this meant that the exercises were too difficult for the people with the lowest joy. Still, the exercises were proving very helpful to people in leadership or who had families. We now knew that if we were low-joy early in our lives, it was possible to become high-joy people. Joy, however, did not spread very quickly, but for the first time Jim and Chris were hopeful that joy could be grown, nurtured and propagated. They began working to improve the exercises.

It soon became clear that Life Model skill exercises fell into two different categories. Understanding the difference is crucial because one kind of exercises requires a teacher, and the other only requires a practice partner. The most common misunderstanding Jim and Chris encountered was the assumption that everyone had the skills, so they only needed to practice. This simply was not true.

Life Model relational skills exercises

The first step in developing a skill is acquiring the skill. For this to happen we need someone who possesses that skill who can also teach it to us. Perhaps we want to greet someone in Hungarian. We cannot practice the greeting until someone helps us learn it. The second part of skill training is the practice needed to develop and strengthen the skill so that we can use it effectively. After we have learned the Hungarian greeting, we practice saying it until we get it right and can use it to interact with others.

It's important to note that there is a distinction between learning a skill and practicing that same skill. When we learn a skill for the first time our cognitive process is very different than the cognitive process involved when we practice the skill. This means that there are two types of exercises, one for learning a skill and one for practicing a skill.

As Jim and Chris worked to improve the exercises, their goal was not to simply train people in skills they could use for their private joy. Private joy helps us, but it does not change a low-joy world. They were seeking joy that would spread beyond the people they could train and without requiring the amount of training that Chris and Jim needed to get this far. They called this "self-propagating" relational skills that would continue to spread from person to person. In order to self-propagate, the training must transfer more than the simple skill itself; it also needed to transfer the motivation and identity that goes with using the skill. For instance, we could easily train people to shake pom-poms, but it is much harder to get the average male motivated to become an accomplished pom-pom shaker.

Acquisition exercises

What motivates us to learn new skills? Transferring the motivation is as crucial as transferring the actual skill. Many of us have learned the skill needed to read the Bible and pray. Some of us learned to be motivated by fear and some of us are motivated by love. Those of us motivated by love use our skill to grow a deeper relationship with God. We are happy to teach our skill to others. On the other hand, if we are motivated by fear, propagating this motivation will not produce a relationship with God.

Consider a more complex example, the motivation involved in becoming a protective grandmother. Anyone who has had a baby knows what it takes to get the baby dressed and out the door in time for a social engagement or trip to the store. We know that the likelihood that the baby will fill its diaper is in direct proportion to the social importance of the event. We also know that the chance of getting something smelly on our baby's outfit is directly related to how carefully we choose that outfit. However, consider what happens in non-diaper cultures. In many non-diaper cultures one must also prepare baby for a trip to town, to meet the people of rank, enter the market, and safely keep mother from being soiled while she carries her baby on her back. The solution is simple for a skilled grandmother; we give the baby an enema. We take a little warm water with our mouth, gently spray the water into baby's bottom and rinse out the poo-poo just before leaving for town. There are a few other parts of the procedure to keep in mind that are not as essential here. A limited amount of skill is required to get the baby ready for the trip into town.

Motivation, however, is a much bigger issue. Who actually wants to give baby an enema with their mouth? The feeling of revulsion we have as we think about the ritual is what makes it hard to propagate the motivation part of the skill. Protective grandmothers are motivated to be sure that the baby and mother are received with joy in town. The grandmother feels good about herself and is motivated to regularly and faithfully practice giving baby rinses. The feeling that the baby rinsing skill is part of grandmother's protective identity is much harder to propagate than the physical skill alone. This sense of motivation and identity must be part of what is propagated along with the actual skill.

Consider what happens if we introduce disposable diapers into this non-diaper society. We gain a variety of economic advantages for selling diapers, ecological disadvantages for disposing diapers and some gains and losses for sanitation. What we do not notice is a threat to the intense personal interaction between the three generations that propagates motivation and identity.

Part of the motivation to become a protective grandmother is threatened with extinction. While we like these environmental changes that let us eliminate mouth enemas, they also threaten the specific conditions under which many generations have acquired the motivation to be protective grandmothers.

We are not too concerned if young girls fail to learn how to rinse the poo out of babies with their mouths. We are greatly concerned if girls lose the motivation that is transmitted by the protective grandmothers who regularly prepare babies for a joyful reception in town. The bonded family context provides the conditions needed to acquire the motivation, character and identity that eventually builds a grandmother. Watching nurses give enemas in a medical center will not produce the same results in children. This example demonstrates how crucial parts of our identities begin dropping out of the transmission process and may face extinction in a few generations. We will study this problem in chapter ten.

Strengthening exercises

Practice helps improve speed, increase accuracy, build strength and decrease the amount of mental concentration needed to achieve success. Practice is good for things we already know how to do. We can practice most skills on our own once we learn them from others, but some skills depend on timing, and we need a practice partner to develop timed skills. With our brain's ability to observe and simulate what others have done, we can learn to do many things we have never practiced doing. Much of learning to drive a car starts in this way. Before we ever take the wheel, we have many ideas of how to drive. On the other hand, since we rarely watch people fly airplanes, we feel much more "lost" thinking about how to fly a plane. As soon as we start driving or flying, we discover the task is harder than it looks and we need practice to become skilled.

Practicing the Life Model relational skill exercises builds "capacity," which is another way to say that it becomes a mental habit. Habits change the white matter connections in our brain in ways that greatly improve our speed and accuracy. With more practice and capacity, we can use our skills longer and under more difficult conditions, much like driving practice allows us to drive in traffic, snow, or while someone in the car is asking us questions.

Bringing the weak and strong together

Chris and his wife, Jen, continued developing Life Model exercises for *THRIVE Training*. Together, they organized the *THRIVE* exercises to maximize training effectiveness. This training format was designed to strengthen and train leaders so they could return to their communities and propagate the skills they had learned.

Although *THRIVE Training* remained highly effective, it was limited at first to bonded partners. How would we help people without partners?

Ed helped Jim take theoretical answers from the Life Model and create *Connexus*™ for people who did not have close bonded partners. *Connexus*™ exercises were based upon the brain's family bond pattern where three-way bonds develop joy. Using three-way bonds made the exercises safer and less intense for training people in churches and communities. In time Chris found ways to create a segment of *THRIVE Training* using these three-way interactions as well. (See more in Appendix D)

The fist part of *Connexus*™ was the *Restarting* module, designed to help traumatized and addicted people begin building joy. *Restarting* worked as Ed hoped but did not produce the full transformation zone experience. A sustainable transformation zone only happens when the weak and strong are together, and the strong were missing.

We knew that strong Christians would only stay in the transformation zone if they could experience God's interactive presence. Most strong Christians lack an interactive sense of God with them. David Takle was studying the difficulties strong people experience trying to sense God's presence. David developed the *Forming* module to help people hear and know God.

Restarting, welcomed the weak. *Forming* was a more understandable starting place for the strong. We now had training for both the weak and the strong but how could we encourage the tender responses needed to keep them together? In most settings, the weak and strong avoid each other. They may attend the same church, go to the same schools, or marry into the same family, but there is rarely joy when they are together.

To bring the weak and strong together with tenderness to weakness, Ed and Jim developed the *Belonging* module. In *Belonging*, both the weak and the strong come together. Now we had a community-training environment with all three conditions of the transformation zone. Ed went on to develop other small group and leadership programs you can find in Appendix D.

With some materials for home and church now in place, Shelia began taking joy to school. Shelia was already familiar with the Life Model and *THRIVE Training*. She understood the importance of facilitating interactions between the weak and the strong in the classroom and was committed to spreading joy in a system that is characteristically low-joy. Because of the joy Shelia experienced with a transformational teacher in her own childhood, she is passionate about propagating joy to the next generation at school.

Shelia was not the only educator interested in bringing joy into education. Dr. Bill St Cyr and his wife, Maryellen, see a marvelous harmony between Charlotte Mason's older education methods and the newer neuroscience. Together they created the Ambleside Schools International so that the entire school would be built on joyful learning.

The Life Model continues making inroads into education around the world. After Darv Smith M.D. and his wife Carol attended *THRIVE training*, they introduced elements into the addiction recovery counselor training programs they created for Youth With A Mission (YWAM) through the University of the Nations. Ed, Jim and Chris have taught in many different YWAM schools. Darv arranged for translations of the original Life Model book, *Living From The Heart Jesus Gave You* into Dutch, Russian, Korean and Portuguese.

Jim works with *Life Model Works* where he encourages theory and application development using a standardized vocabulary. The many applications of the Life Model for joyful transformations can be found at joystartshere.com and in Appendix D.

Why doesn't joy spread everywhere?

We might be wondering by now why joy does not simply spread everywhere. Why isn't there more joy? With a little more thought we might wonder why trauma and predator personalities spread quickly, while protectors are harder to find. If joy is what we desire most deeply, shouldn't we be more aware it is what we want? Shouldn't there be more joy around? To understand the answers to these questions, we need to stop and examine joy theory in more detail so we can use the Life Model together and start some joy.

The Life Model

Most of us recognize that a life filled with joy, shalom, maturity and Jesus-like character is the design and goal for Christians. Anyone who has been around for a while understands that developing godly character, then expressing this character under strain, is easier said than done. The Life Model combines the Bible and brain science to grow a fearless people who love like Jesus. This idealized model is a road map to describe human growth and development across the lifespan.

At the heart of human growth is the issue of our true identity. Who we really are comes from our spiritual DNA in the heart that Jesus gives us. We are not the low-joy people we have become. Our true selves and destiny make us all gentle protectors like Jesus.

Jim uses the word, "maturity" in Life Model materials to describe being fully ourselves at every age, in every situation and every relationship. Because joy means "someone is glad to be with me," it is very important to be right about who "me" is. If others like my fake self but would despise my real self, there will be no real joy. Anything that damages our identity also damages our maturity and damages our joy levels.

Holes in our maturity leave low-joy

To grow a full identity means adding new capacities all our lives. The first Life Model book called *Living From The Heart Jesus Gave You* took a chapter for each of the five elements needed to thrive. The five are: belonging, receiving and giving, recovery, maturity and living from the heart Jesus gives. The Life Model created a comprehensive chronology for human maturity from infancy to death. Maturity stages containing the needs and tasks for joyful maturity are found in Appendix C of this book and other Life Model resources.

There are clear signs when a mature identity is missing. A specific type of pain occurs when each step is not fully completed. Along the way the development of a mature identity could be damaged in two ways, by bad things that happen to us (Type B trauma) and the absence of the necessary good things like joy (Type A traumas). *Living From The Heart Jesus Gave You* concludes that the only way to develop this mature identity is for the weak and the strong to share life together.

If a mature identity means being everything God meant us to be at any given age, then we discover that our actual maturity level is a bit crumpled and less than optimal. If the full picture of our mature identity would make us gentle protectors like Jesus, but parts are missing, we find that in those missing places we become predators and possums instead of protectors. Since we all have missing pieces of our full identity, we discover that predator and possum identities spread much more easily than protector identities. We find that when we have spent a life-time acting like a predator or possum, it is hard to believe we are really meant to be protectors. This is why we need to see ourselves the way God sees us through Immanuel experiences. These Immanuel experiences are also needed in community for joy to start and spread. Discovering that there really is a Jesus-like person in each of us is cause for great rejoicing. The lost has been found!

Propagation of protector and predator patterns

Predator identities propagate without work or help. When we encounter predators it does not take long to learn to hide and avoid (possum) or become one of them (predator) to avoid being eaten in the future. Each one of us has the potential to be a predator. Many of us already are. Because it takes more time, energy, training, and awareness to be a protector than a predator, predatory ways will continue to self-propagate easily. Protector identities are more complex and require training and restoration. Joy is the essential quality to grow and train protectors. Every protector stands in the unique position within a family, church, school and community to be a source of joy, life, and blessing. Protectors can train others to be protectors by responding to weakness with tenderness. We pass along joy building skills where it is safe to be little and weak. Predator traits will self-propagate if nothing is done.

The link between protectors and food

We cannot leave our introduction to the transformation zone without one more observation about the predatory reactions that are so wired into us. Predatory behavior of tracking and capturing was intended to help us find food. Food is also rewarding and uses some of the same brain center used for joy. Predators may not be getting joy, but they are getting food. They begin to use everything that gives them a thrill, from the hunt to the kill to the feast as a substitute for joy.

Protectors know food also has a powerful influence on forming joy bonds. We bond to the ones who feed us. We search for food and drink for the ones we love and for the animals under our care. Meanwhile possums play dead so they will not be considered food by predators. We need a bit of understanding of this "feed me don't eat me" relationship between predator and protector thinking as it comes to food. When we understand this relationship we will discover how food cravings become one of our most common symptoms for low-joy. When we crave joy that we cannot find, we begin to stalk something easier to locate, like chocolate covered, well, chocolate covered anything! Ed calls these cravings BEEPS.

God wants to feed us and meant for feeding to bond us to the feeder. The first sin mentioned in the Bible was choosing the food over the feeder. When we choose food over the feeder, we activate our predatory system where food is more important than relationship. We are meant to be protectors but became predators each time we attached to the food instead of the feeder. Our joyful attachments to others begin by feeding them not eating them. In this book we will learn how to use food to restore a bond with the God who feeds us. We will learn how to feed God's lambs. This is how joy reaches the world through homes, schools and churches.

Correcting what we might have heard about weakness and strength

Consider for a moment what our families thought about being weak. Would mom and dad smile if someone told them they were weak? How about our school experience? Was it good to be the weak one in class? How did teachers treat weakness? When we think about church, does the teaching there reflect what our culture says about weakness or a biblical view that encourages people to show their weaknesses? Do our communities show a tender response to weakness or do they pounce on it?

The most common thing we hear is that some version of, "weakness is bad, and with God's help, we can be strong." Does this teaching sound familiar? How do we explain the frequent failures by the very Christian leaders who teach us to be strong? We need to examine whether God's power at work in us makes us powerful or simply makes it safe to be weak while God is strong.

It is almost universal for human cultures to praise strength and dislike or despise weakness. However, cultures do not agree on what defines weakness or strength. A weakness in one culture might be admired in another. As we go through the three distinctive features of the Life Model in the three sections of this book we will find different ways to view weakness.

The transformation zone (t-Zone)

Pastors sense that transformations would follow if their flock practiced compassion and became involved with the life of the church. Pastors spend their lives trying to persuade people to get involved and stay involved with only limited success. We also tried to persuade people with limited success in *Living From The Heart Jesus Gave You*, which contained compelling reasons for the weak and strong to be together. Few were even willing to try. Words and reason were not enough to transform lives. People who already lived with weakness were encouraged, but those who were in their comfort zone usually stayed there.

Transformation Zone: As stated at the beginning of this chapter, life-changing, maturity-enhancing, joy-spreading changes in character and community happen when three conditions are present at the same time:

1.   The weak and strong are together and interacting
2.   Tender responses to weakness are the rule
3.   The interactive presence of God (Immanuel) maintains shalom

We have all experienced these transforming conditions that bring joy.

t-Zone at home: A screaming baby has made more than one mother feel irritated instead of protective. Jen was not getting enough sleep and her baby would not settle down. As she asked God for help, the thought, "Lay him on his left side" crossed her mind. She could see no reason it would help, but when she obeyed, the results were rapid. Her son was soon asleep. Jen's mood went from irritated to appreciation for God and her baby.

t-Zone at school: James transferred schools mid-semester in fifth grade. His new teacher asked for a volunteer to share a locker with James but no one raised a hand. James felt his face flush as he stood at the front of the room. Chris saw his growing discomfort and felt compassion for James so he volunteered to share lockers. While saying his bedtime prayers, Chris got the feeling that Jesus had orchestrated this event. Chris realized it felt good to be protective. Years later, James would be the first person Chris called when he was bailed out of jail for his DUI.

t-Zone at church: Tim was a restless teenager who frequently gave his youth pastor a run for his money. Tim went for fun on a mission trip to Mexico to build an orphanage. Helping impoverished children changed something in Tim. Observing some hungry children, he felt impressed that God wanted him to help them, and that resonated with something inside of him. Tim started fund-raising for orphans when he returned home.

To keep joy transformations from being a once-in-a-lifetime thing we need to create t-Zones in our communities. Well designed activities, rather than words, are needed to help people enter and stay in the t-Zone. The design must allow the three characteristics needed for transformation and create a way for joy to spread. The rest of this book outlines what is needed in order to stay in the transformation zone.

Part One of this book focuses on how maturity is produced in multigenerational communities. These structures have been with us as long as people have lived on earth but are now changing rapidly. High-joy is something that takes several generations working together to achieve. What was once automatic, now must become intentional in order to replace what is missing.

Part Two of this book focuses on restoring our joy after we have been damaged. This grows from a lifestyle of interacting with God who is with us and restores our relational capacity. Dr. Karl Lehman, a psychiatrist, and Pastor Charlotte Lehman, his wife, coined the term "Immanuel" for this experience of a God who is always with us even in our traumas. The Lehmans met the Life Model team and attended many early *THRIVE Training* events. Karl was a major critic of the model at first, but in time, became the one to develop Immanuel healing for professional and pastoral counselors.

Part Three of this book focuses on the nineteen relational brain skills needed to develop maturity as a joyful protector. These skills are a large part of returning to joy after we have lost joy. More importantly, these skills spread joy to the world through our homes, schools and churches. These protector skills are learned from people who have them and cannot be spread by books or technology. Protector skills are rapidly becoming an endangered species.

We believe that with some careful study, help from God, and support from joy starters around the world, we can find a way to save joyful protector skills. With some help, protector skills will propagate once more.

Joy starts here with us!

How am I doing?

Since transformation begins in the t-Zone I must ask myself:

- When am I living in the t-Zone at home, school and church?
- Where am I weak or strong?
- What weaknesses make it hard for me to have a tender response?
- Am I more gentle with weaknesses in myself or in others?
- Do I bring my weaknesses to Immanuel for perspective?
- If entering the t-Zone means acknowledging my weakness and changing the way I respond to weakness in others, then why do I want to go there?

Joy Actions

Home: Pick something that bothers you at home and take care of it yourself with a smile.

School: Sit next to someone who is alone at school or a school event.

Church: Ask God how He sees the thing that bothers you at church.

Readiness for Transformation Assessment

1. I deeply long to see improvements in myself.

   Not at all 0 1 2 3 4 5 6 7 8 9 10 *Strong need to change*

2. I am often in a room where high and low joy people form relationships.

   Never 0 1 2 3 4 5 6 7 8 9 10 *Frequently each week*

3. I am frequently struck by awareness that God is part of this moment.

   Never 0 1 2 3 4 5 6 7 8 9 10 *Constantly*

4. I regularly help___ people in my life who are less mature than I am.

   0 1 2 3 4 5 6 7 8 9 10$^+$ *Number of people*

5. I work very hard to improve my character and responses.

   Not at all 0 1 2 3 4 5 6 7 8 9 10 *Most of my energy*

6. I have regular contact with___ people who are more mature than I am.

   0 1 2 3 4 5 6 7 8 9 10$^+$ *Number of people*

7. I am not afraid to make mistakes.

   Very afraid 0 1 2 3 4 5 6 7 8 9 10 *No fear at all*

8. I have made a huge investment already bringing change to my family.

   None 0 1 2 3 4 5 6 7 8 9 10 *This is a priority*

9. Other people's flaws fill me with a warm desire to help them.

   Not at all 0 1 2 3 4 5 6 7 8 9 10 *Every time*

10. I actively protect all people from any intimidation or contempt.

   I don't get involved 0 1 2 3 4 5 6 7 8 9 10 *Every one of them*

Total your scores here. _____
Mark the matching spot on the scale.

0   10   20   30   40   50   60   70   80   90   100

Weakness and Joy Bible Study

We experience appreciation when we remember joy from special moments, people and places that bring us comfort and make us smile. Think back on something you appreciate and spend two minutes enjoying appreciation. Next, ask God to make this study interesting for you. Now read the following passage from the gospels.

Scripture Luke 1:26-56 (or Luke 1:13-56) Read then review the passage for each question.

Chapter Four Question: According to this passage, are the weak or the mighty more likely to experience God's joy?

Weakness, Joy and Shalom Questions:
1. Who are weak or strong in this passage?
2. What kind of interaction does God desire between weak and strong?
3. What do we learn about joy and shalom (everything works together) from this passage?

Immanuel Questions:
1. What effects does perceiving "God is with us" have in this passage?
2. Group study activity: God is always present and eager to help us see more clearly. In what ways do we perceive or guess that God is helping us understand this passage right now in the group discussion?

   Note: Thinking about God's active presence may seem strange at first because people generally discuss the past more than they observe the present. Keep your answers short. Feel free to guess. We will do this each week.

Personal Story Question: What experience in your life comes closest to Immanuel (God with us) bringing you joy?

Whole Bible Question: In what stories or passages does God strengthen the weak and weaken the strong?

Wrap-Up Minute: What do you now know that you didn't know before this week's study?

My Life Model Joy Exercises

Start here: Make a list of ten appreciation memories and give them each a one or two word name.

Individual
1. From your list of ten appreciation memories, pick your favorite. Spend three minutes remembering this special memory focusing on the aspects that mean the most to you.
2. Ask Jesus what He wants you to know about His Presence in your appreciation memory. Notice any thoughts that appear. If you get distracted, return to your appreciation memory and begin step 2 again.
3. Thank Jesus for this special memory and anything that might have been a shared thought between you and Jesus.
4. Take 30 seconds to notice how your body feels. If it is a good sensation, notice where and how you are experiencing it.

Group
1. Have everyone from the group pick one of their favorite appreciation memories from their personal lists. Spend three minutes remembering this special memory. Pick three words that describe what aspects of the memory mean the most to you. (Example: Beach, sunset, anniversary)
2. Have everyone share the name of their appreciation memory and their three words.
3. Have each group member return to their appreciation memories then focus on the most meaningful parts of their memory for another three minutes. Each group member ask Jesus what He wants you to know about His Presence in the appreciation memory. Notice what thoughts come to mind as well as what body sensations you feel.
4. Have each group member briefly share possible "Jesus thoughts" along with a short description how their body feels. We suggest a two-minute limit per person.

Part One
Joyful Multigenerational Community

When the righteous prosper, the city rejoices!
Proverbs 11:10a NIV

The Life Model for sustainable joy is based on three things that are not usually found together: multigenerational community, an Immanuel lifestyle and relational brain skills. Take any of these three away and joy levels start to fall quickly. In **Part One** of this book we will look at why we need old people and babies, experienced people and novices and the weak and strong together in multigenerational community if we want joy to grow and spread!

Sustainable joy requires at least three generations interacting in joyful ways. Four generations are even better because this leaves the oldest group to make sure that everyone is playing well together. Community is not about knowledge, technique, education or power but using our combined attention to amplify whatever is good, lovely, praiseworthy and honest, particularly for those who are weak and tired. This is why God put us in families, clans, tribes, nations, languages, cultures and groups of all sorts.

In the first chapter of **Part One** we will examine how joyful community grows. In the second chapter we will see how tragedy develops when community is not multigenerational or joyful. Find the path back to hope.

71

Chapter Five

Joyful Multigenerational Community

The average child will interact with other generations as part of three multigenerational communities. A child's first multigenerational community is as part of a family with grandparents, parents, brothers, sisters and in time, children and grandchildren. The second exchange with other generations is as part of a school system with teachers, administrators, parents and students. The third source for interaction between generations comes from community organizations of which the oldest and most wide spread are religious. For Christians this is church.

Once, and not so long ago, there was a fourth multigenerational institution called the neighborhood. In the neighborhood we could ask any neighbor and be told about our grandparents. The older members might call us "sonny" or "darling" and we talked to most neighbors every day. When someone was sick neighbors helped and brought food. Children played together in the street and in houses. People flew kites. Neighborhoods also had all the same problems as other multigenerational communities. However, neighborhoods expanded to fill every spare moment of life with interaction and relationships. Across the world, neighborhood has vanished almost entirely and is being replaced by the "cloud." In the "cloud" communication is virtual and most is one-way. Cloud people receive a tweet when their favorite singer is walking his dog, predict what the Mario brothers will do and know whether an actress is considering divorce but do not know their neighbors' names. The "cloud" is rapidly taking up all the multigenerational space for interactions that was part of neighborhoods, most of the home space, much of the school space and some of the church space. Joy cannot grow in the "cloud" for very practical reasons we will explore throughout this book.

Joy is relational and, even more than that, joy is an active process that is amplified between people and passed from one generation to the next. Actually, all emotions are relational and amplified so multigenerational groups with joyful relational skills amplify and maintain joy, while other groups who lack these joy skills amplify and maintain distress, fear, anger and misery of various forms. We have all watched how some families are joyful and others look like feuding Chihuahuas. Schools and churches are subject to the same variations in joy. If we are to be joy starters there are no more important places to start joy than through our participation in these three remaining institutions.

Jim's Story

Home was a multigenerational place growing up as my parents were missionaries in the Andes mountains of Colombia, and although we had no relatives for thousands of miles, our home was the center of the spiritual community. My mother had no sense of humor. While she cared deeply for people and was very tender to weakness in others, her relational skills were quite limited and her joy would easily run dry. Later in life we discovered that the right half of my mother's skull was filled with water from a defect she had from birth. The result was that her brain was half the normal size and the relational right half of the brain was displaced by water.

As we might remember from the discussion on joy, babies duplicate the structure, wiring and chemistry of their mother's right brain during the first year of life to learn their joy skills and identities. My mother had water where her right brain was supposed to be. This was the formula for very low-joy development for my brain except for the presence of a multigenerational community in our lives. A young lady named Carmen helped my mother take care of me my first year of life. The pictures of me with Carmen all show a high-joy baby. A constant circulation of joyful people also came through the house each day. Those were violent times called "la violencia" with about 250,000 people murdered (similar to Rwanda) in the first ten years of my life. Perhaps because of the constant danger we were all the more joyful to be together each time we met.

Interestingly, my father received much of his joy as a baby from neighbors. His parents arrived in town under an assumed name and were hiding from any relatives. My grandfather had left his wife and five children to run off with my grandmother when she was sixteen. They were both thrown in jail. As soon as they got out on bail, the two headed for California to stay ahead of the law and settled in the town where their car broke down. They rented a place next the burlesque theater where the dancers of Billy Watson's Beef Trust were delighted to play with my father as a little boy. Joy comes from many sources in a multigenerational community.

School for me included home school, correspondence school, a one-room school house, public education and boarding school complete with physical, emotional and religious abuse. A quick look at my grades over the years will give a direct reflection of the joy levels in the schools. Where joy was low I was failing my classes and where joy was high my test scores tended to be in the top 5% nationally. As a child, this confused me completely as the low-joy schools made it clear that I was a failure and not very capable. I figured that the high-joy schools simply failed to catch how dumb I really was. The highest joy was in the one-room school where I was curious and eager to learn everything that the students several grades ahead of me were learning. Miss Lillian taught this school and, although I am now a grandfather, we continue to exchange yearly letters.

Church is full of stellar highs and lows in my life. Some of the lowest joy and highest joy moments are connected in some way to the communities around church. My mother was conceived because a neighbor forced himself on my grandmother after taking her to church. My father was a young gangster in New York state when an older woman took an interest in him. Her care brought him the love of God and transformed his life. My parents would never have married if Mr. and Mrs. Quail had not been like parents to all the college students and provided them with a home to visit, special meal times, even lending my father their car when he wanted to drive 200 miles and propose to my mother. Much joyful family life was learned at the Quail's home.

As missionaries, my parent's community shared all their donations together in one "common purse" out of which everyone lived. Prospect was
one of the supporting churches and we visited there every five years. Prospect was the same church that reached out to my father as a young man.
However, as the downtown neighborhood changed the church stopped
interacting with the community. The weak and the strong no longer met
in and around the church. Only the strong came to church and year after
year they stayed just like they were. The same people, the same songs, the
same pipe organ, the same clarity about doctrine and, at least to my eyes,
the same clothes. From what I could tell the church had not witnessed a
transformed life in 30 years as the strong stayed tightly together in what
had become their comfort zone. The joy seemed to slowly drain as well.

We would also visit my mother's home church where there was always
a mix of young families, grandparents, children and community activity.
Most stories of transformed lives came from reaching out to people in
trouble. Common ways to reach out were helping rural churches, meeting community needs, or for the youth to take summer mission trips.
During these expeditions to interact with people in need, the youth frequently discovered the weak parts of their own faith and character while
responding tenderly to the obvious weaknesses in others. Looking back,
I could see that people grew and improved their character for a lifetime
when the weak and strong interacted tenderly supported by a multigenerational community.

In our town we had a "loud speaker" church with an amazing sound
system on the roof so the whole town could hear what was going on
inside the church. I walked by many times without going in but, because
we ran the Christian bookstore in town, we came to know many people
from the loud speaker church. People in turmoil flocked to the church;
we could hear the turmoil inside over the speakers. Getting to know
the members revealed that much of their internal turmoil continued for
years, paired with a passion for God. The excitement they called joy came
and went like a storm. I have visited similar churches and found most
participants fall within a fifteen year age difference. Turnover was high
and as many new people joined as left each year. Members had passion
but demonstrated little enduring change of character. New spiritual highs
left no more lasting character change than I saw in the church with a
pipe organ.

What do we mean by joyful multigenerational community?

Joyful multigenerational community is when parents, children, grandparents, teachers, neighbors, friends and church members see what is special in each other and light up with warm greetings. Joyful community grows when people long to be together and hold each other in deep affection. When we share each other's joys, and cannot be kept away when there are sorrows, we have a multigenerational community that is joyful. The sources of joy are carefully protected and cultivated by the strong members much to the delight of everyone.

Joyful community is not something that one individual or leader produces. The desire for joyful multigenerational community is both an individual and community goal. Joy grows out of relationships with those who have more maturity than we have, practice with our peers and giving joy to those who are less mature than we are. Everyone is involved, or at least can be.

Communities can grow in their ability to create joyful environments in which the weak and strong connect with mutual care, maturity grows and belonging flourishes. Stop and think a moment about the low-joy spots you have seen, where people build walls and strengthen defenses. Next, think about the high-joy moments that reveal play, freedom, creativity and people making places where others can belong. Deep in our hearts, don't we all want joyful community?

As we make our way through this book, it will become clearer that a number of relational skills are needed to create joy around us. We rarely notice these skills when we have them. We do not know how we came to have the skills in the first place. It disturbs us when others fail to use these skills at moments when they would flow naturally for us. It is always a mystery for those who lack relational skills how other people manage to get people to like them or to control their tempers. In fact, we tend to think of these skills as people's personalities rather than learned abilities.

Relational skills are learned on the right side of the brain. The right-brain does not watch itself learn and keeps no conscious record of what, where and how we learned. The left-brain generally keeps stories about what it learns that tell us where and how we learned what we know. We will generally remember where we learned to read and write and what language was used in school. We will be able to tell if we ever learned calculus. We are not surprised if we cannot read Arabic if we never studied Arabic. What we learned with the verbal left-brain leaves a memory of the context. In the right-brain we do not keep conscious track of the learning context so we do not think of right-sided relational abilities as "learned" even though they are. We assume that because we can keep things pleasant that everyone else should be able to do that too.

When we cannot keep things pleasant, we do not think, "Wow! My family never taught this skill. I should get some lessons."

With relational skills we restore the relationship. In the absence of relational skills we build ways to manage problems. Problem management styles can become rigid parts of families and cultures that lack certain skills. Each time families lose relational skills there is a drop in joy. We "fall short" or "miss the target" to borrow ancient archery terms that describe how people became less than human. Instead of joyful protectors, we begin to justify our predatory ways and pass on predatory deformities as normal or even desirable. As we enter the "cloud" we attenuate interactions with the people around us to interact with machines and remote people.

So a joyful multigenerational community is a place where skills that maintain joyful relationships are practiced and passed from one generation to the next without most people noticing. In a multigenerational community, the old-timers (with lots of relational skills and more time than energy) interact repeatedly with children. Children work out their social skills while playing with their peers. When the stronger, older child is not tender to a weaker child he hears, "Come here Sonny," and receives a lesson on how to treat others. People with disabilities are included in life because the community understands their disability.

Without interaction there is no multigenerational community. The fact that people of many ages may go to one church means little if they do not have joyful relationships that regularly span three or more generations. It is through this steady stream of interactions that we develop our group identity based on the relational skills we possess.

What is a joyful group identity?

Westerners tend to think of identity as a characteristic of individuals while group cultures tend to regard identity as a characteristic of the group. As our brain develops, the first twelve years are devoted to the development of an individual identity and the next twelve or more to the creation of our group identity. Beginning about twelve years of age, each human brain begins a series of changes that will make us part of a group whose survival becomes more important to the brain than our own. When twenty-year-old people become parents they help their baby find an individual identity based on the group identities of both parents. Thus, our brain development alternates between individual and group identity phases as we develop both identities. Although we rarely think about our group identity in the Western world, we are no longer just an individual, we are a network as well.

Joyful group identity grows where there is regard for the weak. One of the best tests for a joyful group identity is a high concentration of hopeful daughters. More gentle protector skills pass from one generation to the next through daughters than any other way. Joyful little girls, who love the way that babies, women, mothers and wives are treated by both men and women in their culture will look forward to starting joyful families of their own. Hopeful daughters will grow a joyful generation and joyful group identity. One way we can spot hopeful girls is that adults frequently stop to listen with interest to what the girls have to say and the girls expect this response with smiles. Hopeful girls will raise hopeful families. Girls' joy levels let us accurately predict the future for families, churches and schools of the region.

Whether we examine the Bible or the world, we will find people arranged in families, tribes, cities, nations, languages and cultures who see each other to some degree as "my people." This group becomes the select group entitled to tell us who we really are, how we should act and where we belong. We are elated when our team wins and crestfallen when our country loses. Our faces brighten when we meet someone from our high school after 25 years even when we cannot remember them. Mates are almost always found in "my people." Those who have ventured to break this rule can tell us that there has been a price to pay.

A strong group identity gives us joy when others rejoice. We celebrate each other's children, promotions, achievements, smiles and pets. Joyful group identities provide strong multi-generational relationships. The key feature for building joy in a group identity is the way onlookers smile when they see joy. In high-joy groups, onlookers really enjoy the good relationships between other people. Friends and neighbors encourage and support the celebration of life and sharing of sorrows.

From a brain perspective, joining in the joy shared between other people builds strength in our three-way bond structure in the prefrontal cortex that was, coincidentally, one of the best developed parts of Albert Einstein's brain. Our three-way-bond capacity is the basis for stable identity growth, strong character and maturity. Three-way-bonds allow us to genuinely feel a part of the relationships around us. Three-way-bonds help us focus on what is important, calm ourselves and others and make changes when we are upset. Without strong three-way bonds, change is difficult and fleeting. Developing strong three-way bonds is one of the nineteen relational skills of the Life Model.

Since our group identity has power over our brain to determine our individual identity we should not be surprised that God has something to say about it. The New Testament presents us with two iconic group identities that cover all others, the world and the Kingdom of God. The world is viewed as the kingdom of predators where the devil goes around as a chief predator lion saying that power wins. The Kingdom of God is to be a high-joy group identity where protectors thrive and fear does not guide us. Since joy from love is greater than power from fear, those who live for power will lose, while joy will prevail even though the opposite is happening at the moment in every low-joy place on earth.

The Kingdom of God is marked by zones of welcome rather than the zones of exclusion that often surround homes, schools and churches. We do not feel compelled to look good and prove we are important. A joyful group identity invites new people to join, adapts with change, respects the weak and recovers from pain and distress. In the process we discover how to live from the heart Jesus gives which grows in joy with attained maturity. We help each other express the best that God has placed within us while strengthening areas of weakness. The church, as a spiritual family, can now spread into the low-joy places of life.

When the Kingdom of God becomes our tribe and our people then joyful relationships help everyone grow. Spiritual maturity grows in mentoring relationships between spiritual parents and their children as multigenerational community. Character, emotional and relational maturity are not separate from our spiritual maturity rather, the emotional and spiritual aspects are all part of our group identity. The ways that spiritual maturity subsumes all other kinds of maturity is covered in **Part Two** of this book, but here we will notice that spiritual, emotional and relational maturity all grow in the context of relationships. A joyful, multigenerational community is where maturity grows best.

No human community is free from dysfunctions related to sin and iniquity, but living in the t-Zone corrects many of our deformities as joyful maturity grows. We see a decrease in fear and fear-bonded relationships. Spontaneous vulnerability increases because we feel safe, respected and protected. The strong and the weak, the lion and the lamb, can rest together. Protectors pass their skills to the next generation. Weak people find courage to create belonging and joyfully create places for others. Joyful relationships cultivate a "glad to be with you" lifestyle. We will find days for rest, help for the poor, creativity, generosity, diligence, maturity, honesty, hopefulness, investment in the future, training, curiosity, play and other virtues when joy is central to a group identity.

While joyful communities experience all the challenges and temptations of any other group, with a joyful group identity, people continue to delight in one another, remember who they are under distress and live according to their values in good times and bad. When people are not glad to be together the community stops, returns to joy and resolves the problem.

Wherever our homes, schools and churches were low on joy a different group identity formed. When joy levels drop, pain and problems became prominent. Group identities formed around pain and problems. As fear grew, people were defined by what they had done instead of who God created them to be. Tasks, projects, test scores, contributions, accomplishments and failures became a primary way to categorize the importance of members and leaders. Neighborhoods taught children that following the rules and doing the right things brought acceptance and praise. Schools taught that getting good grades on a quiz brought pleasure and satisfaction. Poor grades, disobedience and violating the group identity led to shame and rejection.

By the time babies are a year and a half old, they have figured out that they can get better results by pretending than by being themselves. Although it takes years to perfect, pretending and cheating to get better results, higher scores, sexier looks, faster race times, even buying goods we cannot really afford still leave us with a pseudo-self and pseudo-maturity. Pseudo-maturity hides weakness but also creates fear of being exposed. Since pseudo-maturity always sees weakness as a bad thing, joy will certainly begin to drop. We look good, appear strong and come across as mature when, in truth, we are running on fear. We even strive to look spiritual by focusing on results, power, orthodoxy and whatever is exclusive to our spiritual group identity.

Pseudo-maturity is actually as transparent as the "emperor's new clothes" to anyone with a skill called "mindsight." This skill does not read other people's thoughts but detects what others genuinely feel. Mindsight allows us to create a group mind by knowing other people's feelings and responses. When Dad has a certain look and tone, we know he "means it" and we should respond quickly. This is one example of mindsight but there are many other functions as well. The simplest feature is that we know there is a mind behind a face but not behind a photograph of a face.

Mindsight is a dynamic process created by watching the moment-by-moment changes in micro-expressions in someone's face and body. Movies work to fool our mindsight through music, laugh tracks, sound effects, heightened intensity and close-ups to overcome this limitation in one-way messages from the "cloud." Even when we decode these fake messages correctly, the cloud cannot recognize our responses or interact with us in return. While more sophisticated machines in stores watch our eyes and do recognize our responses to improve sales, this is a predatory pattern seeking weakness to exploit. We cannot learn mindsight without face-to-face interactions with live people we love and trust as we will explore in **Part Three** of this book.

How multigenerational community works

To understand how we pass on relational skills that create identity, we should consider how multigenerational community works. Let's start with one generation. In a one generation community everyone is a peer. Our peers are good for practice because everyone is about as bad at skills as we are. Peers are about as powerful as we are, so harm is less likely. Bear cubs and most small animals fight and play with each other all day without harm. In western society peer groups are increasingly the norm so everyone on talk radio is presumed to know as much as anyone else.

It is easy to see that with two generations there is a large difference in capacity. Put parents and children together, and we create a strong expectation that the parents will keep the children safe and very little expectation that the children will protect the adults. With two generations there are always weak and strong together.

With three generations together the dynamics change greatly. The middle generation will have the most power, the youngest will have the most energy and the oldest will have the most experience with relationships and the most available resources. Here is where we discover if the oldest generation delights to share and nurture weakness or wants to exploit it. We discover if grandma-aged people are critical and judgmental (mocking and humiliating weakness) or joy builders who see the potential God created. We discover if our mistakes become our identity. We will find out if grandpa-aged people see the excitement of little children as an opportunity for some sexual gratification. Are our old people proof that we are predators? Do grandfathers provide genuine joy by seeing all children as special and delightful? Will grandpa build a world where it is safe to play?

When the weak and strong play together the strong hold back their strength so that play will continue. Learning to restrain our strength during play helps the strong learn protective ways, avoid hurting others, restrain powerful emotions, master urges and drives and harm no one. If someone is hurt we share their distress, including any hurt feelings we caused. Sharing the suffering of others regulates our personal predator urges. When we weep with someone we have hurt, we become much more careful about hurting others.

When we make room for play and weakness we create a joyful place around us. When we are being protected and enjoyed, we discover our own abilities to create belonging around us. Most everyone in Ed's *Connexus*™ group was discovering how their lack of joy created weaknesses in their lives and were very interested in growing their capacity for joy. Ed and Maritza regularly scheduled time to play together as a group. Once they cooked out and everyone went swimming. As they floated around, splashing, playing, and laughing, one of the women in the group turned to Ed and said, "I don't know if you know this or not, but the times that you've scheduled outside of group for us to celebrate and play together have meant more for my own healing and recovery than anything we do in group." People playing and being genuinely glad to be together in the midst of weakness helped her catch a vision of her life empowered by joy.

One of the most essential functions of each layer of multigenerational community is to insure the limits and weaknesses of all members are respected. Half of this task is identifying failures to act protectively in oneself and others. Mature members of a family or community will point out their own failures to others. Mature people publicly invite others to help them see their failures as well. When mature people are open about their failures, we can be sure it is safe to be weak. Acknowledging failures also warns younger members of bad examples they should not adopt for their own identity. We should mention that no self-justification can go with the acknowledgment of failures. Mature people openly acknowledge weakness and invite the community to provide correction leading to a change of character and improved spiritual and relational maturity. This is part of how we avoid passing our deformities from one generation to the next.

The other half of protecting the limits and weaknesses of community members is accomplished through sheer delight in watching others grow. The protection of weakness through our delight in them involves all community members whether weak or strong. We are never too young to take delight in others. Even the youngest can pass this gift to others. We are never so weak our joy is not needed. No one can justify pouncing on weakness even when we are hurting. There is always someone who can use our delight to grow their protector identity.

Living in a multigenerational community helps us know who we are growing up to be. We keep growing no matter how old or weak we become provided we participate in building joy around weakness. We cannot stand by and watch, we must participate in order to change and be changed. We all have felt the pull of joy urging us to join and the fear of weakness holding us back from our t-Zone. We will pass on any predator identity and character we developed unless we make some joyful changes in our generation.

Care for weakness keeps weak and strong together in a way that provides the right relational environment for the needy and young to be trained by the strongest and best. Tenderness toward weakness provides the right conditions for protector identities and protector motivation to propagate. This blend of

weak and strong generates growth and hope. Transformations happen when
weakness and strength kiss.

How maturity develops in multigenerational community

Perhaps this would be a good place to discover how maturity grows in a
joyful multigenerational community. Maturity is really nothing other than
being fully developed for our age. When we start with babies it becomes
obvious that different ages have their own weaknesses that are totally normal
at that age. A baby cannot walk. We are not surprised if his great-grandfather
cannot walk either. Adult strength and a baby's mind would create a terrible
menace. When others are fully developed for their age we are delighted. Understanding maturity allows us to see others for where they are and where
they are going to be, based on our mental map of how people develop.

There are six stages of human maturity. The first three favor development
of our individual identity and the last three favor our group identity. These
stages correspond to major changes in how our brain and body operate.

Maturity Stages

1. Unborn = conception to birth
2. Infant = birth to four
3. Child = age four to twelve
4. Adult = thirteen to first child
5. Parent = first child until youngest child is thirteen
6. Elder = youngest child is thirteen to death

We can know how mature we are by comparing our identity to the ideal
for our age. If we have had no traumas we will be right on the mark. But,
where is the mark supposed to be? In some models, called statistical models, we take the average of a sample of people and make that the standard.
However, the Life Model is an idealized model, and we take what God says
about who we should be and add what we know about how the brain and
identity develop. Because of trauma in all our lives, we never reach the ideal
in weaker areas of maturity. But in a joyful multigenerational community we
can acknowledge our limitations, short falls and deformities while pressing on
together toward the high calling of the full maturity we see in Christ. We are
looking for a fully expressed protector personality that is like a good shepherd
for all the little lambs. Good Shepherd maturity includes all the relational
and emotional maturity a human can achieve, together with all the spiritual
aspects of being fully alive like Christ. This maturity shines with righteous-

ness, shalom and joy. A full description of maturity is outside the limits of this book but more about the stages of maturity can be found in Appendix C.

Two types of trauma block maturity

Not reaching the maturity goals for our age leaves us deformed. The ancient word for this deformity is "iniquity." Deformity happens when we are missing something that is essential to growth, like calcium, exercise or joy. In the Life Model we call this absence of necessary good things Type A trauma. Others call it neglect.

Not all trauma comes directly from missing what we need. Some trauma comes from bad and harmful things we did not need. These injuries are called Type B trauma in the Life Model. Predators frequently cause Type B trauma.

Every trauma hinders maturity and lowers joy levels. The most pervasive sign of trauma is that people stop creating belonging around themselves and start acting like predators and possums. Both Type A and B trauma can cause whole families, communities and cultures to lose maturity and therefore lose joy. After 25 years of violence from civil war in Sudan, one of the elders in the South told Dr. Wilder, "The people from the North came with guns but now the guns are in our heads." Predators who came from the North brought trauma and people in the South became predators from the trauma they suffered. The people of the South were struggling to remember how to create belonging. They need to find a joy that will spread. Our dream is to help them find it.

Some signs of pseudo-maturity

Every passing generation increases the chances that something will go wrong and belonging will only be created for "my family" or "our kind" or "our tribe" or "my religion." Once this happens, families, schools, churches and whole cultures become rigid. Weakness is seen as bad and people try to be strong, act strong and look strong creating what looks like maturity but is based on fear instead of joy. Peer groups gang together to gain power and hide weakness. Enforcement predators are put in charge of keeping the group in line while benevolent predators protect "us" from "them." Those who come up short on relational skills, looks, money or power become the despised weaklings. People use weaknesses to disqualify others. Leaders push for overcommitment and people act stronger than they are to avoid exposure. This pseudo-maturity is deadly to joy.

Some signs of healthy maturity

One test for maturity is high emotional capacity. Emotional capacity shows itself as consistency and resiliency under distress. With high capacity we easily remember who we really are and display good character and personal values in the middle of upsetting troubles. A high capacity brain has learned that strong emotions do not erase relationships. Conflicts, accusations, threats, intimidations, crises, misunderstandings and wrongs produce strong feelings and reactions. The high capacity brain has learned to stay relational during distress, protect others, process the distress by telling stories about the event, see some of what God sees and return to joy and shalom.

A low capacity brain will be overrun by fear and use non-relational strategies to make problems go away while a high capacity brain remembers what is important in the middle of distress. We feel the difference when we are with a high or low capacity person during a crisis. A mature person maintains joy and shalom while finding joy in the midst of problems.

As mentioned before, mature communities produce hopeful daughters who raise joyful and hopeful boys and girls. Because of specialization in the female brain, joyful mothers produce particularly joyful brains in children. In fact, if communities want to be strategic, they should take advantage of the ninth month after birth when a baby's brain is growing the fastest. By encouraging babies and mothers to practice joy and smiles in the ninth month, we stimulate the growth of joy capacity under the best growing conditions of a life time. Much of this ability to grow joy is made possible when grandparents provide a secure emotional and financial environment for parents. In return, children spread joy back to their grandparents and parents and anyone in a neighborhood that is free from predators.

Authenticity in a spiritually mature community is marked by high joy, pervasive shalom and a rapid return to joy. We will explore these three factors throughout the rest of this book. First, let us consider God's ideas for a mature community.

Is multigenerational community a biblical goal?

In a joyful, multigenerational community the older generations mentor the younger. This mentoring relationship is what the Bible calls "making disciples" that is, teaching people how to experience the life of Jesus together. "Making disciples" is a biblical mandate. It is clear that one cannot be a disciple in a relational vacuum. Mentoring is a relationship, and becoming a disciple means that we are apprentices to Jesus and to the person mentoring us. There is no discipleship apart from relationship with God and at least one other person.

Sometimes mentoring mistakenly, and exclusively, focuses on helping an individual learn the tools and skills needed to grow their own "personal relationship" with God. When apprentices explicitly or implicitly learn from mentors that the primary goal of discipleship is their own "personal relationship with God," the biblical design for life and relationships is seriously distorted. This thinking leads to the formation of a "me" centered Christianity, in which all things spiritual are thought to be about us, for us and to be consumed by us. Instead of becoming fully integrated into the life of Jesus in the "Body of Christ" that Paul describes in chapter 4 of Ephesians, we tend to view others as a means to help ourselves. Sadly, we become predators who consume "the good stuff" for ourselves, and neglect the role we play in sharing the life of Jesus with spiritual family. We do not become protectors when we cover our own vulnerabilities by remaining isolated. Biblically, the life of God is all about relationships. To fully share the life of Jesus with others we need to recover the biblical mandate for community where young and old, weak and strong are together.

Chapter 4 of Ephesians describes God's blueprint for life and growth in His family. Paul writes:

And He Himself gave some to be apostles, some prophets, some evangelists, and some pastors and teachers, for the equipping of the saints for the work of ministry, for the edifying of the body of Christ, till we all come to the unity of the faith and of the knowledge of the Son of God, to a perfect man, to the measure of the stature of the fullness of Christ; that we should no longer be children, tossed to and fro and carried about with every wind of doctrine, by the trickery of men, in the cunning craftiness of deceitful plotting, but, speaking the truth in love, may grow up in all things into Him who is the head—Christ—from whom the whole body, joined and knit together by what every joint supplies, according to the effective working by which every part does its share, causes growth of the body for the edifying of itself in love. Ephesians 4: 11-16 (NKJV)

What is Paul saying about the development of mature and protective community? Simply, the life of God can never fully be developed in us apart from strong relationships in His beautifully diverse spiritual family. The diversity of gifts is designed to help each follower of Jesus receive and give life, mature and learn to love. Children become adults, vulnerability and weakness are respected, maturity increases, love is given and received so that the life of Jesus becomes a present reality.

Consider carefully the word "equipping" in verse 11. This common way of translating the Greek word "katartismos" seems to imply that "making disciples" means training for ministry tasks. This is an unfortunate impression because katartismos has a much richer meaning flowing from the word "katartizo" from which it is derived. The more complete meaning would include to repair, mend, restore and get going. In other words, relationships are needed for us to be repaired and equipped. Apart from the diversity of God's family, we will remain immature and unstable, and miss the kind of love that is supposed to characterize disciples.

Other stories in scripture reveal just as clearly that the weak and strong members in God's family should remain together even when they disagree. Very early in church history disputes over dietary laws threatened to cause division in God's family. It seems as if the solution favored by both groups was separation, the strong separating themselves to avoid being "dragged down" by the weak, and the weak separating themselves to protect themselves from the strong.

Paul's response in chapters 14 and 15 in Romans is fascinating. Paul acknowledges the clear differences between weak and strong concerning the issue of food. However, Paul clearly wanted the weak and strong to remain together. Instead of trying to help them reach an agreement about food, Paul deals with the tendency of the strong to show contempt for the weak (predator behavior) and the tendency of the weak to judge the strong (possum behavior).

Paul encourages both groups to create belonging for the other. Paul writes, "The one who eats everything must not treat with contempt the one who does not, and the one who does not eat everything must not judge the one who does, for God has accepted them. Who are you to judge someone else's servant? To their own master, servants stand or fall. And they will stand, for the Lord is able to make them stand" Romans 14:3-4 (NIV). To Paul, the problem of the strong showing contempt for the weak (predator) and the weak judging the strong (possum) are the real issues behind their low joy.

Paul writes, "We who are strong ought to bear with the failings of the weak and not to please ourselves. Each of us should please our neighbors for their good, to build them up...May the God who gives endurance and encouragement give you the same attitude of one mind toward each other that Christ Jesus had" Romans 15: 1-2, 5 (NIV). The weak and the strong held valuable roles in building joyful maturity. They were invited to encourage, strengthen and serve each other.

Paul's letters to Timothy and Titus indicate that multigenerational community was a normal part of life within God's family. Paul writes to Timothy, "Do not rebuke an older man harshly, but exhort him as if he were your father. Treat younger men as brothers, older women as mothers, and younger women as sisters, with absolute purity" I Timothy 5:1-2 (NIV). In Titus, Paul says, "Teach the older men to be temperate, worthy of respect, self-controlled, and sound in faith, in love and in endurance. Likewise, teach the older women to be reverent in the way they live, not to be slanderers or addicted to much wine, but to teach what is good. Then they can urge the younger women to love their husbands and children... Similarly, encourage the young men to be self-controlled" Titus 2:2-4, 6 (NIV).

Paul instructs Timothy and Titus how to best relate to men and women who are older, the same age, and younger than themselves, and suggests the presence of three distinct generations was the norm for the early church. Peter and John also write to a multigenerational community. Paul's instructions make it clear that older members of the community were to mentor those who were younger. A multigenerational community where the weak and strong related tenderly to weakness was at the heart of the transformed lives in the early church and creates our transformation zone today. Let us return to our three multigenerational community possibilities today and see what we can do raise the joy in our homes, schools and churches.

Building multigenerational community

Building multigenerational community at home: The simplest way to have a multigenerational home is with food. Having meals together as a family builds a basis for learning to interact together face-to-face. Before inviting other generations to join our meal, we need to practice relating to family members while we eat. Next, we invite older and younger people to join our meal on Sundays, special occasions or simply join us because they are around at the moment we are going to eat. Jim and his wife Kitty made a special point to train their children to engage the guests and provide hospitality. They then invited seniors for weekend and holiday meals with their family. Kitty hates to cook so we can see the degree of importance that hospitality was given in their home.

Keep the food simple and healthy. Rich and complicated meals are a distraction and our objective is to improve the quality of joy, bonding and interaction. We are not having people over for food, we are having people over for joy and the food is only the context. Keeping this in mind, we should plan more deliberately for high joy than for exotic food. Family members can have a contest to see who can find the most different ways to make our guests smile with joy.

Children can also invite their friends and this makes a natural bridge to younger age groups. Consider stepping out of your comfort zone and inviting older relatives to visit in your home. You might go a step farther by having an older relative move in when they are getting too old to live alone. With joy and support these experiences will be transforming. Older couples should certainly consider helping young, single-parent families and families with foster children by providing a family evening, a rest period for the overworked parent or a holiday time together. The purpose is to build the joy levels for everyone involved. Often our extended families offer enough options to keep us busy starting joy across several generations.

Building multigenerational community at school: Most people reading this will be parents, the ones who can add the most multigenerational joy in schools. As parents we can smile and greet each child entering and leaving school when we are there with our children. We build joy with the teachers, aids, janitors, food service workers, secretaries, crossing guards and administrators on every visit. People who build joy find doors open to them when they say, "I think your class would love to meet John's grandfather." In fact, if we regularly create joy around ourselves at school, the teachers will make up ways for us to be involved. Sometimes churches adopt a neighborhood school and look into tutoring and supply simple needs for classes and vulnerable students. It takes time to build trust with a school, but when we are looking to start some joy we like to build trust. We should not overlook the teachers. Helping teachers keep joy going in their lives and classrooms creates huge amounts of appreciation. Expressing appreciation is our best tool for helping teachers and spreading joy. Bringing an apple for the teacher does not work anymore.

Building multigenerational community at church: Starting multigenerational classes is one way churches can build interaction but expect there will be a good deal of resistance. We have experimented for years on ways to get the generations together so the weak and strong interact and found that working together on a meaningful activity is needed. Many churches combine generations on short term trips and work projects. Jim intentionally taught a class of senior adults in order to meet older people and share life. We can work with children and help special needs families. Just going camping together as a group of church families, couples and singles can build joy. Camping trips can pull an amazing age range together and provide an excellent environment in which to be together and still keep our privacy as needed. Young people can give Davidic dance lessons to the old people in retirement homes. Church members of all ages can help seniors with their yard work. Consider gathering several generations to find low-joy targets in the community and plan a joy raid. Perhaps everyone could bring kites to give away on the next breezy day. With a little more planning, we could teach people to make kites and then fly them. Do not gather a group and ask them how to build multigenerational community in church. Instead, gather people who have tasted joy and ask how we can raise the joy level in our community. Soon we will have more ideas than we can use.

How am I doing?

By now we should be asking questions like:

- How mature should I be at this point in life?
- How mature are my emotional skills?
- Do I have people who are more mature than I am who regularly help guide my life?
- Do I have peers with whom I share my struggles and joys?
- Do I have younger people who depend on me for their joy and growth?
- How did my experiences at home, school and church help me build joy?
- How can I start joy at home, schools and churches for others?
- Am I losing joy to the "cloud" in my daily life?

At the center is the question of how well my life fits into the flow of joy from the generation or two before me to the generation or two after me. Is nothing happening? Are we blocked? Are we passing complaints and misery? Where are the resources of "older people" being used or wasted in my family, school and church? Where are joy levels low near where I live? How many generations are involved in the problem or the solution?

The Life Model concludes that if we want positive changes that last, we need to have three or more generations working together. In this way we permit a flow of joy from generation to generation and provide the building blocks for maturity. We all know that infants are guaranteed to lack relational skills, but that being old does not guarantee ability. In many regards our attitudes about emotions are directly tied to our relational skills. People without relationally trained brains tend to distrust, avoid and even condemn feelings. We will finish this section by considering some common beliefs Christians hold about emotions and maturity.

Correcting what we might have heard about emotions

Emotional maturity means that we have developed a life-enhancing response to our emotions rather than responding foolishly when we feel strong emotions. This book is just one of many that includes emotional maturity as an important part of spiritual maturity and Godly character. Rather than discuss how emotional and spiritual maturity are combined, we will consider four common beliefs about emotions that reduce the maturity in many Christian communities.

Belief One: All emotions are caused by thoughts and beliefs

There are two major kinds of emotions in the brain. Being clear about whether we are addressing left or right hemispheric emotions will keep us from disagreeing when we are actually speaking about different kinds of emotions. The emotions that are generated primarily in the left hemisphere are caused by thoughts and beliefs. For instance, if I believe that someone is insulting me I may become angry. If I believe I am stupid I may feel shame. One way to resolve these feelings is to change what we believe.

Right hemispheric emotions are basic responses to life that cannot be avoided by changing what we believe. If someone vomits in front of me, I will feel disgust without thinking anything first. A sudden, unexpected loud sound will cause fear before I can ever think what it might be. Changing my beliefs does not change these basic feeling responses. Right-hemispheric emotions depend on joyful relationships for their resolution, but they cannot be prevented.

The differences between left and right hemispheric emotions are explained in the work of Karl Lehman M.D. and many of our Life Model resources. What makes the left-right difference important here is that gentle protectors have learned the skill of maintaining relationships during the right-hemispheric emotions that are processed through validation and comfort. Left-hemispheric emotions are based on beliefs that are usually faulty and should not be validated. Without proper training, the right-hemispheric emotions lead people to break their relationships when the feelings become very strong. Therefore, right-sided emotions require joy and relationship to resolve where left-sided emotions require truth or action. As the essential emotional skills for managing right-sided emotions disappear from our families and cultures, we are trying harder to change our feelings by changing our thinking when that will only work for half of our emotions.

Belief Two: Anger is a sin

By now, we might be thinking that left-hemispheric anger is often based on false beliefs that create anger. Anger based on false beliefs is sinful. At the same time, the anger response on the right-hemisphere side happens before we have time to think about it first. In the right brain, anger signals that there is a threat that must be stopped, such as seeing a dog attack our child. Emotionally mature people can feel very angry and strongly motivated to protect others and relationships at the same time. This anger is not a sin, but any emotion can lead to sinful actions if we do not know how to return to joy and protect others while we are angry. This is a maturity skill not everyone has.

Belief Three: Shame is bad

Shame presents left and right brain versions, and we need to know the difference. Left-hemispheric shame is usually based on lies and distorted beliefs about our identity. A good test for left-hemispheric shame happens if we were to agree with the shame belief. For left-sided shame responses, agreeing will make the problem worse. So if someone tells us, "I feel such shame about being a worthless person," and we respond, "That is right, my dear. You are worthless." BOOM! We are dealing with a left-sided shame.

On the right-hemisphere side, the emotion of shame makes us want to hide our faces when people do not have joy to be with us. This shame is very helpful when we forget who we are and do things that are not life-giving. Learning what drains the joy around us helps us become better joy starters. When we carelessly drop food on someone's good clothes, they will not be happy. If we go around picking our noses and passing gas, people will not be happy. Instead of joy, people may have any or several of the six unpleasant emotions. We then feel shame from the no-joy looks we receive. This way we learn that we are not bringing other people joy. Without shame, our brain will not learn to change its ways.

Toxic shame is bad and it comes in both left and right brain versions. Toxic shame on the left hemisphere is caused by exposure to anything that is not true about our identities. Toxic shame on the right hemisphere is caused by blocking the return to joy and leaving us in shame that is devoid of relationship. Identity damage begins in just a few minutes of shame with no way to return to joy. We will examine how the return to joy skills are learned in the **Part Three** of this book.

Belief Four: A joyful life means being positive about everything

Joy, as we are learning, means we are glad to be with someone. We have seen that people are sometimes in pain and sometimes happy. We have also seen that people are sometimes their real identity and sometimes a pseudo-identity. We cannot have true joy being with a fake self. In the same way, no one experiences true joy when we put on a mask to be with them. Everything on earth is not wonderful, and we do not have to act like it is. Joy is relational, and we can always have joy when we know we are never alone. Joy happens when the "real me" sets out to find the "real you" so we can be together regardless of how much pain or happiness we are in at this moment.

Being genuine presents problems for women from Texas, men from Northern Europe, people from Asia, teachers, parents, pastors in every culture or any place where weakness is pounced upon. We face challenges reaching joy with our true selves. However, joy is at the core of being Christian so Christians of every variety and culture can set out together to find a way to joy. In the next chapter, we will consider how to make joy a group effort.

Joy Actions

Home: Spend some time away from the cloud putting together kites you can give away as a family.

School: Bring someone from another generation to a school event.

Church: As a church bring joy kites to a school or a low-joy environment. If possible, help people fly the kites.

Environmental Pseudo-Maturity Assessment

1. I am often tired but force myself to keep going.

   I am well rested 0 1 2 3 4 5 6 7 8 9 10 *Always tired*

2. At home, we hide weaknesses from others.

   We are open books 0 1 2 3 4 5 6 7 8 9 10 *No one knows*

3. My life is more shaped by my fears than my dreams.

   Dreams win 0 1 2 3 4 5 6 7 8 9 10 *Fears win*

4. We frequently worry about what others will think of us.

   Not at all 0 1 2 3 4 5 6 7 8 9 10 *Constantly*

5. I motivate myself by remembering what happens if I don't do something.

   I don't worry 0 1 2 3 4 5 6 7 8 9 10 *I push myself*

6. People here act tough.

   Not at all 0 1 2 3 4 5 6 7 8 9 10 *With everyone*

7. I make decisions to keep others from being mad at me.

   No worries for me 0 1 2 3 4 5 6 7 8 9 10 *Consistantly*

8. We spend a lot of time distracting or entertaining ourselves.

   Not at all 0 1 2 3 4 5 6 7 8 9 10 *Most of the time*

9. I feel anxious when I think about disappointing others.

   Not at all 0 1 2 3 4 5 6 7 8 9 10 *I can't stand it*

10. In our family, the same person is always the responsible one.

    We all share 0 1 2 3 4 5 6 7 8 9 10 *Every time*

Total your scores here. _____
Mark the matching spot on the scale.

0   10   20   30   40   50   60   70   80   90   100

My Joyful Maturity Bible Study

Think back on something you appreciate and spend two minutes enjoying appreciation. Next, ask God to make this study interesting for you. Now read the following passage from the epistles.

Scripture Romans 14:1-15:7 Read then review the passage for each question.

Chapter Five Question: According to this passage, how does God want us to protect community?

Weakness, Joy and Shalom Questions:
1. Who are the weak or strong in this passage?
2. What kind of interaction does God desire between weak and strong?
3. What do we learn about joy and shalom (everything works together) from this passage?

Immanuel Questions:
1. What effects does perceiving "God is with us" have in this passage?
2. Group study activity: God is always present and eager to help us see more clearly. In what ways do we perceive or guess that God is helping us understand this passage right now in the group discussion?

   Note: Thinking about God's active presence may seem strange at first because people generally discuss the past more than they observe the present. Keep your answers short. Feel free to guess. We will do this each week.

Personal Story Question: When, in your life, did you sense God meeting you in your weakness?

Whole Bible Question: What Bible stories and verses tell us how God wants us to treat the weak?

Wrap-Up Minute: What do you now know that you didn't know before this week's study?

My Life Model Joy Exercises

At the end of each of the following exercises, notice how your body feels and what changed both during and after you practiced appreciation. (If your answer is, "It felt good," then ask yourself how you know it felt good. For example, "I felt a lightness in my chest, or my breathing is deeper and I can breathe better." Be specific.) When you meet as a group, discuss the results of your individual exercises for chapter five.

Building Appreciation Upstream
1. Think of three people in your life you consider upstream. These are people with more life experience and maturity than you. List three to five qualities you appreciate about their personality.
2. Through face-to-face contact or a physical card, share the qualities you appreciate about their character. If in person, notice how they receive your appreciation. Pay attention to how you feel building appreciation. For card writers, notice how it feels to express appreciation. How do you imagine they will feel reading your note?

Building Appreciation with Peers
1. Think of three people in your life you consider peers. List three to five qualities you appreciate about their personality.
2. The next time you see these people, share the qualities you appreciate about their character. Notice how they receive your appreciation. Pay attention to how you feel building appreciation.

Building Appreciation Downstream
1. Think of three people in your life you consider downstream. These are people with less life experience and maturity than you. List three to five qualities you appreciate about their personality.
2. Through face-to-face contact or a physical card, share the qualities you appreciate about their character. If in person, notice how they receive your appreciation. Pay attention to how you feel building appreciation. For card writers, notice how it feels to express appreciation. How do you imagine they will feel reading your note?

Chapter Six

Multigenerational Environment

There are huge social and global issues threatening the multigenerational community. Since the industrial revolution several new factors have made this far worse. Wars are more extensive. For the first time, weapons of mass destruction can be purchased by cultures that are wealthy from raw materials sales but too predatory to be able to develop such complex weapons on their own. Rapid, low-cost transportation allows people easy movement to cities in hope of work only to find very low-joy conditions. We still have the effects of slavery, sex trade, colonialism, fascism, communism and predatory capitalism exploiting weakness across the globe. To this, we can add time spent servicing debt that keeps many parents out of the home. We are replacing personal relationships with the media and technology cloud, so we text but do not talk. We have a lot more drugs than we did a 100 years ago. People also continue using violence as entertainment. All of these threats to multigenerational community have their toxic effect by lowering the level of our joy. We will examine how we are destroying joy, propagating predator patterns and how we can start joy again. We can reduce the destructive, toxic effects of many threats by raising joy levels and transmitting joyful protector skills to the next generation.

Shelia's story

Low-joy at home: I grew up in Houston, Texas, where the air is humid and the accents are thick. On hot summer days my grandma bought watermelon, and we spit the seeds at each other while running around under the water sprinkler in her front yard. I had a host of cousins to play with, 24 of us on my dad's side. All the generations interacted playfully more often than not. It could have been a great setting in which to learn joy. But my dad had already suffered the loss of baby Grace, and it altered him forever. A few months shy of my fifth birthday, and ten years after Grace's death, my dad, who was on his way home from the oil fields where he worked with his daddy, lost control of his pickup truck on a winding road in East Texas. He died just before my mom and Sean arrived at the hospital.

My dad's death was too much for my mom to take, and for as long as I can remember, she slept day and night. She was in bed when we left for school in the morning, and she was in bed asleep when we stepped off the school bus in the afternoons. She rose late at night, dressed herself up in sparkly clothes and headed off to a local bar where she danced, drank and dated men who were predatory and abusive.

My brother Sean took over most of Mom's duties. He was thirteen. He fed Ella and me and taught us to wash the dishes and do our own laundry. Both chores involved stepstools or chairs for us to stand on since we couldn't reach the kitchen sink or the washing machine. Sean kept us safe and tucked us in at night. He became the man of the house and took care of our mom too. In fact, we all did. When Mom was awake, she banged on the headboard of her bed and demanded things from us: the mail from the mailbox, the newspaper from the driveway, a cheese sandwich, or a glass of iced tea in a glass, glass, not a plastic one, with two squirts of lemon juice. I always took a bite out of her cheese sandwich and wrapped a napkin around the missing piece, so she wouldn't see it at first glance. I think I did this out of anger, although she always laughed.

Often, when anything bad happened in our family, and bad things happened frequently, Mom exclaimed that it should have been her instead of our daddy who died. She threatened suicide and on a few occasions attempted it. One time she parked the car in the garage, turned on the ignition, and waited for the fumes to fill the car. The carbon monoxide also filled the house through a hole in the garage ceiling. My brother Luke rescued her and saved us. I awoke the next day with a terrible headache and nausea. Mom confessed years later that she was only trying to kill herself and had not wanted to harm us. On another occasion, she took too many Valium and attempted to chase after my stepfather who had sped off after a nasty fight. He was one of the abusive, predatory men she met at the bar and quickly married. She pulled out of the garage, backed into a tree, and plowed the car into the side of our house. My brother Luke, who was fifteen at the time, rushed to our mom and somehow got her out of the car and back into bed. Then he ran back outside, slid into the driver's seat, revved the engine, and extracted the car from the crumbling mess of bricks that had once held our home together. I stood and watched in horror.

Our only respite, or so I thought at the time, were our weekend stays with Grandma and Grandpa, which began just after my dad died. These weekends marked my only tastes of routine and "safety." Only I was not so safe. My grandpa molested me. He was a God-fearing man and a dedicated churchgoer, so his actions befuddled me. I adored him so I didn't speak of what he had done. Decades later at Grandpa's funeral, I learned from an older cousin that he had also molested others in our family.

Shelia and church: "Rise and shine, girls! We'll be late for church," Grandma's voice screeched down the hallway into the middle bedroom where my sister and I slept each weekend.

Minutes later Luke bolted in and jumped on our bed singing, "Sun's in the Sky. Grass knee high. Get up, Shelia. Get up, Ella!"

"Hurry up! *Mister Ed* is coming on! GET UP!" he shouted as he yanked the covers from the bed. Ella got up first. She smelled the hot cakes and the syrup, which by now were set on the kitchen table. This was her motivation to get up. I was the last to rise and it was only the sounds of, "of course, of course" that made me budge. The voice of the singing horse rang out from the TV in the den. I grabbed my pillow and headed for my spot on the floor.

"Come on, girls, hurry now. Eat your breakfast. It's time for the *Jimmy Swaggart Show*." That was the signal that we must leave in order to get to Sunday school on time. When Jimmy yelled and slammed the Bible in his hands, we headed for the blue, Ford Lincoln Continental that slept in the garage until the three of us jumped, bounced, and screamed our ways

into position in the back seat. And we were off to church with Grandma
and Grandpa each Sunday morning where we would hear about the
end times, the mark of the beast and the rapture. I wiggled around in
the pew, waiting, watching and anticipating the prophetic message that
surely predicted the end of the world. All the while my sister Ella enter-
tained herself and ate Life Savers unaffected by the inevitable doom that
kept me on the edge of my seat.

My grandma was riddled with anxiety about the last days and the
end of the world. I internalized her fears, but Ella never believed a word
Grandma said. I was convinced by the time I was seven that I had committed the unpardonable sin. Church was not a place where I learned joy.

Shelia at school: Most of my school experience was about hiding my
family life from my teachers and classmates. I quickly became an expert
at acting like everything was just fine. I was an obedient, "goody-two
shoes" type so I fit right in. I was a rule follower, not out of joy, but
because I did not want to be exposed. I was certain that the abuse happening at home made me a "bad girl," and I didn't want my teachers to
know that I wasn't good. Fear motivated me. I worked hard to please my
teachers with a "good" pseudo-self because I wanted them to love me.

I had one teacher in the fourth grade that I never forgot. Her name
was Miss Davis. Fear was not invited into her classroom. In her presence
I only experienced acceptance and love. I remember that I got to school
early each day so I could be there when she arrived. Her face lit up to
find me there waiting. I could not have named it then but I was discovering joy. Miss Davis opened her door early and let me in. I became one
of her helpers. This gave me a sense of belonging and usefulness that I
had no idea I desperately needed. At recess, I kept her within my sight.
I longed to be close to her. I played with my friends, though, so they
would not think I was weird. None of them seemed to want to hang out
with the teachers.

I never told her what was happening at home, but I did bring her gifts
and cards. One time I brought her a candy necklace. She opened it up
and did not hesitate before pulling it over her head and around her neck.
At recess that day, I watched her from the monkey bars and saw her lift
the necklace to her mouth and bite off one of the candy rings. I was ec-
static. She was actually enjoying my gift. It was my first taste of pure joy!
I fell in love with Miss Davis that day, and I decided to become a teacher.

When I was in the fifth grade, I was distraught because I was no
longer in Miss Davis' class. I started acting out in Ms. Dudley's class.

Ms. Dudley did not like me and often punished my behavior. To ease my pain, I wrote letters to Miss Davis. At the end of my fifth grade year, Miss Davis got engaged and moved away. I continued to write to her, and staying in touch helped soothe my attachment pain.

When I was in my 30s, I searched for and located Miss Davis who is now Mrs. Kent. I wanted to tell her she had left an imprint on my heart and I was now a teacher because of her. I called her. When she answered the phone, and I identified myself, she knew exactly who I was! I told her my story and how she had "saved" me. She said she had kept the cards and letters I mailed to her when I was ten years old. She asked me to hold on and went to retrieve them. One was a wedding card she wanted to share with me. I had written a poem in it. 1500 miles apart and 20 years after I had sent it to her, Mrs. Kent read what I had written to her, "A peach is a peach. A plum is a plum, but a kiss isn't a kiss without some tongue." We both roared with laughter. She asked me if I wanted her to send it to me. I respectfully declined, "I think you should keep that one!" I gently reminded her that I had no parental supervision at that time in my life, and that I had no idea from what book I had copied it. Today, 38 years later, Mrs. Kent and I are social media friends. I still want to be just like her when I grow up.

Transformation: My relationship with my mom today is one of tenderness and protection. She told me several years ago that all she wanted before she died was for me to forgive her. At the time, it seemed like such a difficult task I wasn't sure I was capable of granting it to her. Not long ago at a midnight, Christmas Eve church service in Houston, my mom stood next to me. I glanced at her and I felt something akin to compassion. I remembered all the things I knew about her: she drank, slept with different men and eventually ran off with a truck driver. She was a woman who once danced the two-step in bars so gracefully that men flocked around her and begged to be her next partner. She was also the woman who stayed up all night sewing our 1976 bicentennial prairie dresses so that Ella and I could be in the school parade. And she was the woman in the bleachers at all my softball games yelling, "Watch out! Here comes trouble!" She was rooting for me and encouraging my swift ability to steal bases.

As I reflected on the birth of Jesus and my mother's life, something fluttered in my gut, the tears began to fall, and before I knew what's happening, I leaned toward her and whispered, "I forgive you." She raised her head and with tear-filled eyes nodded at me. Since then I've felt only tenderness for her. My mom and I talk and text weekly now, and I will miss her when God calls her home.

What is destroying joy levels?

As we start examining how predators and the fear of predators shape communities and families, we will point out the obvious. We are naturally weak in many ways. To hide weakness from predators, we must pretend to be stronger than we are. We inflate ourselves to look as strong as possible in order to be liked. However, joy comes from someone being glad to be with the real me which might be too hidden for anyone to find. Meanwhile communities punish anyone who might bring predators their way. Communities punish anyone who shows weakness while the growing number of predators exploit every weakness they see. Joy levels drop.

Instead of becoming comfortable with using our weaknesses as a beginning of growth we all begin to feel the push to be stronger than we are. Some of us develop strong ideas others will not question, some strong self-justification, some strong emotions, some create strong fears in others, some want to be super sexy, some work on projecting a perfect image, while others are strongly detached and even cold. Social skills are used to hide weakness, and toxic shame replaces healthy shame. Joy drops as the level of deception and "pseudos" rises with pseudo-identities, pseudo-joy and pseudo-maturity leading the way. In a low-joy world no one is what they appear to be.

The increase in pseudo-joy and pseudo-maturity results in relational pain and problems that directly stunt growth. Low-joy brings a drop in the success at school. Low-joy families raise low-joy children who grow into low-joy adults. Pseudo-joy replaces family bonds as people use BEEPS to regulate emotions and quiet their pain. Bigger, better, stronger and prettier become the goals for our bodies, homes, cars, lawns, churches, sports teams and schools.

Predators use weaknesses for personal advantage. Leo has definite weaknesses in his concentration and motivation. When he wanders off in the middle of another project, Thelma begins a well-known litany of comparisons to "better husbands" and "undesirable people" designed to point out Leo's weakness and motivate him through misery. Joy levels drop each time. Meanwhile, possums will hold up their weakness as a shield or excuse for inactivity. What program leader has not heard a chorus of "I'm not very good" when asking others to help with a church project? The cumulative result is that people begin to hide their weaknesses, hide themselves and amplify distress instead of joy. Low-joy is corrosive so people spend their energy protecting themselves instead of doing creative work.

The problem for people is that we must kill ourselves inside to appear strong on the outside. Our brains can only create a pseudo-me out of some parts of the brain we would use to create a real me. When we create a pseudo-me that is dominant it will slowly take over the operations of our brain. Like an invasive species, this pseudo-me robs the real me of vitality. The problem is that this puffed up and powerful sounding self believes its own delusional lies.

Even if people like the new "pseudo-me mask," joy has been blocked. Instead, strong people are haunted with the feeling that "if people really knew me (all about me) they might not like me." Doubts linger about how well others would like me if I fail. Instead of genuine joy, we attract people who will protect our "pseudo-me masks" and carefully avoid placing demands on us that would reveal who we "really are." We might even warn people, "Don't go there! You are not going to like it if you get me mad!" Any time we have a gathering of strong people, we can be sure there is a high concentration of pseudo-me developing.

What would make a good pseudo-me for home? What would be a good pseudo-me at school? What would be a great pseudo-me for church? When we gather as pseudo-me people, we form a club to support and praise our pseudo-traits. Together we hide weaknesses as much as possible, making joy superficial. "Yes Darling!" Pseudo-me mom thinks, "I am very caring for my family." Pseudo-me teacher believes, "I am a very good teacher and care about my students." Pseudo-me pastor cares for his flock. And none of them is entirely wrong. We usually find real, caring people who hide cravings for sugar, power, sex and attention. We are real, caring people who became shallower than we want to be or even believe we are.

Self-justification is the single most destructive threat to joy

Strong self-justification is the largest threat to a joyful, multigenerational environment. To understand this threat we need to know the relationship between joy and anti-joy in the brain. Our brains are wired to respond with joy amplification to anyone who is glad to be with us. When someone is not glad to be with us, we feel the anti-joy emotion of shame. Healthy shame is how we learn from our mistakes that produce low-joy around us. As strange as it seems, little doses of healthy shame help us protect the joy in everyone around us and keep a high-joy environment. For example, in Shelia's classroom, she often has to correct students. One day as she was teaching, and her students were taking notes, she observed Henry, who had his head buried in a book. She gently and privately asked Henry if he were keeping up with the note taking, since the information was critical to his understanding of *Julius Caesar*. Henry responded with a flushed face and a quick apology. He then closed the novel he was reading and began writing. Henry's sense of shame was not one where he suffered humiliation, but it was a kind reminder to return to the task at hand.

Some people who do not have the gentle protector skill of learning from healthy shame will reject all shame messages. In order to reject all shame messages, it is necessary to justify oneself and make everything someone else's fault. "You had it coming. No, you are the one who is insensitive. You are supposed to be a teacher. You should know better. You always want to be right. I would not react this way if you didn't ..." On and on the self-justification goes. The Bible calls this problem being "stiff-necked" because when people accept healthy shame they hang their heads and those who justify themselves "stiff-neck" the situation. The current term is narcissism. One cannot tell narcissists that they have a problem or the narcissist will react like a predator and bite. Instead of showing shame, narcissists justify themselves. This self-justification destroys joy. In order to avoid the healthy shame message, a narcissist must pounce on a weakness in the other person. What follows is not a tender response to weakness, but the narcissist will justify the pouncing in many ways. By self-justification, the narcissist avoids learning an important lesson about how to grow joy around him or herself.

Self-justification is a form of trying to be strong and "have nothing wrong with me." Like all pseudo-strengths, refusing healthy shame kills joy, stops growth and destroys communities. Destruction will happen whether the self-justified, stiff-necked person is one of the weak or strong members of the community. We will look at examples of narcissistic leaders, but narcissistic followers destroy communities just as effectively. To stay in the t-Zone, the whole community needs to show a tender response to the weakness in others and learn from healthy shame messages about the things that do not bring joy.

Narcissists prey upon the weaknesses and vulnerabilities of others while concealing their own weaknesses. The late Lybian dictator Muammar Gaddafi was a predatory narcissist who raped girls and boys using them as sex slaves. He seemed to prefer school girls and told his victims he was now their father, brother and lover effectively trying to destroy their multigenerational bonds. We have no shortage of narcissists who take the helm of governments, schools, churches, businesses and families, though most go unnoticed.

In many cases, the narcissistic leader is rewarded while the weak bear the brunt of the cruelty. If predators do not freely receive power, they use manipulation, charisma, promises, even force to grab what they want. Read more in Jim's book *The Pandora Problem: facing narcissism in leaders and ourselves.*

Shelia experience will help us spot self-justification and respond with God-sight, shame messages and a tender response to weakness. While this situation was actually much worse than we are telling, it will help us see what dealing with predatory narcissism is like.

Shelia starts a new life away from home

I left home at age eighteen to attend university. No one in our family had attended college. My sister and I were the first. While Ella stayed locally, I moved four hours away from home. I needed a fresh start in a new city.

I was overcome with depression and anxiety about the sexual abuse perpetrated by my grandpa and my stepfather, a secret I had guarded for years. I had not even told my twin sister. I had learned to "look alive" in high school. I was an overachiever, and I had perfected the "performance" of a person on a path to success. I was well equipped with a pseudo-identity, pseudo-joy and pseudo-maturity. I was pseudo-ready!

I decided it best to keep my masks in place. I believed I had committed the unpardonable sin, and the only way for me to be close to God was to do it on this side of eternity. I joined a local church of the same denomination of my grandparents. To my surprise, I found a campus fellowship sponsored by the same group. I met new people and participated fully in weekly services in spite of how awkward and different I felt. I knew I had to be as involved as possible since there was no way I was going to heaven. In my thinking, this fellowship would be the only "heaven" I would ever experience.

Let us pause to consider a few questions. Did Shelia start college with a tender response to her own weakness? Did she expect a tender response from church? Could she see herself with Godsight? Were shame messages directed in the right direction in her mind? Then Shelia continues:

Pastor W and his wife co-pastored the campus fellowship. I was not immediately drawn to either of them, but I loved playing with their beautiful children. This endeared me to Mrs. W. She soon began inviting me to lunch for long talks spurred by her numerous questions about me. No one had taken this kind of interest in me before, so I delighted in the attention. Mrs. W invited me to be a part of her discipleship group and I accepted. Additionally, she initiated a one-on-one discipleship relationship with me. It took me nearly two years, but it was through this personal meeting time with Mrs. W that my heart softened and I chose to share the details of my past, including the sexual abuse. She nurtured me and provided an atmosphere of trust, security and acceptance. As we grew closer I began to see how she was functioning as a "spiritual parent" to me.

As my involvement in the campus fellowship increased, Mrs. W faded out as an active pastor in order to attend graduate school. She assured me that our relationship would continue. Other students would receive discipleship elsewhere. I enjoyed Mrs. W's preferential treatment of me. She was the "mother" I had longed for.

Shelia becomes entangled with a narcissistic predator

Because Mrs. W was no longer leading her women's discipleship group, Pastor W invited me to be in his co-ed group. I refused. He insisted, claiming I needed a male role model and he was a person I could trust. Mrs. W also pushed me to join so I did. Simultaneously, Pastor W initiated an individual (two-way bond) discipleship relationship with me. He stated that his goals were to help me learn to trust men and develop a healthy relationship with a male role model. He often referred to himself as my "big brother." Mrs. W assured me that Pastor W was like a "coach" who would help me if I would just let him. As a result of Mrs. W's encouragement, Pastor W's persistence, and my growing trust in them both, I confided in Pastor W. I told him about the sexual and physical abuse of my childhood. Pastor W was extremely interested in helping me. I had no idea a self-justified predator was "protecting" me.

Within a month of my telling Pastor W about the abuse, he confessed, "I've been in love with you since I met you!" He assured me everything was fine in his relationship with Mrs. W, but that if he weren't already married, he would marry me. Somehow he now saw me as his "source of joy." I was confused and bewildered but admittedly flattered. I had never thought of Pastor W in a romantic way. I did not find him the least bit attractive. But Pastor W's words were smooth and sweet in a Bill Clinton way. No man had ever told me he loved me. I had never had a boyfriend nor had I ever dated. I didn't know what to do so I told him flat out that I did not want a romantic relationship with him. Pastor W agreed with me that nothing could ever happen, and I felt somewhat reassured that he sounded like a protector.

Narcissistic predators "groom" and isolate their victims

I agreed to meet him in a local park, thinking it was a public place where I would be safe. After expressing his feelings for me again, he assured me that he could not act on them. I was relieved. As we walked back to our respective cars, he asked, "Would it violate you too much if I kissed you?" I was shocked and before I had a chance to answer, he kissed me. I yanked my head back and exclaimed, "I just kissed a married man!"

He showed no shame like the shame that burned in me. He simply justified himself and the kiss by saying it was a "goodbye" kiss and not one that would begin a relationship. The exact opposite occurred.

It is a painful reality that the only people who had touched me were my abusers. I carried a notebook in which I recorded his inappropriate behavior. I attempted to end the interactions several times. I refused to have intercourse with him in spite of his repeated attempts.

Four months from the start, I was suicidal and I told Pastor W that I was going to tell Mrs. W. He swore me to secrecy. Another four months passed. Then, on their thirteenth wedding anniversary, Pastor W told his version of the story to his wife. Mrs. W rejected me. She told me to never contact her again. She contacted the church overseers at the state level.

You can be quite sure that the details of what Pastor W did are a great deal worse than anything Shelia has told here. We need to reflect on what we have read. Do you see any self-justification? Was Pastor W monitoring Shelia's weaknesses and isolating her? Was anyone seeing with Godsight? Where were shame messages needed? Should the people who knew Pastor W suspect that his story was self-justifying? Shelia continues:

By February of the following year there was a hearing by the denominational leaders. The hearing took place without me. Pastor W contacted me after the hearing to inform me of the outcome. He was to remain campus pastor but on probation. I was no longer allowed to attend the services on campus. The pastor of my local church informed me I was no longer welcome to attend his services since Pastor W and Mrs. W were also members. He said that I was not to tell anyone.

Once again, I was burdened with secrecy. I felt guilty, shamed, alone and desperate. Three years later I wrote a letter to the national headquarters of the denomination telling my story. I requested that they change the protocol for dealing with matters of clergy abuse.

I received a letter back stating that they regretted how I had suffered, *"due to [my] perception of the discipline and rehabilitation process the [denomination name] have in place for our credential ministers. While it is never our intent to ignore the heartaches of anyone, our only right of involvement lies with the minister in question."* The letter also stated, *"There is always healing available in Christ. He stands ever ready to help when we can but touch the hem of His garment."*

The letter made no mention of changing the protocol nor did they offer to help. I had been a member of the denomination since I was four years old. I was left unprotected and suffered at the hands of three pastors: the campus pastor, the local church pastor and the pastor at the helm of the denomination. While I have never questioned the "healing available in Christ," I immediately questioned whether there was healing available in church.

Three predatory pastors nearly destroyed my life so I never imagined how God would begin to heal the abuse. Jesus, in His uniquely personal way, joined me with Jim, Ed and Chris to write *Joy Starts Here*. Today, I'm experiencing the amazing, gentle protector skills of these three pastors who are instrumental in my restoration.

If you are having trouble with Godsight for Shelia, the Ws, the church or denomination right now you are not alone. Hearing Shelia's story generates intense feelings and makes us all uncomfortable. Yet, many stories like this stay hidden behind the masks in churches. Peeling back masks that cover narcissistic predators raises questions. What is a tender response?" Should we even have a tender response? Who will stop the self-justification? Who will deliver a shame message?

Shelia's church and denomination demonstrate how we avoid people and turn them into problems while forgetting relationships. Strong, self-justified reactions from predators and the institutions that support them, make exposing predatory abuse even more difficult. Fear of these reactions turns us into possums, permitting predatory behavior to propagate unchallenged.

Dealing with self-justified predators

A predatory leader is a weakness like an aneurism on an artery or a hemorrhage from the neck. The tender response to such weakness is a firm and determined effort to make it stop. No self-justification allowed. Study and do the exercises Jim lays out in *The Pandora Problem* if you want to learn how. Jim explains that when people around a narcissist decide that it will only get worse if they say something, it empowers the predator. Changes in the group that plays possum are needed.

Brian wanted to help other people break the destructive cycles that nearly cost him his marriage. As a successful businessman, Brian was respected within his community and felt important whenever people recognized him. Due to his business success, Brian's church felt comfortable putting him in charge of the recovery program. Brian was easy to enjoy as long as he was free to do as he wished. However, Brian left a trail of broken relationships. Brian's inability to receive a shame message without anger frightened his wife and intimidated his employees. Volunteers at the recovery group noticed Brian being sharp, bossy, and mean when things did not go his way. Brian raised his voice to get his way. When church leaders expressed their concerns to Brian, he threatened to leave the church and take "his people" with him. Church leadership developed a strong fear bond with Brian that placed him in control. Brian's church leaders became possums.

Trying to correct a narcissist is like touching a hot stove. We end up blistered with little desire to do it again. The ancients say, "Better to meet a bear robbed of her cubs than a fool bent on folly" Proverbs 17:12 (NIV). Narcissists use blame and shame as primary weapons to protect themselves which quickly drains joy in a group.

Communities guided by joyful leaders, on the other hand, feel the freedom to ask questions, correct, even contribute to the needs of both members and leaders. We find comforting imagery of God's leadership style in Isaiah. "He will feed His flock like a shepherd; He will gather the lambs with His arm, And carry them in His bosom, And gently lead those who are with young" 40:11 (NKJV). Jim worked with Dr. Marcus Warner writing how to develop *Rare Leadership: 4 Uncommon Habits for Increasing Trust, Joy, and Engagement in the People You Lead* for those who would like more on the topic.

Every culture dislikes weakness, so do the weak

As soon as pointing out weakness helps us gain the upper hand, it seems almost everyone joins the fight. Here is a way to win, to motivate, to get revenge, to distract and escape, to "level the playing field," to "show others how it feels" and to be "fair." We make a major mistake if we think that the weak are not capable of attacking weakness as vigorously as predators can.

If causing pain is the way to power then there are few sources as easily available as weakness. Weakness is vulnerability. Weakness is usually easy to demonstrate. Since most people hide weakness, then most people will suspect others have hidden weakness, even without much proof. Furthermore, everyone can do it. People can even use teaching about joy to create a weakness.

Herbie would drop by his pastor's office whenever he wanted something. If his pastor did not drop everything and happily attend to Herbie's desires, he would say, "You are supposed to be a pastor and you teach all about this joy stuff but you don't seem happy to see me! How am I supposed to do it? You are supposed to be my example and you seem irritated to see me." Herbie was good at pointing out people's faults, especially when he felt he was not being treated properly. Herbie had contempt for weaknesses in others that was second only to how he hated weakness in himself. Herbie often felt bad, thought he was bad, or became angry that he imagined other people thought he was bad. It was clear that Herbie had more weaknesses than most people. Herbie had few family members, few impressive accomplishments, limited artistic expression, scarce adventures and few friends. He lacked admiration from others and had not generated a long list of acts of Christian service.

In low-joy communities, weakness is despised and ridiculed. Jessica teaches fourth grade in a low-joy school. Parents who do not like the grades their children receive want to make sure that Jessica takes the blame. Administration and even other teachers join in looking for the weak link and heap disgust and contempt on whomever they think is responsible for low grades, scores or making the school "look bad." Joy levels keep sinking at Jessica's school.

When people look at all these problems and weaknesses, it helps them conclude incorrectly that the solution is to be strong. Let us consider once again why weakness is more than something to get rid of and why weakness is a necessary part of all lasting transformations.

How does weakness become essential?

Tenderness toward weakness has some obvious advantages for us in weak moments, but the greatest benefit comes when we respond tenderly. Dr. Kang is an admired dentist and community leader, but he does not point to becoming a dentist as the thing that transformed him. Dr. Kang points to his five years providing dental care to transient workers as the experience that helped him learn to be a protector. Working as a dentist for people who could not adequately care for themselves started by necessity, not idealism. Caring for people who could not afford soap did more to make him a man of God than learning helpful dental skills. Transformations happen when the weak and strong are together and weakness is treated tenderly. Without tenderness for the weak, the strong will waste their protectiveness on their possessions. This is not the path to joy.

Weakness is essential in joyful, multigenerational community because mutual, joyful bonds require vulnerability. Self-protection in others does not grow joyful community. A community based on mutual self-protection is rooted in fear and not joy. Fear bonds will be life draining and kill, exclude and reject those who do not perform well. This is a breeding ground for religious performance and Pharisaic behavior. However, real caring comes from real joy. We recall that pseudo-me was made from "real me" brain parts that were deceived about who we really are in order to hide weakness. Real character grows when we build joy with weak people. When there is a strong enough joy bond with weak people, the strong will discover they also have weaknesses. Now real transformation can begin for everyone.

Weakness is essential to community because it allows for the growth of a stronger, more stable individual and group identity that includes everyone. Without care for weakness, communities develop higher numbers of predator traits. Biblically, communities should accept and care for the weak: widows, orphans, strangers and the poor. This is not only the object of true religion, it is a part of the means by which true religion changes character.

All the same, there is vulnerability in becoming our true selves. Predators will still take a bite when they can. Recovering predators among us still pounce when they are craving. Pseudo-me masks create rejection, and disdain will create pain. Weak people take pride in finding weaknesses in the strong and each other. Any pastor can attest that both the strong and the weak excel at pointing out her or his faults. While churches frequently have the weak and the strong in the same building, they are usually there at different times or in different corners. Most are willing to point out the weakness in each other when threatened, using overtones that range from concern to derision. There is no joy and no character improvement from these encounters. It is not enough to have the weak and strong together. We need something that will allow tenderness toward weaknesses from all participants.

It is necessary for both the weak and strong to have a tender heart for weakness. Therefore, all the plans by churches and schools to inspire their members to be strong where weakness abounds unravel as soon as weaknesses begin to show in the leaders and participants. Some leaders refuse to accept anyone pointing out their weakness and will quickly turn the tables. Protectors try to stop the scratching and biting, but without joy, we soon find people nursing their tender spots instead of growing tender hearts. Most well-intentioned efforts end in this kind of misery.

When the interactions between the weak and strong are guided by people with mature protector personalities, the interactions are very revealing. The strong discover their areas of weakness when they start to share life and relationships. Once outside the comfort zone they created with their strength, they discover new places to grow. The weak discover that they have areas of strength to share with people they thought were too strong to need them. Everyone discovers that they are strong with weak times or weak with strong times. We have times when we need others to be stronger. There are times to practice our skills with peers where we are all about the same capacity. But, we particularly need times when we can help weaker members of our community to be fully alive.

Weakness teaches us to value and protect our group, our people. Neighbors grow closer during earthquakes, floods, power outages, blizzards and times we need to help each other. Family members turn to each other during times of illness, and churches bring meals to those who are recovering. Physical weakness is a good example of the attitudes we should adopt for other forms of weakness.

Propagation of a joyful identity requires weakness in community to be visible and welcome. When there is joy to share weakness, then weakness transforms community members. Tenderness toward weakness allows church communities to include others who are not yet members of spiritual family. Creating belonging around us is for both weak and strong. Thus, weakness leads to authentic community when our relationships are joyful.

Correcting low-joy, BEEPS and fear

We are starting to see that we can all have predatory moments. We all have times of self-justification. We all have relationships where we find possums. We all have weaknesses that we hide from others. If we get super honest, we have some weaknesses that really annoy us and we have a hard time responding tenderly. If we look into our own cultures and multigenerational tree, we will find a lot of contributing causes to the way we deal with weakness and the weaknesses we have. Perhaps the hardest part is being honest about our iniquities, those deformities that we cherish as a group or family that we think make us strong. Some of these deformities have come to us from our particular Christian heritage as well. Do we have the courage to ask if these things we consider strengths are helping joy to grow and spread from one generation to the next?

Joy starts at home

In the early 1990's, Ed's life seemed to be going well. He was a supervising therapist at a 96-bed alcohol and drug treatment program and was also working two to three evenings a week with Christ-centered support groups in local churches. Then, following surgery to correct an injury to his knee, he developed an incredibly painful disease called Reflex Sympathetic Dystrophy in his knee. The RSD caused such extreme sensitivity that even the air from a ceiling fan blowing on Ed's knee triggered excruciating, burning pain. The disease spread from Ed's knee to every joint from his jaw to his feet. Suddenly, unable to work, concentrate, focus his attention or complete simple tasks of daily living, Ed's career and ministry came to an abrupt end. Ed was soon living in a chronic low-joy state as his health, work and relationships were severely damaged and serious depression followed.

It was not long before Ed discovered a tasty form of pseudo-joy, banana nut muffins and ice cream. Although the muffins and ice cream did not make his condition improve, the sugar in the large muffins and big bowls of ice cream were a pleasant distraction from the pain. Ed began to look forward to "muffin time" as a reward for living through the mornings and afternoons. Ice cream was his reward for making it through the day. Not surprisingly, Ed gained weight as comfort-eating increased and his low-joy state continued. In the ensuing years, Ed gained approximately 60 pounds and developed Type 2 diabetes. His comfort-eating provided temporary relief but could not satisfy his brain's deepest yearnings for genuine joy.

Ten years later, Ed and Maritza attended a trauma conference in Medicine Hat, Canada where they met Chris and heard Jim teaching about joy for the first time. As soon as Ed heard Jim teaching about joy, he realized that he needed to start building some serious joy! He also understood for the first time that the effects of joy and pseudo-joy in the brain helped explain the process of addiction and trauma he had observed for years. Joy was what was missing from his personal and professional life.

Ed and Maritza also realized that understanding joy was not enough; they needed to experience and grow joy together in their relationship. They attended *THRIVE Training* and spent intensive days learning from Chris and practicing exercises to help grow a foundation of joy for their relationship. When they returned home, Ed and Maritza continued practicing joy exercises, and their joy bonds grew. As Ed and Maritza increased their capacity for joy, their appreciation for one another grew, and their relationship became increasingly life-giving. Everything about their relationship, including how they related to Maritza's sons, began to change. Sharing joy with Maritza and with God was immensely satisfying and much healthier (and much less fattening) than comfort eating!

Joy starts at school

Shelia desired to grow joy in her entire school, so she started the Joy Builders Club. She wrote a brief mission statement, "We will focus on establishing an atmosphere of joy and trust through 1) Story-telling, 2) Pausing, and 3) Practicing the art of appreciation. We will keep it SIMPLE." Shelia was not sure the club would work, but she was willing to take a risk. Shelia started small with the vision that the group would grow over time. She sent an invitation to six teachers she knew would be receptive. Shelia understood that a joyful group identity is one that is not rooted in problems and fear so she built her club around creating a joyful lunch period for teachers. She sent out the first invitation, and all the teachers showed up.

When the teachers entered the room, Shelia handed them "pretend" microphones, and they all joined her in lip-syncing the lyrics to a high-energy

song. Laughter erupted. After watching a short portion of a video on vulnerability, she invited each teacher to talk about their response to vulnerability
and times when they have been free to be vulnerable. They connected deeply
in a matter of minutes. The atmosphere was tender and fun.

Joy starts at church

Pastor Eric and his wife became very excited about joy after attending
THRIVE Training. He liked the effects of joy, and immediately identified two
places each Sunday he could spread this joy to his congregation. The first was
the crucial seven seconds after people walked in the front door while the second opportunity came when the congregation stood to greet each other. His
first step was to prepare his greeters to create joy as people arrived.

Using two of the nineteen skills he learned at *THRIVE*, Pastor Eric trained
his greeters to one, express joy with their face and voice and two, recognize
when people needed a breather. New people, in particular, can feel anxious
when entering a church so greeters could provide joy or shalom as needed. After a few Sundays of joy building by greeters, people began commenting that
church felt life-giving, refreshing and much like a "fun family get together."

Pastor Eric coached his worship team to give joyful greetings as an example
for the congregation during the meet and greet time. Then, so people would
understand what was happening, Pastor Eric preached about joy for several
weeks. He urged members to practice joy at home and at church. He also
encouraged his congregation to invite others for lunch after church. He asked
church members to notice and connect with people who were new or who
appeared to be struggling or sitting alone.

Pastor Eric was pleasantly surprised to see how the atmosphere in the
church changed. He watched as faces lit up, people talked, laughed, cried,
hugged, prayed and interacted. The energy levels significantly increased during the joy-based interaction. Mixing the weak with the strong in this way
moved his church into the transformation zone.

Jim and Michel Hendricks have more to say about buiding joy at church
in their book *The Other Half of Church: Chritian Community, Brain Science,
and Overcoming Spiritual Stagnation* for those who would like to read farther.

How are we doing?
- What is our response to narcissistic leaders?
- How does our community deal with self-justified people?
- How does our culture regard weakness?
- Am I strong with weak moments or weak with strong moments?
- Do I hide certain weaknesses from others?

Conclusions about joyful, multigenerational community

We have now met Ed, Shelia, Chris and Jim. Each one comes from a different background with lots of reasons to be low-joy. All of us have come to the conclusion that we were meant to be joy starters and pass joy on to others. We are sure that being a joy starter is at the core of our dream for living as well. We have seen four things so far that must be added to the simple desire to start joy. First, we cannot lay around like possums as the Christians did under Hitler. We cannot be possums at home, in school, with bullies or with narcissists, for political correctness or popularity. Second, being joy starters means we do not let predators go unopposed. Jesus pointedly called out the religious predators of His day, calling them hypocrites, blind guides, snakes and a brood of vipers. Third, to keep predators from reproducing through our children, we must restore gentle protector skills. Fourth, we must start the kind of joy that spreads from wherever we are right now. We spread joy to those who are older, to our peers and the people who are younger than we are. This is a step we can all take to save the multigenerational environment. In the next part we will look at how God helps us start joy.

Joy Actions

Home: Have a family meal and thank God for feeding you.

School: Find one or two partners to help you think of ways to build joy at school.

Church: Share this book with one or two people at your church that you think might become joy starters with you.

Environmental Self-Justification Assessment

1. I protect myself from shame, criticism, hurt or judgment.

    I invite critiques   0 1 2 3 4 5 6 7 8 9 10   *I'm always careful*

2. I do not feel comfortable speaking to leaders about their faults or failures.

    Not a problem   0 1 2 3 4 5 6 7 8 9 10   *Very risky*

3. Other people would be better off if they followed my advice.

    I need advice   0 1 2 3 4 5 6 7 8 9 10   *I'm usually right*

4. We have "swept many problems under the carpet" here.

    Nothing hidden   0 1 2 3 4 5 6 7 8 9 10   *A huge problem*

5. I try to rise to the top and be in charge.

    No responsibility   0 1 2 3 4 5 6 7 8 9 10   *I get things moving*

6. What I disclose in this place will be used against me (or others) later.

    Strongly disagree   0 1 2 3 4 5 6 7 8 9 10   *Strongly agree*

7. It is hard to listen to others because my opinions are usually right.

    I love to listen   0 1 2 3 4 5 6 7 8 9 10   *I make things clear*

8. I am constantly worried that things that go wrong will be my fault.

    Not at all   0 1 2 3 4 5 6 7 8 9 10   *This is my life*

9. I actively oppose letting a critical spirit or negativity develop.

    Not my concern   0 1 2 3 4 5 6 7 8 9 10   *No criticism allowed*

10. People under me say I encourage them to point out my character flaws.

    No reluctance to talk   0 1 2 3 4 5 6 7 8 9 10   *Total silence about my flaws*

Total your scores here. _____
Mark the matching spot on the scale.

0   10   20   30   40   50   60   70   80   90   100

Our Joyful Identity Bible Study

Think back on something you appreciate and spend two minutes enjoying appreciation. Next, ask God to make this study interesting for you. Now read the following passage from the wisdom literature.

Scripture Job 29:7-25 Read then review the passage for each question.

Chapter Six Question: How does Job demonstrate character and spread joy from one generation to the next?

Weakness, Joy and Shalom Questions:
1. Who are weak or strong in this passage?
2. What kind of interaction does God desire between weak and strong?
3. What do we learn about joy and shalom (everything works together) from this passage?

Immanuel Questions:
1. What effects does perceiving "God is with us" have in this passage?
2. Group study activity: God is always present and eager to help us see more clearly. In what ways do we perceive or guess that God is helping us understand this passage right now in the group discussion?

> **Note:** Thinking about God's active presence may seem strange at first because people generally discuss the past more than they observe the present. Keep your answers short. Feel free to guess. We will do this each week.

Personal Story Question: When has your joy been increased by someone from another generation?

Whole Bible Question: What characters from the Bible would you go out of your way to meet or avoid and why?

Wrap-Up Minute: What do you now know that you didn't know before this week's study?

Our Life Model Joy Exercises

Choose as many exercises that time will allow.

Group: Appreciation
1. As a group, take turns sharing three things you appreciate from your day.
2. Discuss how appreciation feels. When everyone finishes, close with three minutes of quiet.
3. Take turns expressing three things you appreciate from the previous week.
4. Discuss how appreciation feels. When everyone finishes, close with three minutes of quiet.
5. Take turns expressing three qualities you appreciate about God.
6. Discuss how appreciation feels. When everyone finishes, close with three minutes of quiet.
7. Close by praying for each group member. Include a blessing as you pray for each person.

Group: Joy Stories
1. As a group, take turns telling a few of your favorite joy memories from the previous year. Each story should be told in under three minutes.
2. Close with three minutes of quiet time.

Group: Food
1. As a group, discuss the role food and drink plays in your life as it relates to your joy levels, managing your distress and recovering from upset. Consider having this discussion during a joyful group meal.
2. What types of food do you consider comfort foods? Why is this?
3. What is the cost of using food to help you feel better?
4. What role do food and drink play to bring comfort in your family, school and church?
5. How can you use food to draw closer to one another and God through shared "breaking of the bread" experiences?
6. Pray for weaknesses and struggles that were expressed.

Part Two
Joyful Immanuel Lifestyle

Rejoice in the Lord always. Again I will say, rejoice!
Let your gentleness be known to all men. The Lord is at hand.
Philippians 4:4-5 NKJV

The Life Model for sustainable joy is based on three things that are not usually found together: multigenerational community, an Immanuel lifestyle and relational brain skills. Take any of these three away and joy levels start to fall quickly. In **Part Two** of this book, we will look at why we need something our family and friends cannot give us if we want joy to grow and spread!

War, trauma, crime, cruelty and many wicked things have deformed human communities so that they no longer reliably produce joy for weak and strong alike. We will not get the Nobel Prize for being the first to notice. Wherever there is damage, life must be healed and restarted. What is missing, killed or injured must be revived so that everything needed for joy will be in our lives and identities. When things are put right, we feel a kind of rest we call shalom. Sustainable shalom, where everything fits together peacefully, is needed for long-term joy.

In the first chapter of **Part Two**, we will look at how Immanuel (God with us) finds and revives our identities through relational interaction with us. In the second chapter, we discover that Immanuel does not work alone but always in the company of God's people. Shalom, joy and restoration are a community practice for home, school, work and church.

Chapter Seven

Restoring My Joyful Identity

We are all underdeveloped and, to be blunt about it, distorted in our identities. With all our creativity and reactivity, we frequently act like less than we could be or want to be. How many times have we thought, "I could have done better!" While performance is simple to critique, identity is much more difficult because our brain is configured to know our identity according to how others see us and not what we want it to be. In **Part Two** we will simply propose that when people install our identities incorrectly, God is available to interact with us and reset our identity.

Ed's Story

For as long as I can remember, I wanted a connection with God. Having learned about Him as a child at home and in Catholic schools, I knew that God was supposed to be important and very loving. I longed to know what that kind of connection felt like. At night, after my parents helped us say our prayers, tucked us in, turned out the lights and closed the door, I would often quietly get out of bed and kneel down to pray. I was sure that God loved me and listened, but I really had no idea how to connect with Him. From time to time I caught small tastes of what I now understand are God's joyful presence and peace, but these always seemed to be "happy accidents" with no predictable, discernible pattern. These seemed to occur more frequently around my mother's smile and joy, family holiday gatherings, moments when I listened to music and occasionally at church, but I had no idea how to regularly experience Immanuel.

While I loved those Immanuel moments, they really did not do much to change my identity or my view of myself. I was deeply loved by mom and dad. I also frequently experienced low-joy and very high performance environments at home, at school and with friends. Failure seemed to equal shame, humiliation and contempt. To avoid being eaten, it seemed best to hide and avoid weakness, if possible. To make things worse, the religion classes taught by the rather strict and seemingly joyless nuns in my early years focused on consequences of sin and hell. I vividly remember the day when Sister told us stories of people who died horribly in fires and whirlpools, simply because they were disobedient. If her intent was to make us afraid, she succeeded!

This fear introduced iniquity into my life and had a powerful effect on my identity. I desperately wanted to connect with the loving God I heard about and saw in my mother's smile, but He also seemed to be just as demanding, humorless, joyless, punishing, blaming and shaming as many others in my life. To survive, it seemed best to hide my weaknesses and vulnerabilities on the inside and to appear outwardly strong by pleasing others and performing as perfectly as possible. My identity was powerfully shaped by fear of being embarrassed, humiliated and shamed for mistakes and failures. I made resolutions to "do better" the next time. I longed to experience Immanuel's love and acceptance.

As time went by, those moments of tasting God's presence seemed to happen more infrequently. My life and identity became increasingly shaped by my inability to live up to what seemed to be impossible expectations and the sense of shame and humiliation that failure produced. As my resolve to perform and appear strong grew, I felt increasingly angry, frustrated and tired of performing. I rebelled. By the time I reached college, I happily began to drink, drug and use a variety of BEEPS to relieve the pressure, manage my emotions and and numb the dreaded sense of anxiety when I tried to connect with others. BEEPS produced a temporary sense of relief that was overshadowed by the inevitable hangover. Furthermore, my behavior while I was using BEEPS violated my own value system and left me feeling ashamed and even more empty. The counterfeit pseudo-shalom produced by the BEEPS was nothing like the loving, peaceful presence of God I had tasted as a child, or the joy from the sparkle I had seen in my mother's eyes.

When I finally "hit bottom" I asked some Christian friends, and God, for help. The moment I asked Jesus for help, I was flooded with an incredible sense of God's presence, joy, and love. I felt surrounded and gently held by The Presence I had been looking for my entire life. Now, God no longer seemed He was a distant but loving God. He was Immanuel, God who was with me, and full of love, joy and shalom. I experienced more of Immanuel's presence and peace as I read my Bible, worshipped and developed new relationships with loving friends at my new Bible fellowship. The combination of joyful interactions with Immanuel and the joy on my friends' faces when we were together began to transform my sense of self. The love of those friends also was invaluable in helping me come to better know and understand Immanuel's presence.

My experiences with Immanuel only increased my longing for more of His peace and presence. I still tried hard to appear strong and conceal my weaknesses from my new friends. I worked hard to figure out what I needed to do in order to "grow in Christ and live the Christian life." While I learned that I was a "new creation in Christ," I still felt very much like the same deeply wounded person who worked hard to appear strong. Looking around at church leaders and my new friends, they all seemed so happy, and I felt like I was missing something. I also discovered that the harder I "worked" at being a Christian, the less awareness I had of God's presence. Looking back on that time, I can see that God loved meeting with me, especially when I was honest about struggles. He did not seem to be nearly as interested in meeting with me when I was trying to act like the human performing machine. My frustration only grew when a nasty split divided the Bible fellowship, as well as many of my new friends.

Several years later, at another church I attended, one of the elders held a class on how to listen to God. That sounded exactly like what I had been waiting for! I wanted to know Immanuel's presence as a lifestyle and hoped this class would help make Immanuel's presence a reality. After about three or four weeks of preparation in class, it was finally time to start listening to God's voice, and I did! It was an amazing and scary experience. Up until this point, I tried my best to study scripture and then try to apply it to make good decisions in life. After the exercise, I suddenly realized that I would now be responsible to actually do everything I might hear God tell me. This was not particularly good news, because I was already trying hard to avoid shame, pain and failure by performing as hard as I could. The prospect of having a new list of "things God wanted" was terrifying because I was fairly sure I would fail. Furthermore, the exercise seemed to focus more on the mechanics of hearing God's voice and not on actually experiencing the joy, delight and love of His presence that I wanted the most. It seemed to me that I was just learning to listen to a semi-anonymous voice that was going to give me a new set of rules that I would not be able to live up to. What could have been a joyful encounter with Immanuel's presence became a fearful, frustrating and empty experience. My identity remained stuck in fear and shame.

Things began to change as I entered training for ministry in the mid 1980's. I began to study the scriptures more closely, and I learned a new form of prayer that emphasized waiting to experience God's presence as well as talking with Him. To my surprise and delight, Immanuel began to make His joyful presence more consistently real to me. I increasingly learned to talk with Jesus about my day, what was on my mind and what was on His mind. Jesus always seemed really happy to talk about everything! On top of that, Immanuel's sense of delight, joy, and love persisted even when I failed, "blew it," or made major mistakes. The more I experienced Immanuel's presence, the more Jesus' joy began to nibble away at my old shame, fear and iniquity-based identity. I still feared failure, but my identity was changing in response to God's presence and grace.

After a number of years of fruitful work and ministry, I was injured and contracted the very painful disease mentioned earlier. As my disease progressed, I found myself sick, alone, unable to do work or ministry, and living in a severely low-joy state. Everything, including life and relationships, felt overwhelming. As my life and relationships crumbled, I came face-to-face with an identity that had been based on avoiding weakness by performing. At that point in my life, I no longer had the strength or energy to try and conceal my obvious weaknesses, and I experienced intense feelings of shame and failure. What remained of my identity crumbled.

Over time, as my condition finally stabilized, I spent a lot of time talking with God about my life, pain and experiences. As I began to interact with God in my weakness I became increasingly aware of God's presence. In the moment of my life's greatest weakness, God's joy and delight began to break through more consistently and intensely than at any point. It did not seem to matter what was going on; I started looking for Immanuel and found Him everywhere! Jesus was not ashamed of me and never responded with humiliation or contempt. Jesus was glad to be with me, my identity was shifting, and I was starting to experience the Immanuel lifestyle!

One day when I was in the hospital, I was so weak that getting out of bed was almost impossible. I was utterly discouraged. Suddenly, to my amazement, Immanuel's loving presence seemed to fill the room. I was astonished as I became very aware of Jesus' compassion, joy and shalom. I clearly heard Him say in my spirit, "Ed, I know you have little strength, and that's really okay with Me. Just hold on to what you have." The sense of Immanuel's presence brought the deepest shalom I had ever known. Tears of joy poured down my cheeks as I knew overwhelming joy. I knew I was loved, enjoyed, understood and valued, at the weakest point of my entire life.

As I processed this encounter with Jesus, I realized that something had profoundly changed. A deep and abiding sense of shalom remained. Instead of feeling shame, hate and fear about my weakness, I felt absolutely and totally accepted. My identity had been shaped by iniquity, fear, shame and the drive to perform. And now, at the weakest point of my entire life, Jesus told me that it was really OK to be weak. His presence in my weakness made me see that I did not have to try to be strong, hide weakness or perform, ever!

What started with Jesus began to grow with others. I began discovering and growing joy in my relationship with Maritza and others. The change in my identity became more pronounced. God, and other people, helped shape my identity and restored me to the heart that Jesus gave me. The joyful, Immanuel lifestyle had begun and would now be passed on to other people!

What happened to my identity?

Families and cultures pass along identities to babies during the first two years of the child's life in a complex face-to-face process that shapes the brain's chemistry, structure, connections and even which genes will be activated. In these first two years babies are programmed with the skills to be human. The newborn child has many potential abilities that might be activated, but only those that are used will be seen. The rest of our potential abilities are largely deleted after ages four and twelve. So here is the bad news. A child's brain will only develop the skills used by his group during the formative years. No one in the family or culture will know that other skills and abilities might have been possible.

Some propose that we leave children undefined so that they can name themselves, and choose their own gender and identity when they are about four years old. There are two fatal flaws in this idea. First, the brain will delete unused nerves at age four leaving the child without the brain cells needed for potential but unused characteristics to develop. Second, the brain does not directly perceive its own identity. Leaving the child to know what the brain cannot see creates uncertainty. Who to be becomes a wild guess.

With a little thought we will decide that we want nearly perfect conditions for the brain-to-brain identity download in baby's first two years. However, if we have ever updated a computer we know that problems are common. The two major ones are: 1) interrupting the transfer and 2) downloading a corrupted file. Interruptions of the transfer process are usually external problems like: war, illness, accidents, work, travel, death in the family, crime, riots, famine, BEEPS, imprisonment, family violence, incest, abuse and any other major life disruption during the formative first two years of life. While the child may appear to be developing normally on the outside, one or more gentle protector skills dropped out of the process.

Second, the people who raise us might lack some skills in their identity "file." In Ed's case, he learned the value of excellence in work from a loving dad who was missing essential joyful relational skills from his identity. Instead of joy, fear, shame, contempt and humiliation became motivators in their relationship. Sadly, this was never his dad's heart or intent. Ed's father's lack of joyful relational skills, as well as an identity shaped around performance, work and fear are seen in the life of his own family and grandfather, at least three generations from Ed.

Relational identity skills are often lost over the generations and centuries. A whole generation may be changed due to war, pestilence, famine, earthquakes, floods or genocide. When people are forced to flee, a new colony grows with only the skills that they managed to bring along. Cultures can develop a kind of characteristic personality style based on shared gaps. These missing skills become part of the family, religious, ethnic, regional or national character for a group identity. What groups are known for their tempers? Who will always argue? Where are wars frequent? Who are hard drinkers? Who lies? What cultures avoid shame? While these generalizations reflect patterns used to cope with missing skills, all human communities have gaps. Each family has missing abilities and everyone received a damaged identity during the transfer process.

Religious beliefs suppress certain skills and parenting fads often shift whole groups of children. When everyone around us has the same cards missing, we never guess our identity could be otherwise. When we are the only ones who seem to be missing skills we entertain deep doubts about our value.

The identity transfer process shapes the brain's relational circuits and functions responsible for developing our identity. Any errors or missing components of identity will disrupt the function of our brain's relational circuits so we no longer understand our identities and relationships the way God intended. The restoration of the function of our relational circuits is accomplished by learning to perceive God and interacting with others. Ed's toxic shame was a derivative of his damaged relational circuits.

While these problems have been around for thousands of years, in **Part Three** of this book we will examine how the extreme changes in the last 100 years are driving a new cluster of skills to near extinction. We will first examine how joyful identity is restored after centuries of sin, iniquity, transgression, calamity, famine, human trafficking, persecution, pestilence, pillaging, peril and sword have taken their toll.

God's joyful presence restores our identities

Many of our abilities are never developed because no one activated them. One of the brain benefits of our spiritual and religious life is to activate parts of our identity that would otherwise get lost. All major religions do this in differing ways. All major religions promote belonging. Confucian philosophy heavily stresses multigenerational community, respect, loyalty and care for the values of the past. Buddhists practice quieting skills. Islam and Judaism activate and restore group skills.

As the world's largest religion, Christianity has the greatest potential to restore joyful identity together with a history of not doing so. The sheer number of Christians is a force that should not be wasted. Combine the numbers with Jesus' statement that high-joy is the reason for His teaching, and we find over two billion people with a mandate to be joy starters. Joyful, sustainable recovery suits the Christian mission.

Jesus expected people to bond with Him in high-joy ways and spread the joy of a joyful God. Joy was the reward. Christians were to lavish joy on all around them especially their low-joy enemies. People who previously had no joy to see each other were to learn new identities that created belonging and love. What is especially noteworthy is that the weak were always to be treated as the most important throughout the Kingdom of God, so that joy would always find its way to the places of highest need.

Right from the start there have been problems getting this to work. Christians continuously change the scriptural descriptions of joyful character into a list of performance standards that they must do in their low-joy state. Performance standards do not allow for weakness and encourage the development of a pseudo-me. This was definitely a significant issue in Ed's life from which it took him years to recover and helped lead to the use of BEEPS.

Let us assume God knows our identity before it even starts to grow. Each part of us is awaiting the signal to be awakened. Our natural families and communities have activated some parts, misshaped other parts, disliked parts and told us what we have done is who we really are. We all have many undiscovered parts, but we have no idea what they are.

Even when we receive a new life in Christ and enter life in the Kingdom of God, we can honestly look at ourselves and notice that many of the characteristics of a Christian are still missing. We often do not love our enemies as one example. Part of entering the Kingdom of God as a little child is the willingness to become someone we have never been before. Such a person has already been awakened in our spirits. Our brains can only see our identity from the past (who we have been) and from the capacities someone has activated in us. We desire something better, but we cannot do it or make it work on our own.

There are, in fact, two ways to awaken a new self. We could have Jesus awaken our souls, or we could have an older and stronger Christian find in us what has grown in him or her. In Ed's case, his interactions with God and with family, friends, mentors and peers were all essential to the growth of his new identity. Interacting with Immanuel became a source of joyful identity change. Through the years, Ed was also blessed with the influence of amazing mentors who also fundamentally transformed his image of himself. The same interactions with God and others can help all of us awaken our new self. The untouched aspects of our identities would be revealed by interactions with Jesus and strengthened by practice in our multigenerational community. Mature people would see in us what God sees. Peers would practice growing our new identities and skills. We would see God's design in younger people who are weaker than we are. In fact, the Life Model exercises were designed to achieve this very purpose. The key to it all is the God who will actively interact with each of us in ways that help us find our real identity. God is always with us, and for that reason, we have called this the Immanuel lifestyle.

What is an Immanuel lifestyle?

The Immanuel lifestyle is one in which we increasingly discover how Jesus does things and invites us to join Him while we enjoy Him. Increasing awareness of God's interactive presence with us begins to enter ways we relate with others, live our lives, raise our children, do our work and drive our cars. It takes very little observation to notice that when we are aware of God's presence and point of view, there is profound peace as we live that moment. Shalom is that sense that God is working everything together in a good way even when we are not sure how. We sense that God is not worried so why should we be troubled?

The Immanuel lifestyle is a biblical lifestyle for we are told to "pray without ceasing" or we might say, "talk with God about everything." Antwan was raised in a culture where adults, particularly men, did not interact with children. When visiting another country, Antwan watched with amazement how a four-year old on a car ride with his father chatted and asked questions about everything he saw, and the father answered. We may be equally amazed that God wants us to chatter with Him about everything we see and ask questions and learn something in return.

Another simple observation is that in all areas where our shalom is gone, so is our sense of God's active presence. The most extreme case is that of Type B trauma, when bad things happen. We feel isolated and alone in our distress. Dr. Karl Lehman has worked extensively on ways to help people recover from these traumas and has named this the Immanuel process whereby we discover that God has always been with us. Aspects of this Immanuel process are included in many of the Life Model resources. While this way to recover from traumas can be used with individuals and groups, Immanuel experiences do not represent a miraculous healing so much as a return to the normal joy-bond between God and God's people. In this bond we see ourselves and the world correctly and therefore have shalom.

The more we understand computers, the more important synchronization becomes. Synchronization is at the heart of networks that work. Nervous systems like our brain require precise synchronization with the right thing at the right time in the right amount or there is trouble. We thought, "God must have talked about synchronization in the Bible," but what word did God use? The word was shalom and is usually translated peace. As we have seen, shalom is everything in right relation, in the right place, at the right time, in the right amount, so that God is pleased. Obviously that we cannot achieve this standard on our own. One of God's leading characteristics is the ability to synchronize everything so that everything works together for good where it should be good. We say, "That just makes sense!" It all fits. Sometimes it all fits in a way we cannot even explain and then we have shalom that passes all understanding. We are also to restore synchronization, as Jesus said, "Blessed are the shalom makers."

The signs of a joyful Immanuel lifestyle include: an increasingly secure bond with God and others and a growing, increasing capacity to remain connected with God when things are difficult. Oddly, this does not usually mean we have God on some kind of telephone line (or cell phone) where we hear a constant commentary or video stream. Instead, we have a capacity to think with another mind in real time we call "mutual mind." Our brains have a mutual mind state designed into them that runs faster than conscious thought and that is reserved for only those beings with whom we share a deep bond.

In the mutual mind state, we cannot tell immediately if a thought is mine or theirs or ours. It is exactly in these mutual mind states that new aspects of our identity can be activated and shaped. The mutual mind state is deeply relational and reserved for "our people" who have our trust and the right to redefine who we are. In this state, we could allow the "mind which is in Christ Jesus" to dwell in us with that certainty that we would be changed. You can discover how our attachment with God produces a mutual mind in Jim's book *Renovated: God, Dallas Willard and Churches that Transform.*

Mutual mind states of joy with God are also the basis for joy between God's people. Paul takes us through this process in his instructions to the Philippians. He starts by saying, "Fulfill my joy by being like-minded, having the same love, being of one accord, of one mind." He concludes by saying, "Let this mind be in you which was also in Christ Jesus" Philippians 2:2, 5 (NKJV).

Mutual mind states with God help us become new people, but they also help us to know how God sees the world and particularly the people around us. This ability to see things as God does is what we have dubbed, "Godsight." It is a stiff workout to learn to see things the way God does. The change is not for the timid and will never happen without joy. While there are many theologians who study documents and theories to develop structures for religion, Godsight is not like that at all. Godsight comes from a life of shalom with God that gives special care to anything that troubles the unity and peace of our experience. Godsight grows by returning to our best connection with God and asking to be shown why some bit of life causes us to lose our peace and break our bond with God. When my neighbor leaves his trash cans at the curb for three extra days and I think how I would like to see them knocked over and spilled on his driveway, my shalom is gone along with my Godsight.

My brain is in sort of an "enemy mode." It is time to restore my bond with God and have my identity corrected. Why my identity? Because I still think that what I like is revenge and pain for my neighbor. That cannot be the mind of Christ working in me.

The growth of capacity, Godsight and mutual mind states with God do not mean that we will float through life blissfully unaware of pain, challenges and problems. My neighbor still leaves his trash out for the week. People still rudely take the parking spot we are waiting for at the mall, and our family members will still do the same things that always make us angry. Rather than take away our problems, the growth of joyful capacity, Godsight and mutual mind states help us grow more joy strength so that we can suffer well. "Suffering well" means that we have the capacity to experience the pain of life but remain relationally connected with God and others. This allows us to suffer and still remain the same relational person over time when bad things happen, just as Jesus, "who for the joy set before him endured the cross, scorning its shame, and sat down at the right hand of the throne of God" Hebrews 12:2b (NIV). Joy allowed Jesus to endure the cross and shame and interact redemptively with those around Him. Joy allows us to stay connected with Jesus and each other through the pain of life.

Immanuel shalom at home

Rodrigo and Lupe had one of their periodic fights about her spending too much time and money on her family, at least from Rodrigo's point of view. He pointed out how hard he worked, how they had their own children, how things were tight and how the house could use more care. Lupe pointed out how Rodrigo had just helped his brother, how her mother had been very tired lately and that it would not hurt if Rodrigo picked up a few things around the house. Well, we do not need the full tour to know that by now neither Rodrigo or Lupe were having shalom. In fact, the joy levels were down, and they were pouncing on weaknesses in a very predatory way. Had Rodrigo noticed, he would have known his shalom was gone before he started the discussion. Had either of them noticed, they would have detected that their shalom was gone for the whole exchange. Although both would tell us they were Christians, neither had any sense of God's presence, creativity or options during the entire fight. Well, they would say they do not fight, so let us call it a "joy robber."

As Rodrigo sat in his room feeling no joy and fighting the urge to get on the internet, he picked up the phone and called his prayer partner instead. His friend's first question was whether Rodrigo could sense God's presence during this important moment and when the answer was "no," they agreed to solve that problem first. Although he did not feel like doing it initially, with his friend's help, Rodrigo remembered several times that he felt close to God, how he had appreciated God's help when his daughter was sick and the joy of children's laughter. This already made Rodrigo feel a little more shalom and sense that God was there.

Now they asked God to show Rodrigo where God was in this situation with Lupe. Rodrigo had an impression he could not quite explain that Jesus knew how important Rodrigo's home was and how hard he worked, so he would not live in the kind of chaos he had growing up. It really felt true to him that Jesus understood and was proud of him. Then Rodrigo had a thought and sort of a picture of Lupe as a teenager when her mother was quite sick. Lupe looked like a frightened little girl. This image gave him a tear in his eye, and he said out loud how much he would like to make it better for everyone. It occurred to him that this realization would have been a much better starting point for his talk with Lupe. Immanuel was with him so Rodrigo went to find Lupe and have another talk, this time with protective shalom in his heart and a tenderness toward her weakness.

Immanuel shalom at school

Latisha felt that the other girls in her second grade class did not like her and did not ask her to play. She would often come home upset. Her mother talked with other mothers only to discover that more than half of the little girls in the class also felt that no one liked them or wanted to play. This poll did not cheer Latisha. Her mother had learned about Immanuel shalom, and it occurred to her to ask Latisha when she was upset if she felt Jesus was in the classroom with her. Latisha said, no. Mommy invited her to sit together and hug. She validated how sad Latisha felt. Mommy asked her if she would like a pear, her favorite fruit. When she saw some steady smiles, Mommy asked if Latisha could feel Jesus here now, and she could. "Let's ask Him to show us where He is in your classroom." Latisha saw Him at her table coloring. So Mommy asked if He seemed upset. Latisha said no, He was happy. Mommy inquired about what Jesus wanted her to know about the children that did not want to play with her. Latisha smiled quickly and said that Jesus told her she could invite them to play with her. When Mommy asked if she could do that, Latisha nodded and happily ate her pear. In the next days, Latisha reported that she liked having Jesus at school with her. Although there was no evidence that the girls in the class became any friendlier with each other, Latisha had her shalom back.

Immanuel shalom at church

Karen was elected as an officer for her small church group. That meant that she was to help run the meetings. However, it soon became clear that Lisa, an older member of the group, considered it her job to run everything while complaining at the same time that she had too much to do. The group was getting tired of Lisa and her controlling ways and complained to Karen, leaving her with the sense that she should do something. Thinking about Lisa, or even what she wanted for the class, would cause Karen's shalom to disappear. Her brain's relational center began to lose synchronization leaving her irritated and with a vague sense she was doing something wrong.

Karen had learned in her *Belonging* class that these signs meant her shalom was gone and that she was not sensing God's presence. A quick check showed this was true. Karen did not feel close to God when she thought about Lisa. Karen sat down and remembered what God had done for her until she felt thankful. Only then did she ask God to help her see the Lisa situation as God did. If Karen could not reach shalom right away she could find someone in church to help her. The important part of the Immanuel lifestyle at church is that Karen needs to find her shalom before she tries to talk through her upset with Lisa. It is important to make sure that God is peacefully with us before engaging with others to solve a difficulty.

Why is joy at the heart of the Immanuel lifestyle?

Joy is the basis for a secure bond with God. Our brain will only build a solidly new identity within a joy-bonded relationship. If we want to be new people, we need a new bond with a "joy-daddy" in the right-brain who has all the characteristics we need to learn. Joy activates the brain's relational circuits in the middle of our identity center, so we can perceive God is with us and interacting with our minds. Joy grows out of a thankful heart.

The kind of joy bonds that are at the heart of the Immanuel lifestyle are a response to the extravagance of God's love and grace. If God was only glad to be with us when we were working very hard to be good, then joy would be totally conditional and performance-based. Because God loves us first, we are able to receive His grace to us with joy. These bonds renew our strength when we are weak and help us share God's joy with others.

How does weakness become essential?

Any pseudo-me identity will have hidden weakness because, like any prosthetic, it does not match the real us. Therefore, weakness is usually present when we begin to ask about God's design for the real us. When we sense a weakness and ask God, "What do you want me to know about this?", we are asking a wise question.

When we are being our true selves, we will have shalom inside, seek harmony with others and feel appreciation. Colossians 3:15 shows us how to put this sense of shalom to practical use in our lives. The verse says, "And let the peace of God rule ["brabeuo"- to be a referee] in your hearts, to which also you were called in one body; and be thankful" (NKJV). So, we are to let God's shalom be the referee and every time shalom is gone we must stop the game and get it back before we can do anything else. Shalom is the indicator (referee) that tells us if we are being our true selves according to our calling. Further, shalom will be accompanied by appreciation (thankfulness) every time.

Jane is agitated with how the young people are leaving trash in the church parking lot. Is she in shalom? Donna is frustrated that the fourth graders are still not lined up and quiet after the second bell when she has been teaching them to line up quietly for a month. Is she in shalom? Arthur is agitated that his son has refused to do what his mother has asked him to do for the third time. Is he in shalom? No, they all feel powerless and frustrated. All are considering how to become more powerful, so they can take control of the situation. But, in their frustration, the shalom of God is missing and the referee is blowing the whistle.

When we are raised by people who did not teach us to seek shalom from God, we will turn to people when we are upset, grab them by the throat, and try to make them give us some shalom. This is codependency and a personality deformity (iniquity). A deformity produces the lack of shalom.

Many things we see as strengths are hardened parts of our lives we use to cover weakness. From the tough guy who does not need anybody, to the overachiever who uses people, all monsters and super-men live without shalom, trying to make life work by becoming more powerful. This is universal and not just something that happens to Christians. The closer we come to God, the more reliable our shalom becomes. On the other side we notice that self-justification goes with looking stronger than we really are.

Whether we live with the self-justification of a predator or the self-hate of a person wearing a possum mask, the results are the same. Shalom is gone and we must hide parts of ourselves that we do not approve. Weakness develops around the areas that we keep hidden because they are the "non-relational" areas of our lives. These are the areas where we do not perceive God's presence. Therefore, another test of shalom is whether we can perceive God's presence.

An Immanuel lifestyle therefore must pass the three tests from Colossians 3:15 in every moment we live as well as all those we remember. The three tests are:

1.   I feel shalom
2.   I desire harmony with God and God's people I know
3.   I am in a state of appreciation

All false strength comes from hiding how we were hurt by others. We hide from relationships or in relationships. This means that attachments must be restored before we will be free of the urge to find power. We need a reality where God is with us, likes us and is for us.

Care for weakness propagates protector identities because we as protectors seek shalom rather than being strong, working hard and justifying ourselves. Shalom brings God's active presence into each situation, and by seeing God's heart, we learn to protect with a tender heart instead of becoming upset. In shalom and care for weakness, we discover what can keep the weak and strong together. We need to make this work in real life, and that requires training that helps us learn shalom, appreciation, joy and Godsight together whenever we feel agitated. What makes this counter-intuitive is that we are trained to strengthen our pseudo-selves and hide our real selves.

What God does with weakness to build shalom and identity

Saint Paul speaks about each of us having an old pseudo-self that is being dismantled and a new true self that is being built. "Do not lie to one another, since you have put off the old man with his deeds, and have put on the new man who is renewed in knowledge according to the image of Him who created him" Colossians 3:9-10 (NKJV).

Our old pseudo-self is the only one our brain knows and is full of deformities (iniquity) and things that are not as good as they could be (sin) that we have long considered to be our identities. Our identity becomes incorrectly assembled with parts missing and characteristics that do not belong to us. Each of these flaws becomes a weakness. So the first way that God works with weakness is to find flaws in our identities and, provided we acknowledge they are flaws, begin to restore us. These flaws are really the secret to why we hurt. When our old identities and lives do not fit the person we were created to be, there will be pain. When God looks at how we were misassembled, we feel known and special. Even why we hurt is special because it shows we are yearning for something better. God also uses what is strong in one person to help us see and heal what is weak in another. So the weak and strong parts of our lives both find a purpose in the Kingdom of God that builds a high-joy environment.

As Christians tried to figure out the old pseudo-self and the new true self using the logic of Western education they concluded that a perfectly logical person would be godly, and emotions were the weakness that made us go bad. Saints became those who could, by their wills, override their emotions, at least in public. Many a saint was hard to live with at home. Those with the strongest wills and most pious determination were able, while they had the strength and mental ability, to override their passions, emotions and desires. Sadly, as capacity to override emotions declined with age, the results became toxic. Christianity became a religion that regarded emotions as the weakness that causes sin. Since relationships were seen as leading to emotions and sins of indulgence, relationships were also a threat to the holy life. To be spiritually mature meant ridding oneself of emotions and possibly relationships as well. Developing emotional and relational maturity was seen as trying to revive the old pseudo-self and perceived as unspiritual.

True spiritual maturity includes every aspect of emotions and relationships but sees them all through the new eyes of Immanuel. God built our brains so they are hard-wired for specific emotions and grow well only in the presence of joyful relationships. The brain design alone shows us that these emotions are built to be regulated by loving relationships. What is needed is a new identity that actually sees people the way that God sees them and therefore feels about people as God feels. We would like to define spiritual maturity as the growing interactive relationship with God in which we are increasingly aware of His presence under difficult circumstances so that our identity, relationships and emotions increasingly reflect the character of Christ.

Emotional and relational maturity are part of our spiritual maturity. When our maturity is only grown from other human beings, we can only awaken in ourselves what they know. When Immanuel guides our maturity, God can awaken in us all the elements of God's design including the ones that have been lost or deformed by human history.

Here is the way to replace what has become extinct. God wants to teach us to see what is hidden behind weakness so joy rules our relationships through the shalom we feel. God wants us to embrace weakness. God is okay with that. This is our design. We are weak and God is strong.

Growing the Immanuel lifestyle at home

Burt and MaryAnn were at it again. No matter how hard she tried, Mary-Ann was chronically twenty minutes late for everything. After reminding her repeatedly throughout the day that they had to leave at 7pm for the impor- tant dinner with his boss, Burt sat in the car at 7:20 fuming. When MaryAnn finally slid into the car, Burt unloaded eight years worth of "why can't you be on time?" He was greeted by tears, resentment and promises to "do better the next time." "Next time?" Burt said incredulously. "There's not going to be a next time if you don't stop ruining my life and get your act together." Burt and MaryAnn shared a hurt, angry, silent evening with each other.

In his quiet time the next morning, Burt was troubled by what he said to MaryAnn. He loved MaryAnn but he also felt justified. "It is just not normal for someone with no children to always be that late," he thought to himself. As he began talking to God about his feelings, Burt felt a sense of sadness. As he explored the sadness further, Burt started to realize that God seemed to share a sense of sadness about the argument and all the hurt feelings through- out the years. "God," Burt said quietly, "I want to love my wife. Can you please help me?"

As soon as Burt finished his prayer, he remembered an old picture of Mary- Ann with her brothers and father. He thought of the chaos of a home with an alcoholic mother. A good day was when nobody was slapped, and nobody went to bed with a stomach growling for food.

Jesus reminded him of the way his wife's eyes sparkled when they first met, and how they still lit up when he came home from work. He saw how hard she tried to keep things organized at home and have dinner ready on time. Burt saw the look of sadness on her face when she tried so hard and yet could not get out the door on time. Seeing his wife's love, her weakness and Jesus' heart for her, all at the same time, reminded Burt of how special she truly was.

As Burt thought about how he had treated his wife's love and weakness, he felt ashamed. As his cheeks reddened with shame, Burt realized that Jesus was still glad to be with him. Jesus even seemed to understand Burt's feelings of embarrassment and frustration at being late to dinner with his boss. Burt felt free to love again. Suddenly, Burt realized that he had forgiveness and love to share with MaryAnn. "MaryAnn," he said as he got up, "I have something to tell you." Godsight allowed Burt to see his wife, himself, their weaknesses and Jesus more clearly. This is the Immanuel lifestyle.

Growing the Immanuel lifestyle at school

Lola, one of Shelia's students, wrote an essay about the problem of bullying on campus. Shelia's heart welled up with feelings of sadness for Lola's pain. She knew that since Lola's life had been damaged within the school system, that Lola would need a safe space in which to heal and restart. So Shelia looked up Lola's schedule and dialed the phone number to Lola's next class. When the teacher called Lola to the phone, Shelia told her that she had read her essay, that she was concerned about her, and that she was available if Lola needed anything. Shelia could hear the disbelief in Lola's voice. No one had ever taken the time to really see and hear her. This broke Shelia's heart, but it also served as the impetus to create a bully-free zone.

Shelia wanted to grow her protector identity in her classroom and at her school. She knew that our brains can only see our identity by remembering the past and have no idea that something else is possible. Students who are weak become targets of bullying, while other weaknesses lead to bullying behavior. Shelia's goal, as an educator, is not simply to educate academically, but to awaken their hearts and provide space for their true identities to emerge and grow. Shelia knew that both a protector and predator will see the weaknesses in both the bullied and the bully. She also knew that no one was going to have joy to be with either the bully or the bullied. The weakness of the bullied often prompted feelings of disgust and contempt, while the weakness of the bully often provoked feelings of rage. Shelia desired to see students the way God saw them.

Growing in the Immanuel lifestyle at church

After his first fifteen-minute Immanuel experience Pastor Ken declared, "I want everyone I know, especially my family and congregation, to feel the depth of joy that I just found!" The following Sunday Pastor Ken shared his Immanuel story to the congregation. He provided Bible examples where people frequently missed God's active presence. Pastor Ken expressed joy for what his Immanuel moment meant, along with his belief that living and interacting with God should be a way of life and worship. In the middle of his sermon, Pastor Ken asked everyone to remember a time where they felt true joy. "I want you to focus on your joy memory for several minutes until I say stop." After several moments to remember joy he said, "Now, ask Jesus if there is anything on His mind for you today."

Pastor Ken noticed the congregation responded with smiles, tears, hugs and even some celebrating. Next, Pastor Ken asked people to briefly share with each other what they experienced. Energy levels quickly rose. A growing wave of joy and shalom spread throughout the room. After this church service, Pastor Ken inserted the Immanuel lifestyle into his staff meetings, coffee times, prayer intercession gatherings, premarital counseling and the weekly Sunday service. Pastor Ken made it a point to have members of his pastoral team trained so the Immanuel awareness would become part of the fabric of the church. The Immanuel lifestyle not only brings people together but works for singles, couples and groups from all ages and backgrounds.

Appreciation and shalom

Shalom and a sense of God's presence go together, but when both are missing, appreciation becomes the doorway back to shalom and sensing God's presence. Most of us can remember a time when we were so upset we felt like we did not care. We did not care about prayer, what the Bible said or what we promised when we got married. This is an extreme case of our minds being out of relational mode and our relational circuits very dim. The opposite state of mind is one of appreciation where we care easily, share well and listen carefully. Appreciation is the best state for perceiving God's presence whether we are alone or in community.

When we need to reach shalom, due to the things that are not synchronizing in our lives, we start by finding appreciation. We use appreciation and shalom as keys for problem solving because they not only get our brains running in optimum states of creativity, but they help us engage with the resources in God and others. Problem solving does not go well individually or corporately without both shalom and appreciation. Without shalom our minds amplify the upset and the problems so the problems get bigger. Without shalom any problem becomes more important than love, attachment and the relationship. In practice this means that as soon as we lose shalom and appreciation, we need to stop, restore our relational circuits, restore appreciation and reconnect with God and others.

Shame and shalom

People will sometimes ask, "Is God glad to be with me when I'm sinning?" In response, we ask, "Is a doctor glad to be with us when we are having a heart attack?" If we accept the fact that we're having a heart attack, the answer is yes. If we want deny that we're having a heart attack and pretend that we're having shoulder pain that leaves us short of breath, the doctor might be exasperated and say, "You are going to die if you don't listen to me." This is because the doctor wants to help our real self, and our fantasy self is denying the heart attack. When God is glad to be with us it is never our pseudo-self, what the Bible calls the "old identity" or "old man," that makes God joyful but the real self hidden behind the pseudo-self. In Ed's case, his trying hard to be good did not give God joy. God was glad to be with the real Ed.

God then responds with "not glad to be with you" to the pseudo-self and with joy to the true self. Shame is the emotion we feel when someone is not glad to be with us. When God responds with "not glad to be with you"to our pseudo-self, He is trying to help us realize that we're not acting like ourselves, or at least not acting the way He intended for us to act. This kind of shame will lead us back to shalom if we look at things in the Immanuel way.

People who avoid all shame become narcissists, stiff-necked and known by their determination to justify themselves. Both weak and strong members of a community may be narcissists, and they will always destroy the community that does not know how to use healthy shame. We will consider this problem in more detail as we move forward.

What do we often mistake for shalom?

Strong people mistake their comfort zone for shalom. The comfort zone we create through our own strength by staying quiet, going numb, keeping peace at all costs, disengaging from relationships (dismissive attachment) and hushing others through tyranny might all look like shalom at first pass. Actually this is what the Bible calls, peace peace when there is no peace.

The possum keeps quiet, avoids upsetting anyone and says he is merely letting it go. A flippant "who cares" that treats all emotions as unimportant and no big deal is also not shalom. "Anything I say will only make it worse," is not shalom. These are ways of saying, "something is not right but I will not do anything about it." Shalom is the assurance that everything is right and nothing more needs to be done.

Groups with the resources to stay in their comfort zone, usually allow comfort to replace shalom. We can stay unchanged for years and even generations and mistake comfort for being blessed. This comfort zone is a courtesy that strong people provide for each other and it keeps any significant transformation from happening. Comfort zones maintain the status quo.

We will not escape this comfort zone unless we really begin to care for a weaker person in a personal way. When the weak and strong are together in multigenerational communities, our character will change each time Immanuel experiences help us to see others as God sees. Joy grows here.

How am I doing?
- Do I justify myself?
- Do I live in shalom?
- Have I gotten past just talking at God and begun to interact with God about my daily experiences and relationships?
- Do I help others see their true selves with Immanuel eyes?
- Is my true self making steady progress against my pseudo-self?

Few places reward the Immanuel lifestyle as much as in the lives of couples. Couples live in an emotional amplification system between their two brains, constantly amplifying every upset when protector relational skills are missing or damaged. Most of us know this all too well. Pounce on a weakness and we will puncture our joy. If we do not admit our weakness, our pseudo-selves slowly strangle our joy. We need to practice seeing weakness in ourselves and our mates through Immanuel's eyes.

As individuals, our goal is to pass the Immanuel lifestyle on to others. We discover what it is like us to be as a band of protectors even when we started out as predators. We help each other see moments where we still respond like predators. We need friends where we can talk about our weaknesses without receiving toxic shame in return. Joy comes from a tender response to our weaknesses and a strong sense of what God sees as our real identity and destiny. We change when our weaknesses are seen in Immanuel moments.

Am I going to invite God to dwell in my weakness? Is shalom worth it?

Correcting what we might have heard about knowing God

Three common fears seem to make it difficult for Christians to consider God is right here with us and wants to interact with us. The first fear is that nothing will happen. The second fear is that we will be misled into replacing the Bible with some mystical experience. The third fear is that we already know what God is going to say.

The first fear, that nothing is going to happen, frequently comes true because we go into an experience with God in a non-relational mode and our brain's relational circuits are off therefore we do not perceive God's presence. When people do have religious experiences with their relational circuits off, they are unaware of themselves during the religious experience so they cannot sort out if the experience was something they made up, came from drugs or some spirit other than God. It is best to learn how to listen to God as part of an experienced, multigenerational community that possesses the relational skills needed to engage with God. Engaging God is not difficult but not all approaches work. Jim and his friends John, Sungshim and Anna provide steps to engage God using mutual mind thoughts in *Joyful Journey*. Chris and Jim add ways to help others in the *Share Immanuel* booklet.

The second fear, that hearing from God is the same as trying to write our own version of scripture, reflects a valid concern that people might replace the Bible with some private interpretation of truth. Most of what we sense from God comes to us through a mutual mind state that is created by part of our brain's relational circuit. In a mutual mind state we are never sure if the thought came from us or the other mind. Mutual mind states are used for shaping our relational identity, calming our emotions and caring for others. When God is in a mutual mind state with us, we are a bit surprised by what we just thought, and on careful examination, we see something new we should consider. Hearing from God in a mutual mind state builds identity but never replaces scripture.

The third fear is knowing what God is going to say before we ask. They think God is going to be angry, disgusted, disappointed or condemning. Fear makes them figure out for themselves what they think God thinks. The strange thing about their answer (on behalf of God) is that it never passes the shalom test. When we answer questions on our own we don't find out anything from God. People who already know what God is going to say never actuall ask God without guidance. They usually will ask God about their fear with a little encouragement.

Knowing God grows from a strong and joyful attachment to God and God's people. When shalom changes who we are, God is with us in this moment and our community smiles.

Joy Actions

Home: Ask God how He sees each member of your family and put words to your mutual mind state.

School: Pick three people you routinely notice at school and ask God how He sees each of them. Put words to your mutual mind state.

Church: Pick three people you routinely notice at church and ask God how He sees each of them. Put words to your mutual mind state.

Assessment Of Immanuel Shalom

1. Every time something bothers me I talk with God until I feel better.

    Very rarely 0 1 2 3 4 5 6 7 8 9 10 *Almost always*

2. When things go wrong at church we still feel peaceful.

    Not likely 0 1 2 3 4 5 6 7 8 9 10 *We have solid peace*

3. I feel God with me.

    Not at all 0 1 2 3 4 5 6 7 8 9 10 *Consistently*

4. Most of the time I feel very peaceful inside.

    Not likely 0 1 2 3 4 5 6 7 8 9 10 *I have solid peace*

5. Prayer helped me see others differently many times this last year.

    Never 0 1 2 3 4 5 6 7 8 9 10 *Constantly*

6. My church family helps me find God's perspective when I am distressed.

    No help there 0 1 2 3 4 5 6 7 8 9 10 *Reliably*

7. I generally like who I am.

    Not at all 0 1 2 3 4 5 6 7 8 9 10 *Most of the time*

8. I can clearly tell of times when God changed my perspective.

    Not at all 0 1 2 3 4 5 6 7 8 9 10 *Many memories*

9. I feel appreciation most of the day.

    Not at all 0 1 2 3 4 5 6 7 8 9 10 *Most of the time*

10. Love often moves me out of my comfort zone.

    Not at all 0 1 2 3 4 5 6 7 8 9 10 *Most of the time*

Total your scores here. _____
Mark the matching spot on the scale.

0   10   20   30   40   50   60   70   80   90   100

God's Joyful Presence With Me

Think back on something you appreciate and spend two minutes enjoying appreciation. Next, ask God to make this study interesting for you. Now read the following passage from the epistles.

Scripture Colossians 3:1-17 Read then review the passage for each question.

Chapter Seven Question: What effects does God describe for our present life when we fill our minds with God's presence? ("Heavenly things" in verse 2)

Weakness, Joy and Shalom Questions:
1. Who are weak or strong in this passage?
2. What kind of interaction does God desire between weak and strong?
3. What do we learn about joy and shalom (everything works together) from this passage?

Immanuel Questions:
1. What effects does perceiving "God is with us" have in this passage?
2. Group study activity: God is always present and eager to help us see more clearly. In what ways do we perceive or guess that God is helping us understand this passage right now in the group discussion?

   Note: Thinking about God's active presence may seem strange at first because people generally discuss the past more than they observe the present. Keep your answers short. Feel free to guess. We will do this each week.

Personal Story Question: Describe a time your attitude, outlook or mood changed after you saw things differently, more like God saw the situation.

Whole Bible Question: What Bible stories tell of unexpectedly experiencing God's presence and the effect produced by knowing God was there?

Wrap-Up Minute: What do you now know that you didn't know before this week's study?

My Life Model Joy With God Exercises

Individual: Shalom Building

1. Can you identify a time in your day where shalom was lacking?
2. Remember one of your favorite appreciation memories for three minutes then take a moment and ask Jesus what He wants you to know that would give you shalom. Put words to your mutual mind state.
3. Can you predict a moment in the rest of your day or tomorrow where shalom-building will be needed? What steps can you take to build shalom in these particular moments? Talk with God about your thoughts and strategies.

Group: Shalom Starting

As a group discuss the following:

1. What you have learned about shalom in your life and relationships.
2. During a regular day how often do you feel shalom?
3. What people (do not mention names), events and situations seem to impact your shalom levels? (Keep in mind shalom is not the absence of distress, conflict or problems. Shalom is the presence of peace and joy where everything works together correctly, the right things are in the right place in the right amount so everything pleases God.)
4. What steps can you take in order to maintain your shalom in those moments?
5. Take time to pray together. Ask for God's shalom. Ask if He has any additional thoughts for you. Discuss your thoughts and observations.

Chapter Eight

A Joyful Church Identity

Since our individual and group identities are constantly diminished by the attacks of predators and the reactions by possums, losses can accumulate. It is not just relational and emotional skills that disappear, extremely important bits of our identities disappear as well. Our identities are left to grow as best they can with incorrect and missing parts. When our gentle protector skills are lost, we all become predators and prey to each other. When all our mentors have defects, how can we rebuild?

Whole cultures have lost the ability to feel shame or anger and stay gentle protectors who still protect weakness. Regions of the world have become known for a tendency to flare and to become aggressive when angry while others work themselves to exhaustion avoiding shame. Escalating problems are evidence of missing emotional relational skills that should regulate the mood and energy of groups. Once we know what we are seeing, we discover the many strange ways people compensate for missing identity and call it normal.

This chapter is about how we restore our identities once our relational skills have been lost. The simplest way to picture this replacement process is to say that we are rebuilding people so that their whole identity and personality resemble the mature character of Jesus. When God is with us through Immanuel life, He both finds the missing parts of our identity and trains us to express our transformed nature.

Experiencing "God with us" changes our individual and group identities. The church begins as a gathering of predators and possums who wish they were not who they are and try very hard at times to stop noticing weaknesses and taking advantage of others. God sees something that we do not see and it brings God joy. Through Immanuel vision and a tender regard for weakness, we discover and share this joy. The normal function of the church starts to develop character and propagate joy to the world as we are transformed.

Jim's Story

My mother only spoke Norwegian until she was school age. She married an English speaker whose grandparents spoke French and German and had her children in South America where people spoke Spanish. I grew up speaking Spanish and English and moved to the United States where I married Kitty who spoke English and Hausa. I was learning Greek when we had children, but our children only learned to speak English. While there were many language skills in the family, most were not passed on successfully.

I can use a slide-rule, iron clothes with a charcoal burning iron and play *bambucos* on guitar. My mother taught me to make clothes from patterns and sew by hand or with a treadle sewing machine. My father taught me to sharpen a handsaw, plane wood to make furniture and take light meter readings to calculate the right exposure for photographic film. My sons shop for clothes and furniture on their smart phones, which they also point at things to take pictures. I have not mastered smart phones.

Skills drop out between generations for many different reasons involving opportunity, need and the ability to transfer that skill. When no one was dancing *bambucos*, my children did not learn the rhythm or the movements. In fact, in just one generation, my children cannot recognize the rhythm pattern or feel any emotion when a *bambuco* plays. Motivation also disappears as they do not feel like they have to move or dance. My children find that traditional Norwegian foods like *lefse* leave them flat and *lutefisk* lowers joy instead of raising it.

What happened to our joyful identity?

Many Christians and their children have noticed that the things of God do not move them, leave them flat and even lower their joy. For about the last 400 years the church has tried to restore Christian character through education, right beliefs and right choices. This would be similar to trying to restore my children to speaking Norwegian by setting standards for speaking Norwegian and explaining these rules carefully to my family. You should speak without an accent. You should use proper vocabulary. You should have correct grammar. You should answer quickly when addressed by others. You should explain yourself clearly and truthfully at all times. I think we all can understand those rules. However, does that make us a Norwegian speaking family?

In the same way, Christians have worked for hundreds of years to perfect exactly what we should believe and the standards we should meet with our lives only to find that few other Christians agreed with them, and no one could actually live up to the standards. Christians have applied several explanations to this failure: 1) more faith is required than what we have, 2) God makes the change through a filling of the Spirit we still lack, 3) we must discipline ourselves in greater obedience to God, 4) we are hopelessly sinful and fallen and only God's mercy will save us in the end, so we can only repent as regularly as possible and 5) Bible standards are nice ideals with little practical application other than to direct our dreams and hopes. We have painted pictures of Good Samaritans helping the poor and tried to improve our attitudes about the people begging for money on freeway on-ramps. While we know we should love our enemies, we look at them with fear and are relieved when they go away or get defeated. Because of the lack of real character change, many simply leave the church. Many who stayed in the church struggle with low joy while others are phony or unpleasant.

By the time I was eighteen I was so sure that Christianity was not working for me that I briefly threw it all out. I had developed a nice Christian mask to hide behind, and it was actually the mask that started me toward God because I was afraid to stop pretending. Soon the pressure of trying to act Christian without believing it really began to bother me so I decided to do something I had never done. Instead of acting like everyone around me, I would read the New Testament and only do what it said there. If there was a God it should work and if not I would escape when I could. As I read through the New Testament three things showed up over and over. First, interact with God about everything. Second, do nothing from fear. Third, love people deeply. I had said many prayers but never interacted with God that I could remember. I did everything from fear. What I feared most was loving people.

This was not going to go smoothly as my actual life was nothing like what I was reading, but it all hinged on whether I could interact with God about everything. In my mind the question was whether God would interact with me at all. I began by talking out loud toward the ceiling like I would with a person and then stopping to listen and notice what came to my mind. I was both surprised and skeptical as things popped into my mind. I noticed that certain thoughts did not make sense at first but then became profound and created shalom as things fit together in ways I had never thought before. Indeed these changes made me less fearful and more willing to love people deeply.

It was right at this time that I met Kitty and we did not like each other at first. Let me say, she really did not like my mask and I often still carried it around. I likewise did not like her mask. Since I was getting close to people to test what I was reading about loving people, I also talked with God about my experiences with Kitty. It was also the 60s and love meant "if you love me you will sleep with me." One day the thought came to me that this "test of love" was more a case of fear as many of the women were sleeping with boyfriends because they were afraid of losing them otherwise. As Kitty and I became more serious, I told her that if I ever tried to sleep with her before marriage it would be the proof she needed that I loved my desires more than her. My interactions with God were producing signs of a gentle protector in me. Although I was very low on human examples, when I would interact with God and get God's thoughts about people, my responses to others began to change. God was building something into me that would become stronger every time I practiced with others. I was becoming a person I had never seen, but the closer I got to people, the more painfully obvious it became that many relational skills were missing.

The complex skills needed to become a gentle protector are even more vulnerable than language and cultural skills when it comes to extinction. Children raised during war may not develop much joy even if their parents were high-joy individuals. Father may be away at war or killed. Mother may be sick or starving during a siege. Terrible news comes every day and, for many, there are terrible sights all around. Children may well be separated from family and experience months or years of attachment pain. But, just as surely as lost language skills do not come back on their own, once relational skills drop out they do not come back on their own either.

The Immanuel group lifestyle - a paradigm shift

If 400 years of helping Christians become better people through correct theology and right beliefs has led us to where we are now, what alternative is there? We wonder if there is anything new we could read or learn that would possibly make a difference. Suppose, however, that we are not changed so much by what we know as by who we love. Jim has more to say about theology since the Enlightenment in *The Solution of Choice: Four Good Ideas that Neutralized Western Christianity* (with Dr. Marcus Warner). Jim develops how we are changed by who we love in *Renovated* and in *The Other Half of Church* with Michel Hendricks. Ed makes who we love the basis for leadership, dsicipleship, and church life in *Becoming the Face of Grace*.

With our brains already wired to allow people who share a joy-bond the power to change each other's identities, perhaps the way to see more change is to build more joy. We as Christians should stop and give this a little thought.

Just imagine for a moment that you could see the real identity inside yourself. Suppose you could look at weakness in others and know when someone had forgotten who they were. Every weakness we saw would become an opportunity to help others discover their true selves. We would only need to see people as God sees them. Now imagine a community of people who lived this way. Older, more experienced community members would help the younger and newer ones discover their identities. Since very new participants would have almost no idea who they really were, they would constantly malfunction, but tender responses to their weakness would invite them back to joy. The older ones would have years of discovering and developing the gentle skill of seeing others for who they are. Older members would not hold anyone's failures, deformities and transgressions as their true identity. Instead, they would recognize these weaknesses as problems that take away joy and shalom.

But how do we see what is behind masks of strength and through the cloud that covers our real selves? The center of such a life would be the active presence of God in everyday life showing each of us what is real. Every discovery would lead to joy and appreciation. Younger members would learn from watching the older members what this new and wonderful identity looks and works like. We would call this the Immanuel lifestyle.

Probably everyone would like an Immanuel lifestyle except for two things. First, interacting with God makes people nervous for many reasons. Since making sure we had all our beliefs exactly right has dominated Christian practice for 400 years, most people worry that they might not hear God correctly. Some wonder if they are "making it up." As we have seen, some people worry that they are replacing the Bible and church with their own private inspiration from God. Everyone knows of crazy people who think God told them something. We do not want to be bizarre. At the other end, we are afraid we will hear nothing and find out we are spiritual failures.

The second factor keeping people from an Immanuel lifestyle is pain. We have our masks for a reason. We crave our BEEPS and stick our head in the cloud for a reason. Every time a relational skill drops out there will be pain as the cause and pain as the result. Discovering who we really are also involves discovering why we hurt the way we do. People do not like going back to face pain.

Worse yet, for the most part we are talking about attachment pain. The pain we feel when we lose a part of ourselves or a connection with someone we love feels like it is breaking our heart or tearing off a limb. Attachment pain makes us vow not to trust men again, to search the world for the right woman, to shoot our children, stalk our ex-wife, crave chocolate and "do it myself" from now on. Attachment pain is used to control others through rejection and threats of abandonment. Threatening to cause attachment pain is a favorite with predators everywhere. When attachment pain is high, joy is very low.

After this short review of attachment pain we begin to see why many of the ways people malfunction is related to attachment pain. When my wife has an affair I must return to my attachment pain to hear from God how to forgive or love my enemies. Learning to be a gentle protector means seeing myself, my wife and her accomplice as God sees us in our weakness and malfunctions. Pain makes us push others away.

What restores a group's identity to joy?

God interacts with us in ways that we can notice. Most interactions with God involve mutual mind states that run faster than conscious thought and therefore cannot be distinguished directly from our own thoughts. As we saw in the last chapter, the single best sign of an Immanuel moment is the sense of shalom when everything fits and makes sense. This sense of everything is right often runs deeper than our own understanding so we are surprised by our sense of peace. Each time we become aware of God's presence with us as shalom, we are seeing things the way God sees them. Because God has joy to be with all of us, when we sense shalom we also experience joy with one another.

The way to restore a group's identity to joy is to increase the number of times we experience shalom, the number of people who experience shalom and the number of times we find shalom together so that the frequency of shalom moments is dramatically on the rise. We can also call these shalom moments Immanuel experiences as they represent the moments when we are aware that God is with us and we share God's mindsight. Even with all our limitations and lack of understanding, we are left with a peaceful sense that all will work together for good even when life hurts.

We might think that Christians everywhere would spend their whole time together seeking little else than to share God's mind, experience shalom, build joy together and tell others the good news of how their lives are being transformed from glory to glory. In fact, most Christians are less familiar with shalom than they are with joy and for the same reasons. Neither shalom nor joy are produced by believing the right beliefs. Neither shalom or joy exist without a relational bond that allows interaction with God and between people. On top of that, we have been taught that when we lose our shalom, we should solve problems to get our peace back. Most of the problems we must solve involve the people who are upsetting us and who, at that moment, we fail to see through Immanuel vision. The fewer relational skills we have the worse it gets. Instead of joy, we find conflicts and splits in the church when shalom is not shaping our group identity.

Another way to think about building a joyful group identity is to notice that since a joyful group identity forms in direct proportion to how many group members have shalom, we want to propagate shalom around our group. Shalom is produced by Immanuel moments and only lasts when we are sharing God's mindsight. So the way to spread shalom is to share our Immanuel moments. Telling clear stories about our Immanuel experiences helps others to, 1) understand what shalom is like, 2) learn how we reached shalom and 3) seek shalom themselves.

Chris and Jim wrote a short booklet to help people share their Immanuel experiences titled *Share Immanuel*. In this booklet they point out that the key to propagation is telling about our shalom experience in ways people can deeply understand. Western culture teaches us to talk about our pain, but people who talk about pain spread pain. To transform our group identity we need to spread shalom and build joy. We can learn how to create appreciation and share the peace with each other by sharing how our lives have been changed in Immanuel moments.

Perceiving God's presence leads to the simple yet profound realization, Jesus is glad to be with me. In Immanuel moments we experience God's grace expressed as, "I am glad to be with you, and I look forward to being with you, so let's visit as much as possible!" When the Creator delights in us individually or together, we discover our immense value. Even when circumstances around us are frightening, overwhelming, painful and hopeless, we find shalom. Stephen, the first Christ-follower martyred for his faith had a clear sense of Immanuel's presence even when being attacked. Stephen was able to see some of what God saw during his final moments as he interceded on behalf of his persecutors. Seeing some of what God sees in others is what Paul advises in 2 Corinthians 5 that we should no longer regard others from a worldly point of view.

Pastor Robert feared one of the ladies in his church. Mary was an active volunteer who frequently raged when things did not go her way. Mary was also a good worker. One day Pastor Robert was asked to confront Mary about a recent, fiery outburst. Feeling intense dread about this prospect, Pastor Robert looked for shalom. He asked Immanuel, "Lord, what do you see as it relates to Mary? All I see is a scary woman who is going to humiliate me." After a few moments Pastor Robert noticed the clear image in his mind of a young, little girl crying and screaming as she threw a temper tantrum on the floor. The girl was all alone with no one to comfort her. Pastor Robert felt the Immanuel impression, "This is what I see." The image transformed how Pastor Robert viewed and interacted with Mary. Instead of a scary monster he saw a hurt, frightened little girl who needed love, acceptance, guidance and grace. His protector skills as a father rose to the challenge. Mary needed to learn that she too could respond tenderly to the weaknesses in others.

One of the remarkable aspects of sharing Immanuel experiences is how it cultivates appreciation within our communities. When we share stories about our appreciation and God moments, we move into a new group identity. Immanuel stories actively illustrate Paul's advice in Philippians to meditate on "whatever is true, whatever is noble, whatever is right, whatever is pure, whatever is lovely, whatever is admirable - if anything is excellent or praiseworthy - think about such things" 4:8b (NIV).

Immanuel experiences restore our group identity by healing unresolved traumas. People with unprocessed Type A traumas say things like, "It's just the way that I am" and "This is how it was back then," as they justify their low-joy state. Noticing the way Jesus cares for others fills gaps in our character. Jesus washed feet, broke bread, served, forgave, healed, blessed and continually demonstrated a different brand of living.

Immanuel moments also resolve Type B traumas, the bad things that happen. Interacting with Immanuel heals the pain that produces predators and possums. Now, our individual and collective identities are no longer root-ed in pain, dysfunction, shame, blame and exclusion. For this reason alone Immanuel training and experiences must be part of the church.

Immanuel moments restore our joy with the God who feeds us, replacing our strong attachments to food. We let Jesus and joy compete for our attach-ments to food without fear and shame. We bring our experiences with food to Immanuel and actually begin to use food in the way God intended, as a means of bonding with Him and others. We ask Immanuel to help us become aware of His presence as we eat and when we think about favorite comfort foods. Jesus helps us grow an attachment with Him that restores food to its rightful place as an aid to attachment with God and other people. Meals become a place of celebration, relationship and sharing joy with Jesus and one another.

As Immanuel-joy replaces an attachment to food with an attachment to the feeder, an interesting change takes place for predators and possums. As Immanuel feeds us the daily Bread of Life and Living Water, we no longer need to eat and be eaten by each other. Predators discover that joy is far pref-erable to power and control. Possums discover gifts to share. Instead of allow-ing their identity to be defined by predators, transformed possums awaken to an identity based on Immanuel reality. Predators and possums alike learn to find shalom and joy in each other's presence as we learn from Immanuel to become gentle protectors.

How does weakness become essential?

Whenever groups who seek God fail to achieve a joyful identity, we can be sure there is uncorrected narcissism in the mix. It really does not matter who has the narcissism for the damage to be done. Narcissists deny faults in themselves and track faults in others. Narcissists justify their lack of tender responses to the weakness in others by pointing out these faults. "The way he answered me on the phone is not very Christ-like and he is supposed to be the pastor," is just one of many ways to pounce on weakness. Where the acknowledgment of weakness would normally foster life and growth, preda-tors punish weakness. Predators frequently scan the environment for signs of weakness that can be exploited for personal gain. While we consider narcis-sism more deeply elsewhere in this book and in other Life Model resources, our point here is that as long as there is a narcissist predator on the loose in a community, people will want to keep their masks strong.

Narcissists must admit their weakness and lack of tenderness to the weak-ness in others for their own transformation. We know Jesus has changed a predator's heart when the person begins expressing value for the weaker members of the community. Narcissists learn that they and their masks are not the same thing. The same Immanuel vision that brings shalom allows the recovering narcissist to see the people who are not happy with them through Immanuel vision as well.

Laying down their swords opens the door for predators to be welcomed into the community of protectors. Giving up control leads to joy with other people. Care for weakness develops protector identities and joins the weak and strong together. Predators start to see what God placed in other people that has not yet been activated.

Predators, possums and all of us actually, must confess that we do not know who we really are in order to enter the Kingdom as a little child. Only then do we discover the way God sees us. Areas of weakness are the areas where God can form us the most.

Correcting low shalom

Although we may fail to notice joy levels are low in church we will definitely notice the agitation and lack of unity that follows. Churches, schools and families where problems become the main topic of conversation and the source of most emotions quickly draw our attention. We feel the tension and the silence as a family in conflict arrives at church. We hear the teachers yelling at students in school, notice the criticism and hear that morale is low. If we could see people's brain function in these locations, we would find that many relational circuits are in the impaired range. If we checked people spiritually, we would find that few to none were aware of God's presence at that moment. Instead of God's presence, each mind would be on the problem. The family that arrives at church in conflict knows the fight is on, "Sit still! Quit fighting! I told you to bring your Bible!" Each family member is ready to argue without noticing that their joy is low, their relational circuits are off, they have lost shalom and have no awareness of God's presence. Further, even at church it would be a rare family that would think, "We are in the right place now," the place that would welcome their weakness and help them learn a better way. Few families or churches would even think that experiencing God's presence right in the middle of conflict would produce shalom.

Shalom, just like joy, is spread best when we learn in groups of three, using the three-way-bond structure in our brain. We learn shalom best when three or more gather together to listen to God about where He is among us and how God sees things. As we compare what we "hear," check for shalom and tell each other what brought shalom, we become quicker to seek shalom next time it is missing.

Our path toward increased shalom starts with discovering what shalom is like and grows by noticing every time shalom is absent. The missing group process requires someone to notice shalom was gone and announce it. We could then stop to feel appreciation to get our relational circuits running again. Together, we would ask God to help us perceive God's presence. When we were aware of God's presence, we ask God to help us see our situation the way God sees it. As people begin experiencing shalom, we tell each other what changed for us that makes everything work together. Our shalom levels rise but this process only works well for our distress when we have practiced finding shalom together when we did not have a conflict or problem between us.

Immanuel shalom

Let us consider a few examples of what seeking shalom together would look like in homes, schools and at church. Hearing the stories of how others found shalom and what changed for them is a great help in learning to find shalom for ourselves. For shalom to propagate we must tell our shalom stories to others as well.

Immanuel shalom at home

Chris tells his story: After 43 hours of labor Jen was feeling exhausted. Two days of waiting and praying combined with agonizing labor pains brought us to a point of desperation. We wanted relief, especially Jen, whose dream of having a natural birth was quickly fading. The addition of pitocin (synthetic oxytocin) by the doctors quickly turned up the intensity. Up to this point none of us realized Matthew, our first-born son, was misaligned. I feared for Jen and my unborn son as I helplessly watched the medical staff scramble to intervene. Miraculously, by the 47th hour Jen was holding our son as tears of joy rolled down our faces.

During the moment of intensity, a two-hour window when the pitocin was doing its job, I was fully aware that I lost my Immanuel awareness and shalom. After the delivery I recognized that the time when strong feelings were present was the time I did not have shalom. Suddenly, I no longer wanted more children. My thought was, "I don't want to go through that again!" The loss of shalom, and the addition of fearful resistance, were signs that I had been traumatized. I turned to Immanuel for guidance. To help me reconnect with Jesus, I thought back on a time when I had been able to interact with Him until His presence seemed real to me again. I prayed, "Lord, I realize I have no idea where You were or what You were doing during the time Jen was in serious trouble. I was afraid for my wife and my son. I felt so helpless and alone. Where were You when I needed You?"

After sharing my grief I perceived God's comforting presence and the thoughts, "Chris, that was scary for you. I was there providing and working through the team of nurses and doctors who were trained to do their job under extreme circumstances. Even though you did not know what to do, they did." This reality brought some shalom to my soul, allowing me to catch my breath.

I still felt tension and fear when I remembered the pitocin hours. The lack of shalom was a sign that there was more. "Lord, thank You for Your team of people. They were helpful. However, I still feel hurt, afraid and angry about the whole ordeal. Why did it have to be so intense? That was so scary, Lord!"

At this point I noticed a remarkable image in my mind. The best way to describe the image is what happens if you face a mirror when there is another mirror behind you and your reflection appears multiplied as far back as your eyes can see. With this image in mind I felt Immanuel continue, "Chris, when the team of nurses and doctors were born, I had Matthew in My mind. When the parents of your nurses and doctors were born, I had Matthew in My mind. When their grandparents were born, I had Matthew in My mind." The pattern continued until I felt overwhelmed by the gravity of the truth. Jesus was affirming that He had my son in His mind all the way through time. He prepared this specific, special team of people to help my wife successfully deliver our son!

Increasing levels of shalom and joy returned to my mind and body. I noticed the longing for more children once again. Instead of anxiety and tension about the birth of my son, I now had a peaceful picture of Jesus providing for my family that is clearly etched in my mind. I shared my Immanuel story with Jen and we rejoiced. Immanuel restored my shalom, and I could share my shalom with Jen and others.

The other person I wanted to receive shalom from this event was Jen's doula (birthing coach), a young woman named Sherri. Sherri rode the intense roller coaster feelings with us. I can still remember the concern on her face when Jen was struggling. Sherri was deeply touched by my story of Immanuel's tender care and hospitality. She received hope and peace from the comforting picture Immanuel painted. Since Sherri does not share our faith, we wanted to share our shalom with her. The look of joy on Sherri's face still makes me smile.

Immanuel shalom at school

Shelia tells her story: My school is a government-funded public school. This may cause teachers to think that shaping a joyful identity and correcting low-shalom in a public classroom is impossible. The public school environment does not need to stop a teacher. I am determined to foster shalom-enhancing experiences where my students have opportunities for connecting with each other, connecting with their community, and connecting with the world at large. One such example involved my school's annual canned food drive for Thanksgiving.

I grew up in poverty, and I remembered that having a few bags of canned goods delivered to my family's front door did not make for a very festive holiday. I was grateful, but I believed that there had to be more creative ways to help families in need. I challenged my students to "think outside the can." My students excitedly went beyond a canned goods campaign and brainstormed possibilities. The students decided to sponsor five families and provide a hearty Thanksgiving meal with all of the trimmings. Some of the students determined that leftover food made the Thanksgiving weekend great so they decided to give enough food for day-after Thanksgiving turkey sandwiches. Each of my five classes sponsored a family.

A local Catholic church provided my students with the names and addresses of five families in need. Since my students were not culinary artists, they decided the best option would be a local market which served all the traditional Thanksgiving foods. They contacted the families to determine the need, planned a menu including leftovers, made a budget and held a fundraiser. They created spreadsheets and faxed the order to the market. To add a personal touch, my students posed for group photos of their respective classes and created five separate poster-board sized, handmade greeting cards. Each class member wrote an inspirational quote and signed the card. The purpose of the card, they determined, was to allow the family to get a glimpse of the students behind the Think Outside the Can Project and to receive 36 personal messages. The day before Thanksgiving, representatives from each class piled into five cars and headed to the market. I went too although my students had taken full ownership of the project. Cars piled high with turkey dinners and fixings headed in five different directions to make their deliveries.

The overall climate in my class shifted during this project. Students were meaningfully engaged in an undertaking that they created and implemented. My students, perhaps for the first time in their young lives, became the strong helping the weak through a collective effort. They produced joy far beyond canned food and boxed potato flakes dropped at the front door. Through caring for and being tender toward those weaker than themselves, their shalom increased knowing they had made a contribution to the greater good.

Immanuel shalom at church

We first learned about Pastor Ken in the last chapter where his personal Immanuel change spread through his life and congregation. Until then Pastor Ken worked hard at his job but felt little satisfaction. He juggled endless to-do lists and a hectic schedule of church activities, staff meetings, speaking events, visits with sick people and counseling sessions for families and couples. At home, Pastor Ken would drift into the "cloud" finding it nearly impossible to leave his smart phone alone when he should be spending time with his family. In spite of his best efforts Pastor Ken was losing joy and shalom until he was just going through the motions of life. Feeling alone and lost, Pastor Ken sought comfort in a large bowl of ice cream each night. Soon the ice cream was not enough. Once his wife went to bed, Pastor Ken entered the dark side of the cloud and surfed internet porn sites. On the outside Pastor Ken appeared happy but deep down he felt himself drowning. To manage his guilt, Pastor Ken drank four to five cans of his favorite soda along with several cups of coffee to go with the sweets stashed in his desk drawer. Pastor Ken's waist started to expand along with his rising levels of shame.

By the time Pastor Ken learned about Immanuel experiences, he was desperate. Interacting with Immanuel made it real to Pastor Ken that Jesus loved him in spite of his malfunctions and deceptions. He understood Jesus to be genuinely glad to be with him. God reminded Pastor Ken of moments during his teenage years where he felt alone in his pain. Alone meant no awareness of Immanuel, no shalom and deep attachment pain. This realization helped Pastor Ken identify a destructive pattern. Whenever he felt alone, he turned to BEEPS for relief. At one point Pastor Ken felt like Jesus conveyed how proud He was of the pastor. Surprised, the pastor asked, "Lord, how can you be proud of me? Just look at all the bad things I have done!" Pastor Ken wept as he perceived Jesus' response, "I am proud of you because you turn to Me for help." These Immanuel exchanges grew into profound moments of healing. An increase in shalom calmed his restless cravings. Pastor Ken quit the ice cream and replaced his soda and sweet treats with healthier alternatives. Pastor Ken asked for accountability with his internet escapades and started exercising. Pastor Ken began to live each day with clarity, joy and peace. Pastor Ken's identity grew and remained anchored in joy instead of work and busyness. Pastor Ken's marriage improved. Soon his Immanuel shalom stories helped his staff and church discover the Immanuel lifestyle. Pastor Ken now writes and speaks about the changes in his life and the shalom and joy that comes from an interactive relationship with the King. Shalom is spreading.

Joy and Immanuel at church

In Romans 12:15 we read that we should rejoice with those who rejoice and weep with those who weep. Churches who share joys and weaknesses are a good place to confide our lack of shalom. When we cannot find God's presence because, like Chris during Jen's labor, our feelings are too intense, we can turn to those who have a stronger awareness of God at that moment, and they can help us. By weeping with those who weep, we learn to help each other stay connected with Jesus when we are in pain. We also learn how to lead each other through low-joy times back to joy and shalom. When we share our Immanuel moments and memories as families and churches, we build our ability to stay connected next time.

To practice group Immanuel we begin by learning to tell our joy stories. A simple way to start joy-building at church is to share appreciation stories. By telling others what we appreciate about God's presence in our lives, we are keeping our relational circuits active. When we express appreciation for each other, we begin to build joy. When the strong appreciate the weak, we begin to change for the better. For some people this will be their first time recognizing joy. We always find joy when we discover God is with us. Telling others how we discovered Immanuel helps our group learn to overcome obstacles and have hope. Sharing joy builds the group identity.

Remember that learning to experience God is with us in our weakness and pain only happens where protectors are recognized, and predators are denied leadership roles or easy access to frightened possums. Leadership must also practice seeing others as God sees them. The problem with predators is that they are very happy to tell you what they think God sees. However, words of predators do not bring shalom. God's words about us always bring shalom.

The effect of practicing Immanuel together is the growth of shalom. Really, the most common reason that we do not return to joy is that we are not accustomed to stop and seek Immanuel-shalom when we are upset with others or even upset with ourselves. We don't notice that our relational circuits are off thus preventing shalom. We do not notice that the people we are with need help with their weakness when they are losing their cool because we lost our shalom with them. When we practice Immanuel together, the first thing we learn is to notice whether shalom is present or missing. When shalom is missing we stop and appreciate Immanuel before doing anything else.

By telling stories of how we found Immanuel and what changed, we help others to recognize shalom or its absence. We also learn the skills needed to improve shalom by practicing together. We learn to quiet together, restore our relational circuit function when needed and affirm each others' griefs through validation and comfort.

If this is making sense to you but you do not see these mature gentle protector skills being learned and used in your church, then you are looking at the need to have the weak and the strong interacting in a way that propagates joy. If your church is already growing a good supply of gentle protectors, you will find the Life Model gives you words and explanations for teaching.

Rowing or sailing

When we have lived in low-joy and had to work hard to please others, we tend to approach God as someone else we must please. Trying to solve the problem of pleasing God on our own is legalism. We must try to do everything at the right time, in the right way and in the right amount and figure out what God wants but without any reference to how God sees the situation. As many people in such a spot have said, "I don't have to ask God how He sees this. I already know!" Ah! But we do not know unless we are as wise as God. When we force ourselves to follow rules as though we could live without sin, it does not produce shalom, feeling special, known, valuable, validated and comforted. For all our knowledge about God, we continue in attachment pain. In this strange way, attachment pain creates legalism.

In *Forming*, David Takle compares developing Christian character to boat travel. "Rowing" is the effort to think the right thoughts, believe the right beliefs, have enough faith and seek the right spiritual experiences. In contrast, "sailing" actively carries us along by the very power of God's thoughts, motivation and character. In "sailing" we respond relationally to God's presence in our daily events rather than trying to think high and lofty thoughts and behave correctly. We find ourselves responding as God does although, admittedly, a bit slowly at times. To our surprise, we begin showing increasing similarities to Jesus.

Does that sound too easy? It is. During real-time life stress it is much harder to experience God's presence. Low-joy, masks, low-shalom and missing relational skills make it even harder. When our relational circuits begin shutting down we do not want relationships, and we have trouble seeing anything the way God does. Even if we think about experiencing God, we really feel like we do not care. In essence, the more we need the help, the less able we are to access the help we need. We would be totally stuck if it were not for others around us who also practice seeing what God sees. This group, known as the church, is supposed to practice the skill of synchronizing together with God in both high and low-joy. At any given moment one of us will be stronger than others, and our tender response to their weakness will make all the difference.

If a group of us were stranded in a snow storm and we took out cell phones only to find the first did not have any signal, the second had a dead battery and the third had a signal and a charge, what would we do? It is easy to figure out because each person was willing to share their current state of low power or poor reception until we found the person with a strong connection. Sharing our weaknesses and strengths allows the whole group to make the phone call that will save us.

Experiencing and passing on the skill of perceiving God's presence during suffering and distress means that spiritual maturity cannot be developed one person at a time. We cannot develop the Immanuel lifestyle in private counseling between two people. While two is much better than one, three people with joy bonds are needed for the best results. While the exact science is more than we will discuss here, the bond between three people operates at the speed of conscious thought allowing us to combine our best knowledge about God with our bonds to God and others. We use both what we believe about God and the bond of love with God and others to restore our relationships. In a three-way bond, our loving experience of God is able to hold hands with our confessions, creeds and conclusions from all the years that we have worked to get our theology right. Let us look practically at how this can be achieved and why it is the way that we build a joyful church identity.

Returning to joy in church

As we will see in the next two chapters, returning to joy refers to how long it takes after something upsetting happens before we are glad to be together again. Returning to joy should take mere seconds for mature people. We develop this ability and speed in a family, school or church culture where we learn to weep with those who weep instead of withdrawing, ostracizing, criticizing or blaming.

Rather than years of emotional reeducation, the Life Model proposes that we learn to return to joy as a church community by first returning to shalom with God through a practice of Immanuel awareness as groups. When we experience Jesus being glad to be with people around us when they are distressed, we learn to do the same. In time, perhaps a very short time, we will not want to leave people alone in their pain.

Yet, to propagate shalom to other people in the church and community, they need to know what happens when we experience God is with us in painful places. This requires learning to tell the story of what changed when we experienced Immanuel and returned to joy. Telling these stories needs to be a normal part of church life.

Before we can complete the picture of church life, we need to examine the role played by relational skills and understand how gentle protector skills propagate. We will examine relational skills next in **Part Three**. This book provides the basic principles for developing a joyful and transforming church but working with people and growing joy require well-planned training experiences as well. Reliance on preaching and teaching the principles in this book will not bring about the change we are describing.

We have developed many resources to help churches learn to return to joy, seek Immanuel and learn to tell the stories so that others will desire the same experience of joy. For training, on-line courses and materials for your group see Appendix D. We have tested methods and developed a structure to bring the weak and strong together in helpful ways. Without structure our pain, distress and problems will quickly be amplified by a large number of people with their relational circuits off. Once people start amplifying distress they only think of each other as the problem. There is no joy or shalom in that!

James the Just wisely tells us that self examination brings life when we put into practice the good things we learn from the perfect law of liberty (James 1). True religion consists of protectors caring for orphans, widows and strangers. This chapter suggests we should examine our multigenerational communities, like church, for the presence of self-justified narcissists. Can we speak of a problem to everyone, including our leaders, without fear that they will jump on our weakness to make us the "bad one?" Most importantly, am I that self-justified person? Can I encourage others to tell me what I do that does not bring them joy? Do I disqualify others from correcting me because of the obvious weaknesses in their lives?

If we have not examined our community for joy and shalom, it is time to think it over. Do we practice finding shalom together? Do we experience Immanuel moments? Do we tell others what has changed about us during Immanuel encounters? Do we really pass the peace (does shalom propagate) when we are together, or do we parade our masks? Who do we help and who helps us when our Immanuel contact is getting faint? These are issues we must consider together as a community if we are to live in the transformation zone.

How are we doing?
- Have we ever witnessed an Immanuel group lifestyle?
- What joyful groups became my people?
- How much do we row or sail in our spiritual life?
- Do we give other people permission to speak into our lives?
- Do we feel shalom during and after interacting with people?

Are we willing to invite Immanuel to upgrade our identity?

Correcting what we might have heard about developing Christian character

Christians agree on the fundamental need for character development that reflects Christ in and through our lives. The agreement and clarity ends there, however. Some approaches focus on pleasing God while others focus on better care for our planet. Developing character that pleases God and blesses people requires relational maturity that can be expressed during good times and bad. The times when we are emotionally overwhelmed provide the most accurate lens to evaluate our character development. Hard times reveal the character of our leaders and community members as well. We quickly discover where growth is needed as we examine our reactions, behaviors, thoughts and words when we encounter misunderstandings, conflicts, hurts, frustrations, accusations, helplessness, wounds and overwhelming times. Let us address common beliefs about forming Christian character.

Common belief: Spiritual maturity is different and separate from emotional and relational maturity: We often consider ourselves spiritually mature because we are faithfully in church and have not heard anything in a long time that we did not already know. Part of what we consider spiritual includes a disregard of what the world thinks of us. If we disregard human opinions, we conclude there is little need to focus on relational or emotional maturity as long as we tend to our relationship with God. Common spiritual disciplines such as reading the Bible and praying, while crucial, do not always translate into relational, joyful character change. We somehow compartmentalize different aspects of our life like spirituality, relationships and identity. Separating spiritual maturity from the rest of our identity neglects one of Paul's points in Romans 6 where we are to offer the parts of our bodies as instruments of righteousness. This offering to God assumes our entire being is involved, spiritually, emotionally, mentally and physically.

While we have constant examples of leadership failure by gifted people who did not combine their spiritual and relational maturity, one of the more famous Christian leadership failures in recent times can provide an example.

A gifted pastor started a church in his basement that grew into a highly re-spected 14,000 plus member church. He lost his church and job when a male prostitute exposed their sexual relationship. He admitted to sexual im-morality, buying methamphetamine and a long-time battle against feelings contrary to his beliefs. He compared his temptations to the struggles faced by dieters who say, "'I'm not going to eat today' and then they eat." This scandal shocked the pastor's church and surrounding community. In spite of his sem-inary education, charisma, theology, convictions and Kingdom aspirations, a major piece of the pastor's maturity was defective. Unlike Pastor Ken we read about earlier, this pastor hid his weakness and pseudo-joy then crashed. Ulti-mately, separating spiritual maturity from emotional and relational maturity creates a dismembered identity.

Common belief: Good preaching should produce change to my identity: My job, therefore, is to believe what I hear. While this idea is rarely ever spo-ken and would not be accepted if a preacher promoted it, many of us live as though it was true. A good number of us pack pews and fill stadiums to hear Christian leaders speak, pray and preach with the hope that miracles, anointing, healing and hope will reach our lives. Over time, we feel discour-aged by the results. Preaching and stadium events often produce profound repentance, change of direction and healing, but they do not produce matu-rity. Shared lives of joy and suffering produce maturity when we live together under the shalom of God.

Common belief: Repentance and obedience is all that is necessary for maturity: Obedience and repentance are essential for a genuine, authentic relationship with Christ. Repentance reflects heartfelt change and remorse over malfunc-tions while obedience displays loving relationship with the Master and a de-sire to honor Him. If obedience and repentance were the only elements of maturity, then we could all become mature on our own. Many of us attempt to do all the right things and become unpleasantly rigid and low-joy. Trying to do all the right things at the cost to joy does not build the same kind of character found in people who regularly seek Immanuel moments and live in multigenerational community.

Common belief: Grace means that I should not have to participate in a group to grow maturity: I am just fine on my own, "just me and Jesus." God in His infinite wisdom chooses to use people as His instruments of restoration even though people have been the source of pain and distress. We tend to avoid groups if we have been hurt, offended, frustrated and overwhelmed by others who lacked gentle protector skills. How can we say we love God if we do not love His people? For much more see Ed's book *Becoming a Face of Grace.*

Common belief: If we can all talk about our feelings and struggles, we will heal together. At the other extreme from "just me and God" is a sort of "therapeutic milieu" view of church. Therapeutic church is increasingly popular and in the most progressive cases they have been able to eliminate the need for God entirely. One of the problems with sharing feelings and struggles in a therapeutic church is that we amplify pain. Amplifying pain does not grow maturity! Some recovery groups have demonstrated more character change in groups that practice honest sharing and self-examination than most churches ever see. The Life Model does not advocate therapeutic churches. We do advocate the honesty that allows people to lower their masks and the gentle response to weakness without which neither therapeutic groups or churches will see lasting transformations. However, it is not the sharing of our troubles that brings maturity. Seeking Immanuel together and interacting with Him in the presence of our troubles transforms us with a shalom and joy that propagates.

Joy Actions

Home: Choose the person in your family, or a friend, most likely to join you in asking Immanuel how He views your family members. Put words to your mutual mind state.

School: Ask the most likely person in your school community to join you in asking Immanuel what He wants you to know about your school. Put words to your mutual mind state.

Church: Choose the person in your spiritual family most likely to join you in asking Immanuel how He views your church. Put words to your mutual mind state.

Environmental Pseudo-Shalom Assessment

1. I "give in" to keep the peace.

   Very rarely 0 1 2 3 4 5 6 7 8 9 10 *Most of the time*

2. We are very conscious of the image we project to others.

   Not at all 0 1 2 3 4 5 6 7 8 9 10 *Most of the time*

3. I do my best to avoid people who annoy me.

   Not at all 0 1 2 3 4 5 6 7 8 9 10 *Consistently*

4. When we pray I'm not sure if God is even listening.

   God feels close 0 1 2 3 4 5 6 7 8 9 10 *God seems far away*

5. I try hard to keep people from being angry.

   Never 0 1 2 3 4 5 6 7 8 9 10 *Constantly*

6. We often find it necessary to portray things as better than they are.

   Never 0 1 2 3 4 5 6 7 8 9 10 *Most of the time*

7. I have trouble getting my heart to match what I know is right.

   Not at all 0 1 2 3 4 5 6 7 8 9 10 *Most of the time*

8. We would rather leave issues unresolved than make someone upset.

   We work it out 0 1 2 3 4 5 6 7 8 9 10 *Most of the time*

9. I often feel like I am "walking on eggshells" around people.

   Not at all 0 1 2 3 4 5 6 7 8 9 10 *Most of the time*

10. I keep my feelings to myself.

    I express myself 0 1 2 3 4 5 6 7 8 9 10 *I'm very private*

Total your scores here. _____
Mark the matching spot on the scale.

0   10   20   30   40   50   60   70   80   90   100

God's Joyful Presence with Us Bible Study

Think back on something you appreciate and spend two minutes enjoying appreciation. Next, ask God to make this study interesting for you. Now read the following passage from the books of Moses.

Scripture Deuteronomy 12:5-12 Read then review the passage for each question.

Chapter Eight Question: What does God expect will happen as we eat together (verse 7) in the presence of the God who feeds us?

Weakness, Joy and Shalom Questions:
1. Who are weak or strong in this passage?
2. What kind of interaction does God desire between weak and strong?
3. What do we learn about joy and shalom (everything works together) from this passage?

Immanuel Questions:
1. What effects does perceiving "God is with us" have in this passage?
2. Group study activity: God is always present and eager to help us see more clearly. In what ways do we perceive or guess that God is helping us understand this passage right now in the group discussion?

   Note: Thinking about God's active presence may seem strange at first because people generally discuss the past more than they observe the present. Keep your answers short. Feel free to guess. We will do this each week.

Personal Story Question: How does food play a part in your joy bonds with God and other people?

Whole Bible Question: What Bible characters were a source of joy to the people of God and to others? How did they do it?

Wrap-Up Minute: What do you now know that you didn't know before this week's study?

Our Life Model Joy with God Exercises

Using Relational Sandwiches To Restore Shalom

Relational sandwiches are a practical design to help us restore shalom and joy while we manage problems and preserve relationships. Before completing the individual and group exercises read Building Relational Sandwiches on the next page.

Individual: Relational Sandwich Practice with God

1. During your daily prayer time this week, practice relational sandwiches with God. Talk with God about your prayer needs, fears or situations. Below is an example.
    A. *Thank you Lord, that You are faithful to all of my needs.*
        Give examples of how God's faithful relationship has been important to you historically.
    B. *I confess Lord that I am worried about paying the bills this month.*
        Tell God how the current event feels.
    C. *Lord, you are the God who feeds, provides and protects. You have taken care of me before and I look to You again for guidance in my present situation.*
        Tell God why your relationship with Him is important for the shalom you need.
2. Notice what changes each time you practice this exercise.
3. Write down the change you notice so you can tell your group.

Group: Sandwiches and Maturity

1. Have group members share their observations of what changed when they practiced making sandwiches with God.
2. Discuss how we tend to mistake gifting, anointing and education for maturity. We want to remember our tender response to weaknesses during this discussion.

Building Relational Sandwiches

Relational sandwiches are a practical exercise designed to prevent problems from becoming bigger than relationships. Psalmists and prophets frequently "make sandwiches" to express grievances, prayers and praise. This structure is a natural part of Hebrew thought and poetry. We use the visual metaphor of a sandwich to describe how we start with the relationship, put the problem in the middle then end with the relationship.

The flow looks like this:
1. Importance of relationship (historic)
2. Current event (problem)
3. Importance of relationship (relational outcome)

The third part of this sandwich is not how you want the problem resolved rather, what kind of relationship you want as a result.

Personal Example:
1. We have been friends for a long time and I like being with you.
2. But, when you cut me off when I am speaking I feel like you are not listening.
3. I want us to have a relationship where we really understand each other. (Notice that we have focused on the kind of relationship we want instead of how we want the problem resolved.)

Psalm 51 Example (NKJV):
1. "Have mercy upon me, O God, According to Your lovingkindness; According to the multitude of Your tender mercies, Blot out my transgressions" (Verse 1).
2. "For I acknowledge my transgressions, And my sin is always before me" (Verse 3).
3. "Restore to me the joy of Your salvation, And uphold me by Your generous Spirit" (Verse 12).

Part Three
Joyful Relational Brain Skills

A wholesome tongue is a tree of life,
But perverseness in it breaks the spirit.
Proverbs 15:4 NKJV

The Life Model for sustainable joy is based on three things that are not usually found together: multigenerational community, an Immanuel lifestyle and relational brain skills. Take any of these three away and joy levels start to fall quickly. In **Part Three** of this book we will look at why we need training, practice and skill if we want joy to grow that spreads!

For joy and shalom to spread, our relationships must express and transmit joy faster than all the negative factors spread damage. Our physical brains are emotional amplifiers and they will amplify whatever is around us. If untrained, our brains will amplify the distress making problems, conflicts, anger, fear and hopelessness bigger as soon as two people are together. When our brains are trained to joy and shalom, we will amplify joy and quiet instead of "getting all worked up." Think about the people we know and we will easily see who is trained for joy and who is not.

In the first chapter of **Part Three** we will look at how we learn to return to joy after something goes wrong. In the second chapter we discover that changes in the last 100 years are rapidly driving joyful relational skills to extinction.

Chapter Nine

Forming Joyful People

We are designed for a joyful identity. Anything less and we become unhappy people. We expect to learn about joy at home, be trained to live in joyful ways with others at school and go to church where whatever is missing in our joy will be restored. Our goal is to pass this joyful identity on to others in the generations that follow us. The world's 2.2 billion Christians carry the message of joy to the world, but we do not have to develop an appetite in others for joy, joy is what everyone wants. We learned in **Part One** of this book how joy passes from generation to generation. In the **Part Two** we discovered how interacting with the presence of God restores our joy and identities. Now we will consider how some very specific relational skills must be handed down as part of becoming human. In the last 100 years major changes in human life have carried some crucial skills down the path toward extinction. While there are a variety of crucial skills, we will focus on the "return to joy when something goes wrong" skill. Something will always go wrong with our joy so the real winners are not those who work hard to keep things from going wrong but those who quickly return to joy afterwards.

Chris' story

I sat at my desk and noticed my stomach start to tighten. My shoulders and back muscles stiffened. Drops of sweat formed on my forehead as my heart rate increased. Today was the first day of speech class at my junior college. Every student was required to take this course in order to receive an Associate's Degree and transfer to a state university. I knew, eventually, I would have to stand in front of the class and give a speech. This terrified me! How would I survive two, three, even four minutes of talking in front of my peers? What would they think of me? Would they laugh or mock me? All joy to be together was gone and I had no idea how to find joy again. My tension levels increased. Suddenly, the teacher announced she wanted to give the class a practice run, so everyone must give a two-minute introduction speech. Panic seized me. I abruptly gathered my things, stood up, walked out of the room and dropped the course. My willpower was no match for these intense fears. Though I looked tough about it, I felt very weak and had no idea that other people had been taught how to quiet fears in seconds and return to joy.

In fact, I lacked two primary, gentle protector skills. One, I did not know how to act like myself when feeling shame nor did I know the way back to joy from "not glad to be together" moments. In my experience, shame left me feeling alone, abandoned and rejected, all because people were not glad to be with me. My brain was convinced that feeling shame meant being stuck in shame which felt like certain death. I did not know how to stay relational and quiet these upsetting feelings, therefore I avoided them. Sometimes I felt angry when ashamed and acted like a predator to make others feel guilty while other times I went possum and felt defeated.

At my school counselor's insistence I signed up for another white-knuckle try with the speech course. Again, I walked out and dropped the class on the very first day! I remember my school counselor's face turning red when I told him. I had to transfer schools and take a loss because I did not have these two relational skills, and there was no one in my entire college who knew these skills were missing or how to teach them!

I took the class at the university. It was hard but I passed. What helped me succeed was watching and learning from the example of stronger students I happened to meet. These students could manage their shame states, although I did not understand at the time what they knew that I did not. Their joyful examples gave me strength in my areas of weakness. I found adults to care, listen and attune with me about my struggles. Tender responses helped me feel seen and validated so I no longer felt alone. People told me stories about times they felt shame and showed me how they could rest in the middle of their upset, even finding joy. I learned to quiet my big feelings. Over time I acquired both of these missing gentle protector skills, which gave my brain the training required for successful recovery. I even discovered Immanuel was with me during painful shame moments growing up. To this day it still surprises me that I have absolutely no problems speaking in front of people and groups. Shame is merely a bump in the road compared to the endless pothole it used to be, which caused me to relationally "bottom out." I feel shalom instead of panic when I encounter shame and recover much faster than ever before. Now I actively train my two sons how to feel shame and recover to joy so they do not have to experience the years of anguish that I endured. Having two boys under the age of three gives me a lot of opportunities to practice the skills so they learn each one. I find it ironic that my only challenge with public speaking these days involves keeping my talks within the time frame allotted, as my tendency is to run over!

How joyful brain skills shape my relational identity

Joy is a mutual-mind state. A mutual state is created, developed and sustained by two minds being securely connected to each other in spite of the emotions at play. In a mutual mind state we feel so deeply understood that our mind allows the other mind to tell us who we really are, resulting in a settled sense of security. Creating a joyful identity requires ongoing practice.

Joy is our natural state; it creates our identity; it is the basis for bonding and joy is what gives us our strength. Joy strength develops through an actual brain structure that is formed and grown in loving relationships. Joyful bonds create our ability to act like our true selves when we must face pain. The strength of our brain's joy structures sets the limits on how much we can stand before we start into a trauma breakdown. But it is not simply a matter of strength, our endurance is also a matter of skill. If someone gave us a 100 pound sack and we immediately stacked it, we would be much less tired after 120 sacks than if we held each sack one minute before stacking. We would stack 12,000 pounds either way, but by holding each sack a minute we would also have carried 100 pounds for two hours while a fast stacker would not.

In the same way, the longer it takes us to return to joy, the more emotionally exhausted we become.

Consider an additional exhaustion-producing factor. If we have a habit or history of attacking the weaknesses in others, they will leave us holding our feelings when we are upset. If we feel alone in our feelings, the first thing to check is whether we are critical of weakness in ourselves and others. Transformations do not happen under criticism and relational brain skills do not develop.

What are relational brain skills?

There are many relational skills we learn. Some skills are closely tied to culture. We learned to be polite, or some of us have. Other skills involve learning to control ourselves. We learned how to sleep through the night without wetting the bed. We learned how to guess what people are thinking, at least part of the time, how to smile, when to wait for someone to speak, how to calm a friend who is upset, stay inconspicuous, avoid irritating other people and many related skills. Of all these skills, we have identified nineteen that are crucial to the formation of our identities. Without them we cannot operate our own minds and bodies correctly. Instead of improving our speeches in class, we are feeling out of control as Chris did and expecting to die in front of a group. We cannot cope with emotions as others do.

Explaining all of the nineteen skills is beyond the range of this book, but we provide a summary in Appendix B. For the moment we will pick three skills and illustrate life with and without those skills then study the "returning to joy" skill for the rest of this chapter.

Skill Nine, knowing when to stop: Someone with skill nine can recognize warning signals in themselves and others that tell them overwhelm is fast approaching and it is time to pause and cool down. With skill nine we can quiet our distress to "catch our breath" and stay in relational mode to avoid going over the top. With skill nine we observe when others reach their limit, or are about to, then pause so both of us can rest. Sometimes we are not so subtle in our responses to overwhelm cues and pauses so we say, "You look like you are about to lose it, what do you need?" We may ask, "Are you ok? Do you need a break? You look upset! Let's stop." We interpret visual and auditory cues that tell us they are reaching their peak so it is time to disengage. This crucial step may only last a few moments but it provides safety and prevents intensifying the distress. We rely on mindsight to put ourselves' in others shoes to accurately gauge how they are feeling and determine what they need and when to stop and rest. We honor others as we respect one another's limits and endurance.

Without this skill of knowing when to stop, we simply overwhelm others and feel overwhelmed ourselves. We blow past the subtle and obvious cues that lead up to the more drastic signs of overwhelm such as someone crying or even losing it. People end up feeling guarded around us while we end up feeling exhausted and alone. Our face, voice, words, intensity and invasion of personal space makes others feel like they cannot let down their guard. We push through warning lights when we fail to interpret the overwhelm signals that inform us they need a break. We rage at others, hit, keep our voices raised, demand answers from people who are not speaking, insult, abuse, injure and sometimes kill. People will say that we "exploded." The strong will speak up saying, "You are intense. Can you stop please!" The young, elderly and weak will shut down. Not stopping always lowers joy levels.

Skill Thirteen, Godsight: Someone with skill thirteen finds peace by seeing what God sees even when circumstances and emotions say otherwise. In other books, Godsight is also called "heartsight" because we see God with our hearts, *i*Sight when the "*i*" stands for Immanuel (God with us) and, "eyes of Heaven" because we see what God with us sees. We discover a life filled with hope, direction and shalom when we turn our sights to God and ask, "Lord, what do you want me to see here?" Our resources may be diminished, our capacity drained and our strength gone, but skill thirteen reminds us our Heavenly Father is still close and personal. David would poetically describe Godsight with, "Yea, though I walk in the valley of the shadow of death, I will fear no evil; for You are with me..." Psalm 23:4a (NKJV). Stephen put it this way, "Look! I see the heavens opened and the Son of Man standing at the right hand of God!" Acts 7:56 (NKJV). While there are plenty of examples to choose from, Godsight is perceiving reality the way God sees it, free from distortions. We discover a joyful God who interacts and participates in our life, our sorrows, our relationships. Someone with skill thirteen sees people as God sees them, even when people are a source of frustration and pain. Immanuel graciously pulls back the curtain to share more than we previously thought was going on. We learn there is a relational God who loves and cares for us during good times and bad. Synchronizing with Immanuel's view and values is how life is meant to be.

Without this skill of Godsight we see and remember malfunctions and distortions. There is neither shalom or true and lasting recovery from pain. Our focus remains on the hurt and pain people caused by their actions or inactions. We get stuck on offenses, hurts, unforgiveness, bitterness, frustrations and wounds when Godsight drops out. We experience anxiety, fear, unrest and much turmoil. Conflicts do not resolve as we remain stuck on who and what hurt us. Phrases such as, "How dare they! Who do they think they are?" justify our right to stay hurt. We grow accustomed to seeing and focusing on what our senses report. But there is always more to a situation than what our senses tell us. When people, even the ones we love, cause us pain, we lash out or retreat. Unprocessed pain robs our present and ripples into our future unless we use Godsight. It is all too easy to miss the God who is with us, who engages and interacts with us and the world around us. While we may know theoretically God is with us, this is not Godsight. Saint Paul's life changed when he encountered the living God although he spent most of his life studying about God. Without Godsight we remember painful events with hurt instead of shalom where everything fits together for good.

Skill Four, create appreciation: Someone with skill four expresses joy everywhere they go. People who use appreciation stay in relational mode and return there quickly if their relational circuits fail. We use skill four to help others return to relational mode as well. Someone with skill four stands out by making people feel seen and celebrated. Skill four creates belonging so the weak start to engage with the strong. Skill four conveys, "I appreciate this about you!" and turns the tide of a bad day, a sour mood and a sad demeanor. Appreciation expresses God's hospitality in such a way that we remember what is important about ourselves, other people or a situation. Appreciation connects people by introducing the most ideal mental state the human brain knows. With this in mind, we use skill four to add meaning, express love and remind people of their true value. We might say, "I feel seen by you!" when someone uses skill four. Noticing what we appreciate trains our brain to focus on the good things and, when activated, brings us together. As appreciation levels increase, problems start to shrink and life becomes more manageable.

Without knowing how to create appreciation, we miss what is important about situations and relationships. We end up feeling pessimistic, bitter, even resentful. Worse yet, we feel disconnected and critical of others. Problems become the most important thing to focus on, discuss and remember. When skill four is underdeveloped we stay busy, distracted, overwhelmed and disconnected in such a way others around us feel diminished. With low appreciation levels we say things like, "I just don't care." Negative emotions dominate our world and reality. Without skill four, we grow accustomed to non-relational strategies of living and interacting. It does not take very long to notice the world is a few quarts low on appreciation.

We need the full spectrum of relational skills in order to grow healthy families and joyful communities. Growing and propagating relational skills brings life, joy and purpose. With relational skill, we can pass each skill on to the people we love. Growing relational skills does not happen by chance.

Why is joy so essential for propagating relational brain skills?

Joy provides the ideal format and motivation for learning new brain skills and strengthening existing, weaker skills. Whether we are learning to drive a car, give a toast or shop for groceries, everything feels better when relational joy is in the picture. Joy adds the reward, provides the safety and increases the momentum to learn and grow new gentle protector skills that become the relational fabric of our life and character.

When relational brain skills are missing something else grows in their place. BEEPS play a major role in replacing brain skills and artificially regulating and quieting upsetting emotions. Joy will therefore create an extra level of protection against BEEPS for those who lack skills but do have loving relationships.

The major reason joy is essential for propagating brain skills is that these skills will not spread without a bonded relationship, and joy provides the bond. Let us take the skill of "knowing how to stop" that we just examined. If I do not know how to stop, and I cannot read the non-verbal signals correctly or activate the correct parasympathetic, vagal nerve branch in response to the signals I do see, then it will not help me if someone orders me to stop next time. It will not help if I want to stop next time. It will do me no good that someone else can stop. The skill does not propagate on command or even verbal instructions.

Western Christians with Western educations have long tried to pass character skills through instruction, lectures, Bible studies, sermons and promises to do better. All that would be good if I knew how to stop but just did not want to. Then, once persuaded, I would change. But for those who are weak and do not have the skill, no choice can activate the correct parasympathetic, vagal nerve branch and make them stop. We could hold a year of Bible studies on scriptures that say I should stop my anger before I hurt others, but I will be no better trained after the study. I will only learn how to stop from a joy-bonded relationship with someone who can stop. For skill propagation there must be joyful relationships. The strong and the weak must be together with tenderness toward weakness. Without joy there is no propagation of gentle protector skills. None.

How do we propagate relational skills?

Plants propagate many ways, some from roots, some from cuttings, some from seeds but each must have the right method or it will not work. For relational skills to propagate from one person to another requires specific methods as well. The more crucial gentle protector skills propagate by 1) a bond between the people, 2) active, face-to-face, real-time engagement 3) a mutual mind state, 4) repeated cycles using the skill until the untrained mind learns it and 5) telling the story of the interaction when we want people to propagate the skill intentionally.

We do not have space in this book to go into this propagation series in detail. People with the skill can demonstrate it like they could "whistling." Those who do not have the skill will not learn it from a book no matter how much detail we give. We need interaction between someone who can whistle and one who cannot in order to propagate the skill. We need more interaction for learning skills than for practicing them.

We learn relational skills by interacting in real time with people we care about who already have the skills. One hundred years ago face-to-face interaction was one of the few options available for personal exchanges. These days we have a wide variety of options for our convenience. The world has changed in ways that greatly reduce the number of face-to-face, mutual mind interactions we will have in a day. To make the problem perfectly clear, even our best technology blocks the mutual mind states required for skill propagation. The better technology allows skillful people to practice, but it does not allow unskilled children or adults to learn new skills. Therefore, advances in technology are currently wiping out the normal transmission of brain skills and driving gentle protector skills toward extinction.

How many families sit together looking at smart phones, watching television, texting, calling and posting their lives on social media? All of those forms of "the cloud" are 100% barriers for propagation of the critical relational skills. The cloud rewires the brain, particularly for low-joy people. A technologically wired brain has a difficult time resting and shutting off. This lack of rest drives joy levels lower.

Texting LOL or "laugh out loud" does not have the same effect as hearing someone we love break into laughter. Is there a person in our life with a laugh that is contagious and makes us smile? These feelings are the result of real-time interactions. The transfer of skills depends on an older generation with the skills interacting with younger and weaker groups who lack the skills. We need to have a lot of interaction with the skilled population that is rapidly disappearing.

It is common for entire families to lack specific skills because no one in the family learned the skills in the first place. Such loss can go back for several generations. Families pass on anger, alcoholism, narcissism, drug abuse, violence and neglect and vulnerabilities when essential relational skills are missing. Someone must be the joy starter to bring joy back into low-joy families, schools and churches.

How does weakness become essential?

Without a need to care for the weak, the weak and strong would simply not interact enough to propagate any relational skills. Baby sea turtles hatch and head out to sea without any parenting. Unlike baby sea turtles, we are weak and cannot raise ourselves. If the weak could take care of themselves, relational skills would disappear in one generation. Our joyful desire to help the weak creates the interactions that propagate whatever skills we possess. If we have no relational skills beyond joy then our joy to help the weak will at least propagate joy.

Blessedly, weakness is not rare and what weakness is more besetting than our tendency to forget our true selves? A tender and protective response to our failure to be ourselves invites the presence of Immanuel to show us our identity and the path back to joy. Tenderness and Immanuel are crucial if we want to train others to return to joy. Paul said it this way, "Brothers and sisters, if someone is caught in a sin, you who live by the Spirit should restore that person gently" Galatians 6:1a (NIV).

It only takes a few spectacularly humiliating experiences in a family, school or church community to create a population of turtles in their shells. However, when the strong share their own weaknesses and failures to "act like themselves," it encourages others to do the same. Building joy skills requires all the members of the group to be careful with the weaknesses they witness. Many people raised with low-joy find the first thing on their faces or out of their mouths is a low-joy response to the weaknesses they see. Many cultures are so shaped to punish weakness that everyone pounces on faults. Parents pounce as they are "preparing their children to face the world" rather than fitting them for a joyful, multigenerational community of hope. It is easy to hate ourselves for our weaknesses.

Now let us see if we can tie together a whole series of things we have learned. First, we are all born weak and unskilled into families that have some skills but not others. Every time there has been some kind of trauma to our ancestors, there is a corresponding likelihood that gentle protector skills were lost. Each time skills were lost, we were left with more of our predator brain structure exposed. Because it requires less skill and training, the predatory brain will propagate every time protector skills are lost. As predators increase, our cultures fail to respond tenderly to weakness and joy levels drop.

What protectors do with weakness to propagate joy skills

Protectors generally approach others by showing them a weakness first. They do it so smoothly that most people never notice simply because protectors are so fearless and unconcerned about their weakness. At the same time, protectors keep the attention on the other person. For example, when Jesus approached the Samaritan woman at the well, as a powerful man who could change her life, the woman met a hungry and thirsty traveler who needed the water the woman could provide. We have all watched powerful leaders sit down, listen and say, "I need help understanding something. I wonder if you could explain…" and they present their need to understand, exposing that they do not know everything they need to know. The weaker member has something of value to contribute.

Protectors also invite others to give shame messages about why they might not be so glad to be together. "Tell me what you don't like about me, this situation or what I control," opens the door once trust has been started. Some predators also use this strategy to eliminate discontent so there is often fear in telling a strong person what we do not like. This is why the transparency of the protector is crucial to any progress. Gentle protectors are known for their transparency. Protectors present themselves in vulnerable ways that expose weaknesses they could just as easily keep hidden.

Protectors speak about the importance of the relationship and group identity more than they speak about problems. Let's say Camp Crabtree has a problem with the cooks. A protector will start with something like, "We are the cooks who determine how appreciative these campers will feel when they think back on Camp Crabtree," and after telling them the problem say, "we are the kind of people who care about these things." We have called this a relational sandwich. At the center of protection is remembering that we protect relationships from problems that steal our joy and shalom.

The returning to joy skill involves six different emotions

We may recall that the brain is wired for six unpleasant emotions that we will amplify or avoid if we do not know how to ride them back to joy. These emotions are sad, afraid, angry, ashamed, disgusted and hopeless. The skill of "returning to joy" must be practiced with each of the six emotions individually. Without learning to return to joy, everyone is dangerous when they are upset. Some will pounce and some will withdraw but both cause damage. The best we can do without this skill is warn the people we love, "Don't make me upset!" and "Don't go there!"

A gentle protector knows how to return to joy and will tenderly help others if one or both of them have any of the six emotions. If we use sadness as an example, when a gentle protector sees someone who is sad, he or she will want to come close, understand, validate and comfort the sad person. The protector will feel an active pull inside to draw close even if the protector is also sad.

Anger is a more difficult member of the six emotions. Still, a gentle protector who knows how to ride anger back to joy will see someone who is angry and want to come close, understand, validate and comfort the angry person. This would be true even if the protector was angry. If we do not know how to return to joy from anger, this example will not make any sense. Inside we will feel that we should get away from angry people or keep others away when we are angry because anger leads to hurt not joy. For the untrained brain this fear is valid. Without training, anger will lead us to propagate predator and possum patterns rather than joy. It is not uncommon for people to find their mind refuses to believe that anger can be anything but dangerous.

Someone who has learned the return to joy skills will be able to maintain a keen interest in seeing the other person the way God sees him or her, reaching shalom and experiencing God's presence during the anger. The protector will feel like a resource and value the relationship while actively engaging with the angry person. However, if the angry person does not recover relational circuit operation, protectors will also take action to prevent and reduce harm to everyone if possible. This is like dealing with an out of control driver. Being careful does not mean we must be afraid of cars, only that there are times to get out of harm's way and times to become safer drivers.

Among the six unpleasant emotions is one called shame. Because shame is anti-joy and yet still necessary for our development, we must return to our discussion of the topic. Shame is what we feel when people are not glad to be with us. Shame is pain warning us when we do not act like ourselves. We do not have joy when someone fails to be their real self. Let us say someone starts to speak to us in a nasty way. We are disgusted and they feel shame which teaches them that their true self was not speaking. We can have joy helping them find their true self again because, with Immanuel's help, we can still see who they really are.

Toxic shame results from a failure to see someone's true self. We tell them lies about who they really are, "You are a total liar." We mistake their malfunction for their identity. Toxic shame also develops when we give appropriate shame but prevent return to joy for longer than a minute. We quickly become weak without joy, and to keep someone from returning to joy for more than one minute, is not a gentle and tender response to their weakness. Many people withhold joy and relationship to create attachment pain so they can get their way and stay in control. This is a predatory response and not tenderness to the weaknesses of others.

As we have learned, people who refuse to receive shame are called narcissists. In the language of scripture they are called "stiff-necked" because
they refuse to show shame. Most narcissists use their anger and contempt for
weakness to control people around them through toxic shame. Narcissists
want to be treated as though they always bring joy even though they do not.
Any group that cannot return to joy from shame will eventually be destroyed
by a narcissist.

Many cultures have developed from low-joy roots where shame was something to avoid rather than a road back to joy. In these cultures few people have
the skill of returning to joy from shame. Just for fun, let us say we came from
a shame-avoidance culture. No one we know would even guess there is a skill
we can use to return to joy from shame. Our whole culture works very hard
to avoid shame. We often use the fear of shame to control behavior in others
as well as ourselves. Avoiding shame now powers much of life and shapes our
values. It will be a delicate job raising joy levels and still protecting the values
in our culture.

What do we mistake for return to joy

People who disconnect emotionally look as though they are handling
things relatively well so it is easy to mistake disengaging for return to joy.
An absence of distress on the outside does not mean someone knows how to
return to joy from their upsetting emotions. People with dismissive attachment patterns think everything is fine as they isolate in the cloud and various
hobbies. "Settle down! Quit overreacting!" they will say to make the distress
someone else's problem. Once distress is past or bearable again, they come up
for air and interact. When dismissive individuals interact with protectors who
have return to joy skills, there is a delightful discovery that emotions will not
smother or swallow them. They no longer need to avoid or minimize distress,
rather, they learn to share emotions and return to joy.

Taking care of other people and smiling is also not the same as returning to
joy from distress. Trying to appear happy is not the same as returning to joy.
Pressing other people to help us feel better is not returning to joy. Protectors
who use the gentle protector skills can disarm the fear that drives a false self.
Protectors help those who are accustomed to using other people to help them
feel better return to joy, rather than appear happy.

Fear of rocking the boat to make sure no one gets mad is not returning to
joy. Individuals who are afraid will placate, people-please and work diligently
to ensure the relational boat does not tip over lest someone fall into the waters
of distress. Fearing upset leads to stuffing emotions and hiding what we really

feel. On the outside this looks like strength and stability. Joyful people who quickly return to joy from distress do not fear distress or upset because it does not last. Interaction and training from a protector who has the return to joy skills brings strength and trust. The protector's consistency, emotional availability and non-anxious presence creates the sturdy bond to grow new skills.

Returning to joy

Since joy means being glad to be together then returning to joy is what we need when something goes wrong at home, school and in church. Once someone is upset with us we need to know how to restore the relationship back to joy so we can solve the problem together.

Returning to joy at home

We depend on a family pool of skills for getting back to joy. Each of us might share the skills that our parents and close relatives used with us. Every time people from two families marry there is a chance to pool together the skills each family has used. The bride's family is very tender to anyone who is sad, where the groom's family sees sadness as a weakness. This will bring a conflict to the couple as his "hardness about sadness" and her "joy behind tenderness" compete to see if he will learn skills from her, or if his trauma will be passed on as a missing skill for their children. The children may or may not learn return to joy from sadness.

Continuing our example, the woman's family did not know how to return to joy from anger. In her family all joy was gone when someone became angry. Problems that caused anger always became more important than the family relationship. There was a real danger of being hurt. As a mother she is now very motivated to avoid anger and warns the children not to make her angry. She is teaching the children that there is no return to joy from anger. They should fear and avoid anger. Father's side of the family did different things when they were angry but the outcome was the same. No one in this family is going to be glad to be together when they are angry. Anger will always drive joy out of this house as long as the skill is missing.

However, both families come from farming backgrounds and it is not hard to feel disgust and stay in relationships. The women are disgusted by cleaning babies, cleaning vomit and dealing with diseases, but they help each other and feel tender care for the sick and injured people. The men must tend cattle and go into slimy and filthy places to make their living. They even eat some disgusting things and laugh it off with each other. No one in these families would imagine that disgust would keep people from being glad to be together.

To their friends and neighbors, Brian and Shelly look like the perfect family. Both have good jobs, drive fuel-efficient cars and they own a nice house nestled in a safe neighborhood. Their three children are active in sports and a variety of school activities. They have a lot of friends and socialize on weekends. Brian is a hard worker who loves his family. Shelly grew up in a loving family that ended in a messy divorce. Shelly has a low tolerance for weakness and relies on predator threats to control her children. Shelly demands order and quiet so she can watch her television shows in peace. She finds it hard to say kind words to her family even when they are trying hard to please her. When Brian points out her failure to hug, nurture or show affection to him and their children, Shelly justifies herself with, "Everyone should know that I love them and that's all I have to say." The conversation ends there.

Brian deals with his problems like a good possum. He stays quiet and disconnects. Every so often he responds to overwhelm by going predator and explodes into fits of anger which overwhelm everyone. He justifies his rage with, "I've had enough!" and tells everyone to "shut it" so that he can "hear himself think." Usually this happens after a hard day at the office or one too many beers. Deep down Brian feels tired and hopeless about life and his marriage.

Their oldest daughter Tina is becoming rigid and controlling. Tina does not accept a shame message. Because Tina is both pretty and popular at school, she uses her personal power to create rejection and hurt others.

Brian and Shelly were introduced to return to joy and gentle protector skills at a *THRIVE* retreat. Reluctant at first, they began to warm up to the exercises and started building joy. During one exercise Brian asked Shelly to forgive him for his angry outbursts. Shelly surprised herself by crying. It was not safe for her to show emotions growing up. The weekend turned out to be joyful, even healing. Their children noticed, "Mom and Dad are much more cuddly since that church weekend." Brian and Shelly have plenty of work ahead of them but family joy levels are higher. Tina confided to Shelly how she had been hurting her school friends and feeling sad. This led to Tina apologizing to her friends and new smiles at school as well. As a family, Brian, Shelly and Tina are learning to keep relationships bigger and more important than their problems.

Returning to joy at school

The average Western child derives limited benefit from the relational skills on either side of the family. Since we would predict more divorces in couples where there is low-joy, and at least one in the couple has trouble getting back to joy quickly, it is likely the children with the higher risk factors are already in single-parent homes. The biggest chance to learn something new comes with school. At school children are exposed to peers, teachers and possibilities they would never have imagined at home.

Because many children discover joy for the first time at school under the powerful influence of a teacher, teachers become a strategic source of relational skills for each generation. Teachers must show joy to be with a child or there will be no relational skill transfer. Some of the best teachers choose the career because one of their teachers brought them joy and gentle protector skills they never experienced at home.

Suppose my fourth grade teacher Ms. Flowers smiles each time I enter class and remembers my name. Ms. Flowers remembers what I have done well and is pleased, but she also carefully finds out my weaknesses. She knows that my spelling is bad. She knows that I do not know how to multiply by nines. She knows that I usually miss when I kick the ball. The other children all know this too and they laugh, but Ms. Flowers does not like them to laugh and teaches them to be respectful. She was very happy teaching me how to do everything I am weak at doing. Ms. Flowers, however, is most remarkable because she gets angry at me and the other children but no one gets hurt. "Amanda!", she would say, "You have been a wonderful class leader all week. I am angry that you would lie about doing your work when you didn't! Please tell me what happened. It is important to do your work and important that we can trust each other." As we explained before, this is what we call a relational sandwich.

By demonstrating over and over to the class how to be angry and still be glad to be with the children, Ms. Flowers was teaching return to joy from anger. Think how much more effective schools could be if they worked deliberately to learn and propagate joy skills. Ambleside Schools International deliberately structures their schools to practice and strengthen the gentle protector brain skills. Children with high levels of joy and shalom learn everything much better. Chris and Jen's two sons attend an Ambleside School and are learning relational skills that increase maturity and develop character. Chris often says his sons have received a better education by fourth grade than he did by the eighth grade.

Carol, a teacher we have met, works in a school where fear, shame, and anxiety are prevalent. She must be intentional about keeping her relational circuits on and not losing sight of the person God created her to be. Carol, like all human beings, often forgets to act like herself when faced with big emotions, especially fear and shame. She wants to be a protector even when interacting with her bosses. This is difficult since many of these professional relationships are not rooted in joy. It is hard to remember that the relationship is more important than the problems that arise. Carol makes it a habit to ask herself one question, "What would it be like me to do if I weren't so angry, afraid or anxious right now?" This question resets her nervous system and her relational circuits come back online. Carol now has a choice to act like herself in spite of what those upstream from her say or do. This is not as easy as it sounds; it requires that Carol keep her own joy at a high level and stay connected with others. She interacts regularly with her three upstream mentors as well as her few supportive colleagues, all of whom are delighted to be with her regardless of her emotional state.

Carol discovered she is able to effect change more proactively by working downstream, through modeling and teaching relational brain skills to her students. One way Carol emphasizes how relational brain skills work is during times when Steven disrupts the learning process. Carol has been known to correct the behavior in an abrupt manner. Because her relational circuits are off, she loses her relationship with the offending student as well as the rest of the class.

After quickly quieting herself, Carol models transparency by explaining her internal process to the class. "When Steven disrupted instruction, I got angry and snapped at him to behave. At that moment, when I snapped at him, the problem with Steven grew bigger and more important in my mind than who Steven is to me, a precious student. This means that my relational circuits went off and I could no longer be my true self." Carol was able to repair the situation with Steven and the whole class by being transparent and vulnerable and apologizing for her abrupt reaction. What Carol accomplished by walking the students through her invisible, internal process was to make it a visible model for them to adopt for themselves.

Additionally, by reminding Steven that the relationship between them is more important than the problem he caused by being disruptive, he realized he was a valued member of the class community. This interaction resulted in fewer disruptions for Steven. This type of intervention and modeling takes time, patience, grace and a lot of courage, but for Carol, the goals were clear. She wanted to grow her protector identity to foster a collective joyful identity and train her students to keep their relational circuits on. The only way Carol was able to sustain her efforts was to remain in close connection with those upstream and downstream from her. More on staying relational can be found in Chris' book *The Joy Switch*.

Returning to joy at church

There is one last chance to return to joy if our family and school did not teach us and that is at church. Jesus said, "These things I have spoken to you, that My joy may remain in you, and that your joy may be full" John 15:11 (NKJV). Surely if there is any place in the world that builds joy and knows the ways back to joy it will be the church and its people. Joy starts here with Jesus, His mission and all His followers. In fact, we would be right to guess that the main point of this book is to remind the 2.2 billion Christians in the world that joy starts with us. Christians are the largest religious group and almost one third of the world's population. If all Christians were joy starters, we would only have to reach two people each to have the whole world full of joy. Joy is the birthright of the followers of Jesus and the deepest desire of the human brain. Joy should catch fire if we could learn to 1) build joy, 2) return to joy when something goes wrong and 3) see others the way that God sees them. These are just three of the nineteen brain skills we develop through the Life Model.

Chris writes: We were standing in line to board an airplane when the announcement was made that our plane was full. Because this was the last flight, I knew we faced an overnight stay. One passenger in line suddenly lost it. In a rage he threw his bags and spewed profanities. His raging voice echoed in the terminal. Passengers scattered. This guy was no longer in relational mode. As I made my way over to the ticket desk, he walked around the terminal screaming at anyone in uniform. I could see his red face and his intense emotions were scaring people. By this time his eyes were bulging and he was sweating profusely. As he neared the ticket desk, I felt compelled to reach out to him. I knew this man was drowning. He needed some serious help returning to joy so I took a deep breath and walked up to him. For a moment I wondered if he would knock me out.

"You are really having a bad day, aren't you?" I asked affirmingly. "You are __ __ right I am having a bad day!" he fired back. We locked eyes for a few moments then I said, "Well, I am a pastor, a follower of Jesus and I would be honored if I could pray with you." I was pleasantly relieved when he muttered, "Ok, yeah, sure." Standing in the middle of the terminal we bowed our heads. I put my hand on his shoulder, we took a moment of quiet (skill two). Then, I invited Immanuel to share our distress and bring some vision (skill thirteen).

I noticed tears running down his face. "You see," he explained, "I have been traveling for medical help because I was recently diagnosed with serious cancer. This flight cancellation takes away my precious, limited time with my wife and daughters." For a few moments we shared sadness then he said, "Wait! I have to do something." He retraced his steps and apologized to every single airline employee he offended. After several minutes he returned. "I have been feeling like I need to get right with God," he told me. "I wonder if this whole ordeal is God speaking?" A sparkle of joy appeared in his eyes as his face muscles relaxed. The next morning I saw him boarding the flight with a smile and a brand new Bible under his arm.

When protector skills are strategically used, every personal encounter becomes an opportunity to practice and propagate skills. With practice and training, we can effectively share joy and demonstrate return to joy in each of the big six emotions.

Learning return to joy at church means that people will need to bring their weaknesses to church in a way that is right out in the open. This will only happen when we respond tenderly to weakness instead of condemning, withdrawing, critiquing, moralizing, exploiting and amplifying problems. We do not want to make church into a place where people can go on remaining stuck in their problems without hope of transformation. Here is where the Immanuel experience makes all the difference. In joy, we discover that we are someone new who does not need to live the old way.

Life Model resources for home, school and church

Joyful relational brain skills have stayed under the radar until recent discoveries in brain science articulated what most of us already knew at some level but lacked the words to explain. We now have a language for propagating protector skills in our schools, churches, families and communities. A few questions below provide some guidance for growing protector skills on a deeper level.

How can I learn to identify people who already have gentle protector skills? As we develop the language and identify the context for what is involved to grow the nineteen protector skills, we search and locate people who have the skills. People who already have the gentle protector skills are caring, warm, inviting, approachable, relational and joyful. We recognize these individuals because they are consistent and transparent. Protectors are genuine and comfortable in their own shoes. Protectors create belonging and stay attentive to opportunities to share their joy. The strong do not hoard nor do they take from the weak. The strong give generously. The strong hold up when feeling tired, overwhelmed, hungry, accused, upset and pretty much any of the big six emotions. The strong tend to greet others in the lobby at church, look out for the elderly and play with the children. Sometimes they are the quiet ones preparing coffee in the kitchen. We can even ask our church leaders, "Who do you know in the church as the top five reliable, joyful people?"

How can I learn the skills? When we lack certain skills we can search where the strong encounter the weak. We identify local activities that may provide the context for practicing skills. Many churches offer small groups for deeper, joy-filled connection. Schools offer clubs and groups with a specific focus. We identify the people who frequently step up when a crisis hits. We notice the protectors who help strangers feel connected. Getting to know people with gentle protector skills is as simple as having tea or coffee, eating lunch, even joining a prayer or a small group. We can engage the strong in a discussion and explain why gentle protector skills must be learned. We invite protectors to share how they learned and formed their protector identities. We approach the strong by creating belonging and spreading appreciation around us.

We have developed specific Life Model resources to take relational skill training to the next level. Our families and churches do not have to create the training that is needed. See Appendix D for more information on these training options.

How can stories propagate skills? Interactive stories are one of the best ways to propagate protector skills, so we must learn how to share stories. Personal stories are one of the ideal ways to enlist protectors. People enjoy hearing stories, especially if stories bring joy and return us to joy. With practice, all of us become trained story tellers who propagate joy. Stories should be short and focused. We want to tell our personal experience, demonstrate the emotions we feel, and show our enthusiasm for joyful, Jesus-like life and character within our community. Stories must give listeners enough details to understand the context for what we are saying. Stories improve with practice and feedback so we invite listeners to share how they felt. While there are varying degrees in the quality of skill training, we can increase the depth of our stories with practice.

If churches are to make a difference, they need many mature people with relational skills who are ready to engage with weaker members of the community for some very focused character building exercises that combine the best of scripture with what we know about propagating gentle protector skills. We have been developing materials for churches to use so that those who are willing to enter the transformation zone will have good results for their troubles. There is nothing sadder than people working hard and sacrificing to carry out a ministry in ways that block the propagation of joy skills because they simply didn't know what they needed. We have a variety of resources through our website www.joystartshere.com or in Appendix D that can be used to increase our joy propagation at home, school or church.

How am I doing?
- What happens when I feel angry, sad, afraid, disgusted, ashamed and hopeless?
- How do I respond when others around me feel the six emotions listed above?
- Do I increase joy levels when someone is upset?

Who are the people who can help me improve my return to joy skills? Where are the resources that I need?

Correcting what I might have heard about training my brain
Much of what we read about the brain is an updated version of what the Western Church has been overusing the last 400 years. The solution of Western culture the last 400 years is that we should make better choices by thinking better thoughts. For more see *The Solution of Choice*.

The brain is used for thinking and choices so this seems totally logical and has instant appeal. The new literature on the brain has picked up the observation that emotions are fundamental to the brain and body. The brain requires emotions for processing experience properly so many new books add emotions as the new ingredient to the old solution of thinking better thoughts and making better choices. The new load for our thinking and choices is that if we choose our thoughts carefully, we will control the emotions that run our brain and body system. Thoughts and choices become the solution to controlling emotions. That is not what we are teaching in this book. For more on this discussion see *Renovated*.

One example of adding the new brain science to the old "think and choose" solution can be seen in the book *Who Switched Off My Brain: controlling toxic thoughts and emotions* by Dr. Caroline Leaf. She describes her solution by saying, "Consciously controlling your thoughts is not just the first step in this process; it is the main step" (p. 107). Leaf sees thoughts and choices as the center of our identities. She describes identity this way, "Because we each make choices based on our thoughts and attitudes, we create responses different from one another. This creates the uniqueness of every person..." (p. 33). While this sounds good and our choices do affect us, our identities are not formed by choices but by the bonds we experience. Who we share mutual mind states with and who we love will shape our choices more than the other way around. Attachments are at the center of our identities. It is very hard to make changes by simply thinking and choosing differently. Try to change the character of how young adults eat by telling them to think more about nutrition and make better choices. But watch what happens when they begin to love and attach to someone and we will see thoughts, feeling and choices changing in a hurry. Think of anyone who fell in love and how they change schools, politics, friends and are suddenly interested in Japanese art!

The brain is much more concerned about who we love than what we think. Emotions and attachments rapidly change our reality. Leaf correctly states that, "You won't believe it unless your brain's limbic system (the seat of our emotions) allows you to feel that it is true" (p. 36). The attachment system in the emotional right hemisphere of the brain has the direct control of our identities and emotions and it is only indirectly influenced by thoughts and choices. It has much more say about what we will think or choose than the other way around. This executive control center is heavily influenced by joy and shalom that grow from attachment and relationships.

While there is every reason to think good thoughts and make good choices, these are not the secret to developing mature Godly character. Training our brain's relational identity center to live in joy and shalom works directly while thoughts and choices can only work indirectly and inefficiently to transform identities.

Joy Actions

Home: With Immanuel's help, think of a time you did not return to joy then apologize.

School: With Immanuel's help, think of a time you did not return to joy then apologize.

Church: With Immanuel's help, think of a time you did not return to joy then apologize.

Environmental Pseudo-Return-To-Joy Assessment

1. When I feel ashamed I want to be alone.

   I open up   0 1 2 3 4 5 6 7 8 9 10   *I withdraw*

2. People make me angry but I don't let them know.

   I work for change   0 1 2 3 4 5 6 7 8 9 10   *I hide my anger*

3. Fear often limits or directs what I do.

   Not at all   0 1 2 3 4 5 6 7 8 9 10   *Consistently*

4. I know people who smile at each other but secretly carry a grudge.

   No one does this   0 1 2 3 4 5 6 7 8 9 10   *Everywhere I go*

5. I would rather be hurt than be alone.

   Rather be hurt   0 1 2 3 4 5 6 7 8 9 10   *Rather be alone*

6. Some people at church have not spoken to each other for years.

   Everyone is warm   0 1 2 3 4 5 6 7 8 9 10   *Huge walls*

7. When I am upset I turn it over to God and try to forget about it.

   Not at all   0 1 2 3 4 5 6 7 8 9 10   *Most of the time*

8. Our family tries to look like everything is fine when we are in public.

   Very transparent   0 1 2 3 4 5 6 7 8 9 10   *Try to look good*

9. I work hard to avoid being embarrassed.

   Not at all   0 1 2 3 4 5 6 7 8 9 10   *Most of the time*

10. I don't like the way I want to act when I am angry or afraid.

    I set an example   0 1 2 3 4 5 6 7 8 9 10   *I don't like what I do*

Total your scores here. _____
Mark the matching spot on the scale.

0   10   20   30   40   50   60   70   80   90   100

Forming Joyful People Bible Study

Think back on something you appreciate and spend two minutes enjoying appreciation. Next, ask God to make this study interesting for you. Now read the following passage from the prophets.

Scripture 1 Samuel 1:1-2:26 Read then review the passage for each question.

Chapter Nine Question: Consider how each character in this story responds to the feelings of others. How does each raise or lower the joy levels? Who made the problems larger? Who made the relationship better?

Weakness, Joy and Shalom Questions:
1. Who are weak or strong in this passage?
2. What kind of interaction does God desire between weak and strong?
3. What do we learn about joy and shalom (everything works together) from this passage?

Immanuel Questions:
1. What effects does perceiving "God is with us" have in this passage?
2. Group study activity: God is always present and eager to help us see more clearly. In what ways do we perceive or guess that God is helping us understand this passage right now in the group discussion?

> **Note:** Thinking about God's active presence may seem strange at first because people generally discuss the past more than they observe the present. Keep your answers short. Feel free to guess. We will do this each week.

Personal Story Question: What gentle protectors (people or characters from the Bible, books or media) have been an example in your life?

Whole Bible Question: What Bible stories tell of tender responses to weakness that changed people's lives?

Wrap-Up Minute: What do you now know that you didn't know before this week's study?

My Life Model Joy Skills Exercises

Individual: Relational Mode
1. Every day during the week, take a moment to go through the list to see if you are in relational mode.
2. *If you answer YES to any of the following scenarios, your relational circuits are OFF. Everything related to relational conflicts will turn out better when your relational circuits are back ON.* *
    A. I just want to make a problem, person or feeling go away.
    B. I don't want to listen to what others feel or say.
    C. My mind is "locked onto" something upsetting.
    D. I don't want to be connected to __ (someone I usually like).
    E. I just want to get away (flight) or fight. Or, I just freeze.
    F. I more aggressively interrogate, judge and fix others.
3. Take three minutes to remember your favorite appreciation memory. When you finish, go through the list again and see if anything changes.
4. Notice times from your day (or the previous day) when you were clearly in relational mode and times you were clearly out of relational mode. What patterns emerge?

   *This checklist was inspired by Dr. Karl and Charlotte Lehman and modified to use in THRIVE Training, Belonging The Joy Switch and many other places.

Group: Return to Joy
1. As a group, discuss what patterns emerged from the Individual Relational Mode exercise?
2. As a group, discuss ways joy can be restored and what would be the benefits for home, school and church?
3. What are the benefits when the relationship remains more important than the problem?
4. Individually take three minutes to remember a favorite appreciation memory or Immanuel moment. Talk with Jesus about these topics. Is there anything Immanuel wants you to know today? Share your thoughts and observations with the group.

Chapter Ten

Saving Joy Skills
From Extinction

Many skills have headed toward extinction. Spear hunting, cleaning game, spinning, sharpening saws, milking, penmanship, canning, hand sewing, top spinning, baking, woodworking and even kite flying were all skills that almost every child learned or at least watched and understood. As useful as these simple skills were at some point in history, most will not be missed. However, there is a set of specific brain skills needed for human identity that depend upon human interaction patterns for successful propagation. No single human interaction provides more opportunities for relational skill propagation than eating meals together. We are designed to bond around food. A century ago, children and most workers had time off at noon to go home for a meal with their families. They already enjoyed a cooked breakfast together and would have an evening meal together as well. They would sit at the table facing each other and talk with no television or radio. There was usually only one light and heat source in the house so fall, winter and spring evenings for the whole family were spent in the same room. This is a huge amount of face-to-face interaction time with family in which to learn relational skills. Those interaction patterns have changed dramatically in the last one hundred years, and it is likely that family interaction time for children now is less than one percent of what it was. Children now do not even know someone who lived and trained their social skills one hundred years ago. With the relational environment shrinking to less than one percent, common skills that previously existed are now facing extinction.

Shelia's story

My dad was only a part of my life as a living member until I was four and a half years old. His absence remained a palpable "presence" even though we hardly spoke of him. What remained of my family after Grace's and my dad's untimely deaths were my emotionally absent mom, two older brothers, my fraternal twin sister and me.

My mom was low-joy and ill-equipped, so my dad's parents played a significant role in our upbringing. With my dad's death, these grandparents represented the connection to any joy and relational skills from his side of the family. While they did provide for some of our basic needs, such as regular meals, extra money, clothing and a place to learn about God, they were not able to teach us necessary relational skills. My grandpa molested me soon after my dad died, and my grandma was often overcome with fear and anxiety. They blocked relational joy for me through both their words and actions on the many weekends we spent together.

Back at home after our weekend getaways, I fought with my twin sister Ella in an attempt to deal with my rage at Mom, which was unspoken. I was so afraid that Mom would kill herself that I walked around on egg shells for fear any disruption would send her over the edge. "It's not that bad" became my defense against just how awful it really was for me.

When I was eight years old, my mom came home with a man named Jerry and declared she had married him. He was an evil man and a predator loose in our house. He was a mean drunk. He hit Mom and verbally assaulted her as well. He whipped me with a belt so hard that I had bruises up and down my legs. He also violated me sexually. Ella was the quieter one, whereas I was a real smart aleck so he attacked me. He wreaked havoc on our family for six years. He left when Ella and I were fourteen. By this time, my brothers were married and out of the house. Ella and I took over paying the bills, and when we were fifteen, Ella secured a job at a local shoe store. I joined her a few months later, and we worked there the remainder of our high school years. We had to work to supplement the two social security checks she and I received each month.

I was quite successful at school, but I rarely, if ever, felt any real joy. Most of what I accomplished was designed to build my mask of strength and hide who I believed I really was. I was too preoccupied with fear and worry to have any real fun. Somehow I managed to perform academically and landed in the top five of my senior class. I was a varsity cheerleader in spite of the fact that I could never get my jumps up high or the moves sharp enough. Cheerleading was my sister's forte`. I felt clumsy and inept. I was not the cheerleader type, but I owned a varsity letter jacket, which "proved" I was good at something.

Ella and I wore our strong masks well, so my mom decided that since we "had everything under control," it was okay to run off with a truck driver. She left Ella and me to live alone for many weeks. We did not know if she were alive or dead until she unexpectedly returned one day in January. She missed Thanksgiving and Christmas that year, but I was so happy to see her when she returned that I never spoke of what she had done to us.

My mom felt so fragile to me that I ignored and suppressed my rage toward her and instead began to direct it at myself. This anger turned inward resulted in an undeniable self-hatred. My internalized rage soon resulted in a deep depression.

I fought with Ella. We hit each other, pulled each other's hair, scratched each other and destroyed each other's things. We would make up quickly and pretend we had never been mad at each other. We had no idea how to return to joy. I was adept at playing the role of possum in our relationship, which has always made me feel and look pathetic. Building joy together was not in our minds. We needed our pseudo-identities and pseudo-maturity to survive and "look good." Even though we pretended nothing had happened, this pseudo-shalom was no comfort. I cried myself to sleep most nights.

Without joy, shalom, return to joy and protector skills from my family or church, school provided a hope for some escape. It would still be many years before I would learn about joy. My life had been a witness to the devastating lack of relational joy all around me.

In recent years, Ella and I have talked about the details of our childhood and its impact on our relationship both as children and now as adults. We've cried together and expressed our love and appreciation for each other. We've made some progress in our ability to communicate

about difficult memories and the painful feelings associated with them.
We've also been able to disagree on some details about our childhood
and fill in the gaps for each other. I've learned that the best way for me to
continue to heal is to be tender toward my own weakness and to respond
tenderly to my siblings and my mom.

What brought relational skills to the brink of extinction?

There are many reasons why relational skills are not passed effectively from
one generation to the next. Acquisition problems arise when the right conditions are not present to get a skill started. Strengthening problems prevent a
skill from developing to useful levels like when children can read but with
such difficulty that they will never read a book. Implementation problems
block people from using the skills they have. Propagation problems prevent
people from passing on their skills to others. We have already considered one
propagation problem caused by the drastic drop in the number of relational
interactions within bonded relationships each day.

There are many social factors that hinder the propagation of gentle protector skills. Some of these are slavery, human trafficking, war, working conditions from the industrial revolution, trauma, BEEPS, loss (attachment pain),
moving to cities, single parenting, commuting, education for test scores and
data acquisition, raising children in front of televisions, shanty town violence,
excessive time with machines, genocide, (exterminations for tribal, political
or religious reasons), cultural/religious/political attacks on weakness or family
bonds, AIDS, epidemics, controlling groups through anger and fear, pornography, gang violence, child abuse, domestic violence, men dominating
women, cultures of narcissism, self-justification, deviant parenting patterns,
political correctness, tyrannical governments and various ideologies that reduce the number of tender interactions between the weak and the strong.

Entire cultures can come to despise weakness thus becoming rigid and
low-joy. A huge drop in peaceful protector skills follows when cultures begin
to exterminate the weak. Nazis viewed the extermination of Jews as the means
to remove a weakness. Weaker groups die in vast numbers during political or
ethnic mass murders, but the killers do so at the cost of becoming predators
and producing generations of damage for those who are not killed.

Environmental and cultural factors leading to fearing, despising, hiding and
manipulating weakness block transmission of joy skills. Gentle protector skills do
not get passed to the next generation very easily and what is left is our hard-wired
predator thinking. Predators also target and kill real protectors making them an
endangered species. Tyrants of all kinds hate protectors.

But we might say, "Haven't these problems always been with us?" To a large extent that is true. Joy skills have always been far too rare. The last century, however, introduced some rapid changes that are now bringing joy skills to near extinction. We are faced with threats that have never been present in human history. Not only are conditions becoming far worse for joy-skill transmission, the people who still have the skills to pass along are aging and their numbers are dropping rapidly. We are in a crisis.

Face-to-face interactions are becoming rare

It takes no imagination at all to see the difference between our world and the world one hundred years ago where families ate together and spent much of their time in the same room. It was a world where relatives lived nearby. The cloud did not exist. People spent most of the waking day interacting with people face-to-face. Although there were plenty of low-joy places in the world, and problems with propagating protector skills were common, the sheer number of face-to-face interactions gave the skills a decent chance to spread.

We might not think about it if we have never lived that way, but disability and weakness were cared for by families and communities. Most people could no longer work by the time they were 45 years old, and these older people made themselves useful around the home and community by watching children, keeping gardens, doing crafts and repairs or by entertaining others with stories. The old and the young were constantly interacting in ways that used relational brain skills. The children picked up the skills just by being around them all the time. No interactions were interrupted by a text message from the cloud.

The last century has brought new challenges to the interactions of weak and strong and added a whole new dimension to the problem. The weakness facing every child entering the world is the near total absence of relational ability. Relational ability is something that inherently weak children once learned from the aging who were considered weak in their working ability but who actually had rather strong relational capacity. The old men and women of the village who could no longer go to the fields were left home with the children. Old people whose bodies were not strong enough found their joy from interactions with children in circumstances where care for the weakness of others was a constant factor. There was little entertainment other than what they provided for each other.

Media and entertainment: Entertainment now occupies huge amounts of time every week. Time spent on-line, watching television or movies, playing computer games, texting, listening to music over headphones and preoccupation with email, news sources and computers now adds to the time spent driving or working. These distractions from interaction with others are not just for adults anymore. Children are watching machines from infancy. Where 60 years ago children spent virtually all of their time interacting with others, playing and comparing abilities, they now spend the majority of their time focused on machines that have no relational skills or awareness of the child's presence. Babies are watching television; they have movies in pre-school, day care, church, at home, and with baby-sitters. The cloud is absorbing our lives.

Even if the child is watching people interact, the child will not be acquiring the relational skills because these skills require mutual mind states that machines and movies in particular cannot achieve. Mutual mind states that are strong enough to propagate relational skills only develop during face-to-face interactions with people who have the skills. Mutual mind states can only develop between two people at a time. No teacher can do mutual mind states with two students at a time. It is both a time and relationship-intensive process requiring many interactions to acquire a clean copy.

The neuroscience literature since 2003 shows requirements for successful transmission of gentle protector skills are quite strict. Television, computers, movies, books or video games cannot spread relational skills. Media has gone from being the message to being the method for much of our training and education. Joy skills do not propagate through media, internet, webcams or even telecommunications. We cannot raise babies into human beings by internet or television any more than we can make babies that way.

But the problem is not simply that babies and children are in front of screens for hours, so are the older people. Even if children want to engage, the grandparents are watching television in their retirement homes. Even if media could transmit relational skills, they are not what is generally displayed in programming. Predators are abundant and media is a useful source for developing predator strategies.

Because of the reasons given, joy skills are not being propagated at home because the weak and strong from different generations no longer provide constant care and practice. Gentle protector skills are not generally taught in school. Schools rarely even do much to strengthen these skills. Relational skills are rarely taught in most churches, because for many Christians, the weak and strong are rarely together in a way that promotes relationships and transformation. Most people in church are staying in their comfort zone and promoting their pseudo-self to stay safe. We should also notice that most people who consider themselves Christian rarely see church as a resource for their skills or relationships.

Mobility: The invention of the internal combustion engine has allowed people to escape places of low-joy. Millions have left the farm, the country, and the neighborhood to find work elsewhere. Travel means leaving behind the weak, old and very young. The strongest move to cities, new countries and jobs where they have a better life. However, in moving away to find a better future they must leave behind the constant interactions between old and young, weak and strong that occupies so much of the day for the weak. Tender moments become an occasional event each year or whenever workers return home.

Work environments are often low-joy and not weakness-friendly. Employers prefer strong workers. Many jobs take the worker's strength in exchange for pay and then discard the workers when their strength is gone or, worse yet, destroyed by the work itself. Even ministries whose goal is the care of the weak may be harsh with the lives of their staff members. Christians and their organizations frequently demand that their workers and leaders be mobile and free of weaknesses.

Cultural mobility has allowed people to leave problems and liabilities behind. Having children became a weakness one could avoid along with being married. Both children and marriage create a long-term "liability" that could result in needing to take care of someone's weaknesses. In fact, any long-term commitment to people will leave us dealing with weakness at some point.

Professionalized care: Those who do stay as families in Western society find that in order to work, the young must be placed in schools and the old placed in homes. The weak are often placed in institutions and their care has been professionalized. Not too far into the industrial revolution, babies began to be nursed by wet-nurses, the sick by health care providers, the old by nursing homes, the dying were in hospitals and the dead put in funeral homes. Even the housing and feeding of people with chronic weakness became the burden of government rather than families, churches and neighborhoods. While these factors constantly shift, what does not change is that there is less and less ongoing interaction between weak and strong. Chances for relational skills to propagate are lost.

Professional care-givers often possess specialized skills but not for propagating joy. Government workers and programs are not set up to develop tenderness toward the weak, they are motivated to reduce costs to the government and keep their budgets. Schools were not designed to produce gentle protectors but rather strong workers who would be free of weakness and stay productive to society.

Fast food: We all know that cooking real food takes a long time. What we do not notice is that during these long periods of food preparation, the generations interacted with each other, children bonded with people instead of food, participants appreciated the effort and waiting for the meal taught craving control over appetites. Cooking causes injuries so people practiced quieting distress, problem solving and returning to joy. With fast food at home or out these interaction times are gone. Whether it is due to less time cooking, central heating, lights in every room, entertainment, mobility or loss of resources, the effect of all these factors is the same, a dramatic reduction in the opportunities to see, learn or practice relational skills. Skills that once propagated on their own are more endangered than the polar bear.

Our lack of awareness: More importantly, what we are discussing here is virtually unknown to the last two generations of humans in the Western world. People who are now three generations removed from the relational world so common for children prior to WWII think that what they are doing is the same as what has always happened. After all, don't they come home from work, take the children to soccer practice and dance lessons? Don't they watch television together? Don't they text each other regularly? What could possibly be different? Sure, they have heard the stories their grandparents tell about how life used to be, but the old days do not sound appealing.

Old folks also do not know what was accomplished during all those hours that were "wasted" dealing with weakness. They worked hard to avoid weakness and make a better life for their children. No weakness or suffering would be passed on to their children who would all be healthy and strong. The elderly cannot put into words how relational skills were learned, but they can see something disappearing in the "young people today." Some even guess it is related to the way life required more from them as children. But these war and depression era survivors want to be strong so who would ever guess that it was the constant exposure to weakness that allowed character to form, emotional control to be learned and gentle protector skills to develop. Old people sense they are weak now but see there is no value in their weakness anymore. They only see an eventual move to the nursing home where they will watch television if they are not lucky enough to go out with a decent heart attack.

Care for the weak is the pivot point for relational skills

Located above our eyes, the ventromedial prefrontal cortex has the very important job of figuring out the least harmful solution to every situation. This damage-control system in our brain needs to be trained with the full range of joy skills. Part of damage control is our ability to return to joy. Return to joy is how we go about saving our relationships when others are not glad to be with us. When a classmate says, "your hair looks stupid," we feel our joy leave the room. Now, the ventromedial prefrontal cortex will have to look at what we have learned from our role models at home, school or church and then decide what to do. We could answer rudely, we could withdraw, we could tell the teacher or our mother. Our brain's identity center considers the examples we have seen and tries to figure out the least painful solution. The control section is non-verbal so it does not consider what our parents told us or what they said in church; it considers examples it has known and observed. Our brain might never have learned that the best solutions bring us back to joy. So we might shoot back, "You are too stupid to know," and our friends might laugh.

But, did we act like our true selves and reach shalom by shouting back? Did we open the door to return to joy with the classmate who insulted us? Did we learn to be a gentle protector? If we did not learn to think about our identity in those terms, our ventromedial prefrontal cortex damage-control computer did not consider them as options. However, this clever computer can be taught to look for options it does not yet have. Even when we do not have the entire set of gentle protector skills, we can position ourselves to find new protector ways with an identity that says, "I respond tenderly toward weakness." When we are people who are tender toward weakness, then every encounter with weakness makes us want to learn better responses, provided our relational circuits are running.

Even without proper return to joy skills we can think to ourselves, "There must be a kind and tender way to respond." If God is always here with us, an Immanuel experience will help us acquire a new response. We can acquire these skills from God because Jesus will redemptively bypass the gaps left by our families, schools and churches to teach us the way back to joy so that we can then practice this skill with others. Sometimes we will find answers by asking our "tribe" to show us possibilities, examining scripture, reading the biographies of gentle protectors or even taking some Life Model training.

Suppose that we totally forget to check with Immanuel or our relational circuits go off as soon as our classmate says our hair looks stupid. We can return to the event when the lack of shalom shows up later in the day and the comments keep running through our mind. Perhaps when we get home, we can ask our family how they would have answered or sit down with God for a quiet time of review to learn a better way. We can learn skills before, during or after an event when our identity wants to be a gentle protector and we do not yet know how.

Perhaps we are still wondering how the hair comment represents weakness. The comment itself was aggressive and hostile. The hair bully was trying to be powerful. How then can this be weakness? However puffed up the hair bully sounded, true strength comes from joy. Certainly the hair bully has a weak level of joy! Joy is what fuels our brain and our spirit. Whenever we hit a low level of joy, or people suck the joy out of life, we have landed on one of the largest weaknesses a person can have. Tenderness would urge us to start joy here.

What can we expect as relational skills disappear?

As relational skills decrease we can expect a long series of shifts in how people relate. These shifts will remain fairly invisible to the generation where the shift happens. For them, "this is just how people are." Without relational skills, power will become more attractive and the phrase "that was powerful" will justify almost anything. Increased interest in power will result in lower joy levels while people will fight for their rights. Revenge crimes will increase because without relational skills, people become problems rather than the people we care about, and revenge represents power to a predator. Lower relational skills will always mean increased violence and predatory behavior.

Emotional intensity will increase in whatever people do together, from how they dress to how they speak. People will "display" their emotional intensity and aggression without shame. Self control will decrease along with common sense. Of course, joy levels will drop as the ability to quiet oneself is lost. The wealthy will begin to find "quiet" retreats to demonstrate their wealth as quiet becomes increasingly rare. At the same time, powerful people will rise above the "common laws" and become increasingly exclusive.

Autistic-like behavior and reactions will increase and maturity levels will drop. Attachments to food and other BEEPS will increase along with weight and health issues from BEEPS. Family meals will disappear. Medications and other non-relational solutions will increasingly be needed to control emotions and focus attention. People will have little to no idea what satisfies them or how to sustain joy, so joy levels will drop.

The logic of relationship will be replaced by functionality. For example, instead of "she is my wife" indicating a bond, anyone who can perform the functions of a wife will be of equal value as "wife." Professionalism will replace tenderness or kindness as the standard of care between people. This will increase the view of people as disposable when they cannot render value. All of this will carry us to lower joy levels. Let us consider some specific issues.

Rise of pseudo-return to joy

One of the more detrimental effects of disappearing relational skills is pseudo-return to joy. As Shelia and Ella discovered, they had to act like nothing had happened. Shelia pretended that she was fine when her mother returned after vanishing for three months. This looks like joy but something is wrong beneath the surface. Walking on eggshells is another way Shelia described pretending that emotions and problems did not exist. Unhappy emotions do not build relationships when genuine return to joy skills are missing. Interactions no longer end in joyful, peaceful, glad to be together moments. Joy levels drop.

Managing problems instead of restoring joy

Mass management of people and their problems becomes the focus of public life when relational skills are scarce. Solving problems take priority over restoring joy. Who will have control becomes more important than uniting the country. People use their energy and resources rigidly to avoid as many problems as they can. More laws and rules are seen as the way to solve social issues. One social issue we will consider in detail involves schools.

Schools manage problems rather than raise human children: Schools will spend most of their time trying to manage violence and predatory behavior by children, parents and staff, while denying there is a problem. Inside the classroom everyone will compete for attention. Without relational skills, power goes to the one who gets the most attention. Schools will take over most of the feeding of children, thus making sure that children bond with food instead of people and increasing the epidemic of obesity and related health issues.

Predators at school: Children who have not learned to return to joy work hard to increase their power. They put other people down. Some use guns or knives, but most children rely on words, shame and attachment pain as the bullets. Frequently children will fantasize about revenge when they cannot return to joy and focus their predatory impulses on a pet, a younger sibling or by bullying other children.

In a school setting we see a variety of responses when individuals have not learned return to joy skills. People stuff emotions and rely on name-calling, teasing, and of course, bullying. Possums bury what they really feel so others cannot see the depth of their pain. Weaknesses stay hidden.

Bullying dramatically drops the joy level in schools. For the victim of bullying, hallways turn into tunnels for cruel jokes and torment. Cafeterias become the dreadful period for being mocked. Locker rooms become a nightmare. The bathroom may become a hideout, or the place where we are cornered. Lisa remembers being confronted in the bathroom by a pack of predator girls. She still cringes remembering the dread. Cyberbullying, a growing trend that spreads far beyond the walls of a school, sometimes includes parents as predators.

In schools, the power of belonging and growing a group identity motivates people to fit in, sometimes at extreme costs. One must look good, sound right and act a certain way to be part of the "in" crowd. To be excluded feels like death. To be left out is to live in a world of agony. Attachment pain colors reality and creates fear. Julie still feels the sting from her friends in high school who liked to call her Miss Prudence. All of Julie's friends knew this term was an insult.

People who lack return to joy skills frequently rely on BEEPS in the form of food and sugar. Obesity is a growing problem but telling children the importance of healthy eating does little to train the brain's relational control center. Children find comfort with artificial joy.

People exclude the weak for their own gain because they long to feel special. Feeling special ironically describes what people feel in genuine, joy-based relationships. Joy is ultimately what everyone wants and needs. Mike was not the predator-type but his fear of rejection drove him to join others in poking fun of Trina. Trina lived in an impoverished home and her clothes were neither clean nor stylish. Deep down Mike still remembers the expression of pain on Trina's face when his group tormented her at recess.

At school Tim would frequently tease Nathan about his weight. It seemed Tim creatively used every opportunity to remind Nathan and other classmates how big Nathan was. What people did not know was that Tim endured similar taunts and abuse at home from his stepfather. Tim's teasing left Nathan feeling powerless at school, and at home Nathan started emotionally abusing his younger sister.

Mark still remembers how frightening it was for him in high school to see his peers, many who were involved in gangs, bring guns to school in shoe boxes. Fear and tension ruled out any hopes of joy and peace. Now that Mark is grown up and his children attend school, he feels relief knowing metal detectors are in place to prevent guns from entering schools. One problem remains, however, metal detectors do not change character. Even without guns, students behave in threatening ways to prove they are powerful.

Gangs

Where weakness is no longer permitted and relational brain skills disappear, we start to see the kinds of monsters we can grow. Gang life is what happens when relational brain skills are missing and the need for belonging goes unsatisfied. We see individuals join gangs about the same age they would be forming a group identity. Twelve and thirteen year-olds often join gangs out of pressure and to fill the deep longing for power, joy, acceptance, respect, belonging, love, protection and connection. When our joy is low or non-existent, it feels good to have peers who are glad to be with us, even if we are breaking the law and deadly in the process. Gang members frequently refer to themselves as family which adds strength to the bond and bolsters loyalty.

Sadly, these basic needs could be met if gentle protector skills were learned at home, school and church through men and women protectors. If return to joy skills are missing or underdeveloped by the time children reach grade school, we have a new opportunity to learn gentle protector skills from our teachers, peers, coaches and other parents. Schools become fertile ground to cultivate and learn gentle protector skills or a hostile playing field where the strong use their power to rule the weak. Unless people of joy begin to propagate joy in our schools and churches, joy will continue to drop and hostility will grow.

Self-justified behavior

Predators offer seemingly justifiable reasons for their cruel behavior such as, "He deserved it!" "He's a know-it-all." "It was her fault we lost the game so I need to teach her a lesson." "He is stupid." "She looks ugly." The more efficient predators always seem to have their own valid-sounding reasons to justify attacking others. In the first Life Model book, *Living From The Heart Jesus Gave You*, we pointed out that this self-justification is called the sarx in Greek and is always contrary to God's ways. Living by self-justification always brings death rather than joy.

Pseudo-identity

Our true identity is always relational. When our identity becomes attached to ideology, religion, problems or success and power, we develop a pseudo-identity that we will perceive as our real self. We function in this pseudo-identity to look happy, feel important and belong. Sadly, this facade is a house of cards that eventually collapses under pressure. With the loss of relational skills people will spend increasing money and effort to create their image and keep it looking good.

Church without relational skills

Churches implode in one of three ways when return to joy skills drop out. First, divisions arise due to malfunctions and immaturity. The inability to return to joy means leaders in particular lack the gentle protector skills to manage what they feel, stay relational and recover from upset. Emotions quickly become amplified and problems spiral out of control.

Second, without relational skills people set up rules while others feel controlled by these rules and rigidity. Personalities who lack return to joy skills fail to flex, adapt and recover from upset. Instead of exploring useful, relational, joyful solutions to solve problems, rigid leaders rely on control that drains joy, restricts movement and robs creativity. During times of crisis and transition, those who make and follow the rules best will win but at the expense of having large numbers of people leave the church.

Third, fear propagates under the guise of spiritual guidance, service and ministry. Leaders who are motivated by fear tend to react and make decisions that restrict people and options. An inability to return to joy shows up as a lack of consistency and may even appear as a lack of integrity. In the end, the church will neutralize itself trying to keep everyone happy and comfortable. This church will stay in their comfort zone until they die.

The result of all three scenarios is a lack of transformation in people's lives. Without relational skills the weak and strong do not share life, and the faithful are left wondering if there should be something more to their faith. Ultimately, young people lose faith in the church as a real resource.

Rise of narcissism

Declining social skills practically mandate an increase in narcissism. Not only is the inability to return to joy from shame and to learn from our mistakes increasingly common but, without the relational skills needed to work together for joy, we are each left to look out for ourselves. Some people with tender hearts toward weakness will choose to look out for others and ignore themselves, but this only trades one disaster for another. Narcissists hide their own weakness and exploit the weaknesses they find in others while bathing their operation with self-justification. See *The Pandora Problem* for more.

Increasing number of unresolved conflicts

Churched or unchurched, educated or uneducated, city or country folk will all find the best intentions and strongest convictions are no match for strain and distress when it comes to missing gentle protector skills. As of 2012, newlyweds in the US can toss a coin and match the odds of their marriage lasting eight years. Divorce, church splits and unresolved ruptures between families and groups expose the toll missing skills have on our lives and relationships.

Bitterness, resentment, stubbornness, custody battles, church splits, alienated friends and endless lawsuits follow a trail of unresolved conflicts. Almost all unresolved conflicts represent a lack of the relational skills needed to return to joy. The weak always suffer the most in these situations. Blame, shame, entitlement, and quarreling demonstrate a lack of maturity and the painful absence of return to joy skills. The outcome is tragic. In families especially, children grow up fatherless and motherless as the family unit ruptures from strain. Low-joy sets couples up for marital disaster. Children learn at a young age that they must be bigger than they really are which fosters pseudo maturity. Low-joy cycles continue for generations, but the pain does not end there. Child abuse and domestic violence propagate as the powerful lash out at the weak people closest to them, creating more predators and possums.

Unresolved conflicts are also spreading on a global scale. For the first time in history wealthy predator cultures can purchase weapons of mass destruction that they could not create on their own because their social fabric lacks enough social cohesion and hopefulness to develop sophisticated weapon systems. This has made terrorism and counterterrorism a road to power for many predators. One culture's benevolent predator is another culture's pirate, terrorist and revolutionary. Predator culture with its characteristically low-joy will propagate unless we put protector skills back into children and cultures. Protectors arise from relational skills and tenderness toward weakness.

Increasing BEEPS

Divorce, death, an affair, an unavailable parent, and abandonment create a dull ache that leaves us feeling alone, unwanted, hurt and overwhelmed. Attachment pain originates at the subcortical level of brain functioning, deep inside the emotional control center, the limbic region of our bonding circuits. This area creates and synchronizes our reality so when we hurt from attachment pain, our entire world and reality is filled with pain. Attachment pain is felt intensely and consumes our entire life and relationships. Attachment pain leaves us wanting to go away, disconnect, numb, veg-out, even die. "I cannot live without you!" one could say to describe the feeling. Does this sound like a song or two that plays on the radio?

Attachment pain appears indirectly with strong cravings and powerful urges. We are strongly motivated to avoid painful feelings we have not learned to manage. Painful feelings tell us we are about to "lose it," or even cease to exist, unless we find quick relief. It does not take long for children to discover that candy bars, chocolate, donuts, soda, pornography and sexually acting out provide temporary relief to pain which opens the door for using BEEPS as a way of life. Attachment pain is the dominant force behind food and sexual addictions. We gravitate toward pseudo-joy as a rush to make us feel better as we try to avoid the lonely feelings that seem as though they will swallow us alive. When seeking relief, we are not so much concerned with finding true joy as we are with finding a shut-off valve to stop the pain. True, meaningful, relational joy is ultimately what we need for lasting relief. Along the way we learn a great many unhelpful lessons from attachment pain such as, "Love hurts." "If I get too close I will get burned." and "I'm safe as long as I do not become too attached." These lies lead us to non-relational sources of pleasure and comfort.

Homes, schools and churches as targets for those who lack relational skills

There is a steady stream of attacks in schools and churches, making them the target of numerous mass murders. Home is the most likely location for violence. The level of domestic violence, abuse and murder reveals predatory behavior inside and outside of homes. The actual violence is often triggered by attachment pain. Think of murders and school shootings that started with resentment, bitterness, disconnection, affairs, loss, jealousy and other evidence of attachment pain. Very often the perpetrator felt wronged and weak.

Schools and churches are not usually the cause of violence but they have become the targets, perhaps because they are supposed to be places of hope but actually have little to offer angry, young people who lack social skills. School shootings demonstrate the opposite of gentle protector skills. The number of school shootings, knifings and killings suggest that schools deserve some attention. There is a long history of school shootings around the world with eleven in Canada, twenty in Europe and more elsewhere in the world. School shootings have been going on for over 100 years with many of the tragedies in recent years.

The United States has had well over 150 school shootings not to count knifings, hostage situations and other forms of violence. Unresolved attachment pain and failure to return to joy are behind many of these incidents where the attacker targets a specific person to kill. The cases that involve mass killings generally reveal an attacker who was trying to be powerful, was self-justified and who carefully prepared and even studied predator strategies to make the attack more powerful and effective.

Matthew J. Murray was a gunman in Colorado who targeted both a school and a church in 2007. This 24-year-old is described as someone with poor relational skills. It is hard to find any shooters with good relational skills. Murray's computer was reported to contain considerable amounts of pornography indicating that he was subsisting on pseudo-joy from BEEPS. He attended a Youth With a Mission (YWAM) training school where he was asked to leave. He returned to that same school to start his shooting rampage. Murray was home-schooled by Christian parents and his situation tragically reflects how it is possible to have home, school and church experiences without developing the character of a gentle protector.

We want to be very careful to say that it is our determination to be tender toward weakness and not the lack of relational skill training that determines if we will become a predator or protector. While a few schools like Ambleside International are working to build gentle protector skill training directly into every aspect of the school day, most homes, home schools, schools and churches are not prepared to train children in the relational skills needed to be protectors. People with no religion are increasingly bringing their children to Christian schools hoping they will learn character. Increasingly young people without emotional maturity and social skills are seeking programs like YWAM, religious orders, Christian schools and missions to learn how to be human, have joyful relationships and add structure to their lives. While most of these groups are prepared to teach how to selflessly serve and give away what we have to others, it is a whole different issue to fill the relational maturity void in applicants. The epidemic of youth without relational skills is just beginning as relational skills continue to fade into extinction.

Allowing weakness to restore our return to joy skills

Respect for weakness lets us form relationships with people who need skills not just with the ones who already have them. Recognizing weakness helps us determine what protector skills are in short supply where we live. When people are unable or reluctant to act protectively with anger, sadness, fear, shame, disgust or despair, we now see a weakness in their identities. The same goes when people get stuck on problems and forget relationships or when they amplify the upset over the problems they encounter. We are particularly aware of weakness when people attack, criticize, shame or exploit the weaknesses of others. Here are the storm clouds that bring low-joy. When we see low-joy as the weakness it really is, we can become joy starters and look for others who will join us.

Weakness also becomes our strong point. When we recognize that we are all rather small, weak and vulnerable people who need tender treatment for joy to thrive, we avoid the kinds of excesses that chronically drain joy from our society. Trying to be strong and "do it on our own" drains joy and starts us on the road to being predators. Recognizing our weakness calls for constant contact with Immanuel to restore us to our real selves and stay tender toward each other.

Respect for weakness lets us train others at the rate they can learn. People learn joy and relational skills according to their capacity and ability. When we work people too hard or fast, they stop learning and start avoiding. Those who seek to restore joy must first let others rest and then return to rest each time people become tired.

It is encouraging that we can propagate return to joy skills through sharing our weaknesses. With practice we learn to share our weaknesses and express vulnerabilities to those we trust. What emerges is a secure bond built on trust and transparency. Weaknesses no longer remain hidden or masked. We cherish the weak among us as God's gifts. We rejoice when people return to relationship instead of isolating or pulling away. We start noticing Immanuel's presence in our life and story. We respond to vulnerabilities with care. Observers now find the courage to let down their guard. A community of faith and hope grows into a community of love as people share their pains, sorrows and sufferings.

Joy is central to a Christian life and identity. Joy is the growth hormone for the development of relational skills. As one third of the world's population, if we Christians were to start joy where we live, we would make a difference in our homes, schools and churches. Could we invite the other two thirds of the world to join in joy?

Correcting narcissism and anger

We cannot overemphasize the deadly nature of narcissism. It is even more important to invite narcissists and their communities to a new kind of life. Narcissism is a way of looking strong and justifying ourselves instead of learning from healthy shame. Narcissism is the biggest contributor to low-joy and the loss of community. Gentle protectors must protect the community against narcissism by demonstrating what true maturity and glad-to-be together life looks and feels like. We not only talk about joy, we create belonging for the weak. Protectors see people as more than their malfunctions. Gentle protector skills such as Godsight convey, "We are more than the sum of our mistakes." Joyful character creates belonging and is developed by strong, joyful people who cultivate and spread joy among the weak. This means narcissists and predators will be shown that their attacks on the weak are not to be justified. Narcissism is not valued in the redemptive community of love. We help one another grow into the life God has called each one of us to live.

As narcissists, we must learn return to joy skills, and people who have an identity anchored in anger must learn how to return to joy. While angry people are accustomed to using intimidation to get their way, protectors remember there is more going on beneath the surface. Protectors guide the angry ones to acknowledge they are weak and extend the invitation to stop pretending they are strong. There is freedom in a humble acknowledgement of weakness.

Returning to joy at home

Parents are in the best possible position to grow gentle protector skills with their children. Parents with relational skills can proactively "download" gentle protector skills, ensuring their children learn and use all nineteen skills. Similar to practicing a musical instrument, relational skills take time to develop. Parents who use their skills show children and guests "this is how we do it" during moments of distress, fatigue, excitement and conflict. Children learn best by mom and dad's example.

Parents who discover missing skills can learn new skills from other parents then practice their new skills at home. Gentle protector training spreads to the local community as parents invite friends and families over in order to interact, exchange joy and recover when things go wrong. Home becomes a transformation zone through a healthy blend of the strong who already have the skills with the weak who lack the skills. As the two groups interact, protector skills are trained "live" under a variety of conditions.

Growing and practicing protector skills can be as simple as an evening meal and time of fellowship. There is good reason for eating and interacting together being one of the most mentioned activities in all of Scripture. Food should lead to bonding. Jesus frequently used stories when enjoying a meal with others. Every Friday evening John and his wife Amy host a pizza night where John's children invite two or three friends over for interaction, pizza and games. This is a high-energy time filled with fun, laughter and joy. John and Amy started this family tradition that now extends into their community. They purposefully share stories about the workweek and school. The group practices relational skills and takes some time to pray for one another. The joy levels stay high as stories include emotions that give listeners practice at returning to joy. Most of the time the interaction is so much fun that the group forgets they are learning new gentle protector skills and strengthening existing skills. John and Amy are creating a legacy of joy for their children and community.

Returning to joy at school

Shelia's desire to propagate joy and grow protectors led her to design a senior project where her older students identify the roles of possums, predators, and protectors as they relate to bullying in school. Shelia taught the seniors how to grow their protector skills while recognizing their own predator and possum-like responses. The 36 students in each of Shelia's classes divided into six teams of six students. The goal of the project was for the seniors to activate their protector identities and teach the ninth and tenth grade classes about the harmful effects of school bullying, while also teaching them about ways to behave tenderly toward the weak. Each team took their presentation "on the road" to ninth and tenth grade classrooms for a three-day bullying education seminar. This meant that each team of six seniors conducted the seminar in three different classrooms on three separate days for a total outreach to nine classrooms. Shelia teaches three senior classes, and her goal was for students to reach out to 54 classrooms of underclassmen to spread the message about bullying and its effects.

This project afforded the seniors the opportunity to "start something that matters" on campus before they graduated in May. The seniors were excited about how they could use their stories about bullying to teach the underclassmen to make their school a more joyful place. The project was more than a campaign against bullying because it included teaching about predators, possums, and protectors and ways to return to joy and stay relational. Since Shelia had just added these components to the curriculum, students were learning key concepts about relational functioning that they had not encountered before. Each team was also required to engage the students they taught in at least one meaningful appreciation exercise. The hope was that the outcome would propagate joy while informing students of practical ways they could begin to regulate their own emotions, whether it was anger, sadness, or hopeless despair.

This ten-week instructional process was a huge undertaking that required courage on the part of Shelia and her seniors. It required students to read multiple research articles, view multiple informational videos, identify predator, possum, and protector behaviors, and practice ways to stay relationally connected through returning to joy. Each team created 1) a visual presentation to inform their younger classmates, 2) a video to engage and challenge them to see relationships as bigger than problems, and 3) a minimum of one appreciation exercise to help students begin to practice the relational brain skills needed to combat the epidemic of bullying on the school campus. Having seniors actively teach the underclassmen how to return to joy by staying relational and expressing tenderness toward the weak began the process of propagating joy throughout the school. And, if it were up to Shelia, this would become the new norm!

Returning to joy at church

Churches have many means of bringing the weak and strong together. In the deserts of northern Mexico, an orphanage brings abused children together with dedicated caregivers. Both young adults and older couples live together with the orphans in long-term, stable homes. This community deliberately keeps the weak and strong together whether within the orphanage, church or community. In every context they show tenderness toward the weak. Training is an ongoing part of the community with deliberate joy, shalom and gentle protector brain skill practice. While many of the staff have discovered weaknesses and traumas in their own lives during this process, tenderness is not reserved for the orphans alone so everyone is helped to heal and transform. This community transforms together. The orphanage includes a school where learning shalom and seeking the Immanuel presence of God when things do not go smoothly is a frequent practice.

A church in Canada created a restaurant to provide work, housing, community and training for young women who found themselves pregnant. The weak and the strong share life with compassion for weakness and transformed lives for both.

In Southern California, a Los Angeles area church group had the idea of making their class into a transformation zone for joy. "The response was amazing! People lingered after class chatting around the tables about what they learned and their lives until we left at ten. It was the most excited response I have ever experienced," the leader said. "The best part was seeing people grasp their need for the transformation zone," she concluded. Schoolteachers in the group immediately applied the concepts to their classes and began figuring out together how to help low-joy children. One veteran teacher, who was ready to quit teaching due to behavior problems in the classroom, was so changed that in a few weeks he reported liking his job. Group members shared that they no longer pounced on the weakness of their children, spouses and family members. "Many were dealing with an awakening of strength and weakness in their lives. It's upside down of what we have all learned," the leader reported. This is life in the transformation zone. The weak and strong interact with tenderness toward weakness and guidance from Immanuel. Transformation will continue and joy will spread while they stay in the "t-zone."

In North Carolina, Ed's church asked him to develop an entirely new small group ministry, and allowed him to design the "Life Group" program and train it's leaders. The church leadership team challenged him to develop a program that relied entirely on Scripture instead of brain science and an exclusive focus on joy.

In response, Ed developed and implemented a life group and leadership training program that is entirely compatible with most churches and ministries. These new groups focus on sharing grace together to grow stronger, deeper, and lasting relationships with God and each other. The groups include all of the essential T-Zone ingredients. The groups have been running now for five years and focus on sharing grace during each meeting. These groups even survived the COVID-19 challenges. Through running these groups Ed developed three books that can guide any group beginning with *Becoming A Face of Grace*. Find out more in Appendix D.

Church schools provide another option for adding the nineteen gentle protector skills and helping children learn love, joy and the Immanuel life-style. What if every student learned return to joy skills for the big six emotions before they finished third grade? Sunday School offers an ideal window for groups to learn and practice gentle protector skills. Summer Bible camps, women's studies, young mothers clubs and many church activities could become places for transformation.

How are we doing?
*   What changes have we observed in the last one hundred years in our family, school, church and culture?
*   Where do we think these changes are taking us?

What signs do we have in our family, school and church that gentle protector skills have moved toward extinction? What is our part in recovery?

Correcting what we might have heard about salvation
The general tendency for Christians is to think of salvation in terms of the after-life. In the after-life, salvation becomes admission to heaven. For others the focus falls on being saved from hell and the punishment that all sinners deserve. Many extend this thinking to try and follow God's rules on earth so we are not punished later. What we would like to discuss briefly is not the means of salvation through Christ or the method of salvation but the purpose of salvation. Salvation is about eternal life. Eternal life does not mean life after we die. Eternal life means "life all our life." Salvation is for all our life, both now and later. Salvation is about leaving our pseudo-self immediately in favor of our true self. Salvation means discovering how to be alive and stay a source of joy to God and all those who love being alive, beginning immediately. While we are beset with weaknesses now, it is not our weakness that prevents us from experiencing our salvation, it is our attempts to be strong that keep us from new life. Salvation is our ongoing acceptance of God's tender response to our weakness made possible by God's great strength and gentle protection. On our part, we do not hide or deny our deformities, short falls and non-relational moments with God, but in admitting them, seek to return to joy and learn from the God who is with us about how to live the same way with those who are non-relational or weaker than we are. Salvation is joy that starts

now and here. The good news we spread is that this life of joy is open to all who would be like Jesus, whose life was called "great joy to all people." Jim has written more about salvation in *Renovated*.

Restoring our Christian capacity to change lives

Historically, Christians have helped the weak in many ways by advocating for children and starting many of the world's schools and hospitals. We now need schools and hospitals for the soul. The main point of this chapter is to highlight the recent and rapid loss of ability to relate as human beings. The media we watch, the way we can travel and the loss of multigenerational community and dramatic reduction of engaged interaction is bringing gentle relational skills near extinction by greatly reducing the direct interactions between the young and old in daily life. Where Christians once helped people learn to read and heal, we now must train the world in joyful relationship skills. If we fail to do so, we face a steep rise in predator levels across the world, in all homes, schools and churches. We are watching this happen.

We cannot afford to build our comfort zones. We try to hide our lack of character by staying with people we like and asking God to help make us stronger. For our lives and character to change, it is necessary, but not enough, to have the strong and weak together. Spiritual and emotional maturity only develop when there are frequent and extended joyful interactions. Being glad to be together during weakness happens when we see each other through the "eyes of heaven."

The unchanged character in most Christians starts from a lack of joy to be with God or joy to be with people. Let us be first to enter the transformation zone.

- Let us express our joy.
- Let us stay in joyful contact with the weak. Joy strengthens weakness.
- Let us find Immanuel every time our joy or shalom gets lost and return to joy.
- Let us sustain joy at home, school and church.

While our best network for spreading gentle protector skills is definitely through churches, the most strategic target is schools. Christian teachers, parents and students are everywhere, and the best way to take joy where it is needed is to bring joy to all classrooms. There are secular attempts to change the culture of schools by training relational and emotional maturity skills. These programs are showing tremendous impact, but these programs will continue to be the exception in schools. The impact will be greater if teachers, parents and students bring joy with them and work to spread the joy in every class they attend. Joy is always personal so let us give joy to every student, parent, teacher or administrator we meet. Learn something about joy so we can help others catch the dream. After all, joy is the most powerful of all human motivations and everyone needs some.

Let us find some low-joy place and get involved bringing joy. We will check with Immanuel every time we lose our joy or shalom. We will invite people with relational skills to join us. Our character will change as we bring our weakness to Immanuel instead of trying to be strong. Trying to be strong will kill our joy. Avoiding our weakness will kill our joy. God put us right where we are because that is the best place God could imagine for us to start some joy. Joy starts here.

Joy Actions

Home: Think of the people in your life who are in the transformation zone who would be inspired to start joy. Share this book with them and start some joy.

School: Find a teacher, administrator, parent or student and share the vision of this book. Start some joy.

Church: Give this book to the children's pastor or youth leader who would be inspired to start some joy in your church. Start some joy.

Home, School and Church Assessment

You might be wondering where to start. Because home, school and church are the three most common places for our identities to be formed and transformed, we have created way to compare their readiness for transformation. To use this tool you must consider what home, school and church you will evaluate. We designed this tool to evaluate the home where you now live, the school you, your children or grandchildren attend (or you work) and your current church. The comparison of scores may help you decide where to seek transformation first.

We are aware that many people live alone, are not involved with any schools and have no active church life. You can therefore pick a category like "school" and substitute "work" answers. "Friends" can replace "home" and any social network can fill in for "church." Simply answer all the questions using the same target group.

A second way to use the home, school and church assessment is to evaluate how your life developed. In this historical use, you can rate your childhood home, school and early church experiences. Once you decide your three target groups, complete the questions on the following page.

Home, School and Church Assessment

1. We often speak about how this place has changed our lives for the better. (0 = *not at all* to 10 = *constantly*)
Home 0 1 2 3 4 5 6 7 8 9 10 School 0 1 2 3 4 5 6 7 8 9 10 Church 0 1 2 3 4 5 6 7 8 9 10

2. It is easy to find things to appreciate here each day.
(0 = *not at all* to 10 = *consistent appreciation*)
Home 0 1 2 3 4 5 6 7 8 9 10 School 0 1 2 3 4 5 6 7 8 9 10 Church 0 1 2 3 4 5 6 7 8 9 10

3. I expect people will say kind things about my weaknesses here.
(0 = *not at all* to 10 = *everyone is always kind*)
Home 0 1 2 3 4 5 6 7 8 9 10 School 0 1 2 3 4 5 6 7 8 9 10 Church 0 1 2 3 4 5 6 7 8 9 10

4. We regularly become more joyful when we come here.
(0 = *not at all* to 10 = *everyone every time*)
Home 0 1 2 3 4 5 6 7 8 9 10 School 0 1 2 3 4 5 6 7 8 9 10 Church 0 1 2 3 4 5 6 7 8 9 10

5. When things are going wrong here I still feel peaceful.
(0 = *not at all* to 10 = *consistent peace*)
Home 0 1 2 3 4 5 6 7 8 9 10 School 0 1 2 3 4 5 6 7 8 9 10 Church 0 1 2 3 4 5 6 7 8 9 10

6. When I see people who are hurting I want to bring them here.
(0 = *not at all* to 10 = *very strongly*)
Home 0 1 2 3 4 5 6 7 8 9 10 School 0 1 2 3 4 5 6 7 8 9 10 Church 0 1 2 3 4 5 6 7 8 9 10

7. Here I can interact with people who have more life experience than I have. (0 = *not at all* to 10 = *easily*)
Home 0 1 2 3 4 5 6 7 8 9 10 School 0 1 2 3 4 5 6 7 8 9 10 Church 0 1 2 3 4 5 6 7 8 9 10

8. What I am expected to do here has value.
(0 = *my energy gets wasted* to 10 = *what I do is really worthwhile*)
Home 0 1 2 3 4 5 6 7 8 9 10 School 0 1 2 3 4 5 6 7 8 9 10 Church 0 1 2 3 4 5 6 7 8 9 10

9. What we do here has a positive effect on the people around us.
(0 = *not at all* to 10 = *daily*)
Home 0 1 2 3 4 5 6 7 8 9 10 School 0 1 2 3 4 5 6 7 8 9 10 Church 0 1 2 3 4 5 6 7 8 9 10

10. I feel understood here. (0 = *not at all* to 10 = *by everyone*)
Home 0 1 2 3 4 5 6 7 8 9 10 School 0 1 2 3 4 5 6 7 8 9 10 Church 0 1 2 3 4 5 6 7 8 9 10

Home total _____ School total _____ Church total _____

Home	0	10	20	30	40	50	60	70	80	90	100
School	0	10	20	30	40	50	60	70	80	90	100
Church	0	10	20	30	40	50	60	70	80	90	100

Disruption of Protector Skill Propagation Assessment

1. The way I have been treated makes it hard to trust people.

    I am very trusting 0 1 2 3 4 5 6 7 8 9 10 *I trust no one*

2. People with lots of problems stay to themselves in my church.

    They mix well 0 1 2 3 4 5 6 7 8 9 10 *They stay isolated*

3. How many people taught me better ways to get along with others?

    0 1 2 3 4 5 6 7 8 9 10+ *People*

4. Most days I spend___ hours watching shows and movies.

    0 1 2 3 4 5 6 7 8 9 10+ *Hours*

5. Asking others for help is a sign of weakness.

    Not at all 0 1 2 3 4 5 6 7 8 9 10 *Strongly agree*

6. People ridicule or reject me if I ask for help.

    Not at all 0 1 2 3 4 5 6 7 8 9 10 *Most of the time*

7. In the last day I have spent time in person with __ people outside of work.

    0 1 2 3 4 5 6 7 8 9 10+ *People*

8. Someone at home spends __ hours a day on computer-based devices.

    0 1 2 3 4 5 6 7 8 9 10+ *Hours*

9. How much has alcoholism, addiction, mental illness and disease disrupted the last 3 generations of my family?

    Not at all 0 1 2 3 4 5 6 7 8 9 10 *Severely*

10. War, crime and abuse has disrupted the last 3 generations of my family.

    Not at all 0 1 2 3 4 5 6 7 8 9 10 *Severely*

Total your scores here. _____
Mark the matching spot on the scale.

0 10 20 30 40 50 60 70 80 90 100

Saving Joy From Extinction Bible Study

Think back on something you appreciate and spend two minutes enjoying appreciation. Next, ask God to make this study interesting for you. Now read the following passage from the epistles.

Scripture Ephesians 4:11-5:1 Read then review the passage for each question.

Chapter Ten Question: What changes in identity and character will God's joy-bonded children (verse 5:1) learn and introduce into their human relationships?

Weakness, Joy and Shalom Questions:
1. Who are weak or strong in this passage?
2. What kind of interaction does God desire between weak and strong?
3. What do we learn about joy and shalom (everything works together) from this passage?

Immanuel Questions:
1. What effects does perceiving "God is with us" have in this passage?
2. Group study activity: God is always present and eager to help us see more clearly. In what ways do we perceive or guess that God is helping us understand this passage right now in the group discussion?

   Note: Thinking about God's active presence may seem strange at first because people generally discuss the past more than they observe the present. Keep your answers short. Feel free to guess.

Personal Story Question: Where in this passage did you sense low-joy in your life and want God to visit your weakness?

Whole Bible Question: Across the Bible, what stories tell of someone who learned a better way to treat others from God or God's people?

Wrap-Up Minute: What do you now know that you didn't know before this week's study?

Our Life Model Joy Skills Exercises

Individual: Return to Joy from Shame

1. What thoughts and behaviors do you notice in yourself when you feel criticized or judged? How does this feel in your body? (For example, "My chest tightens or my stomach aches.")
2. Who has permission to correct you? Who does not? Why?
3. What fears or resistance do you notice when others try to give you feedback and correction?
4. What aspects of your presence, personality and character do not bring other people joy? What is the best evidence to support your conclusions from family, school and church?
5. What reasons are given when other people are not glad to be with you? How well can you place yourself in the shoes of other people when they are upset with you? In other words, can you see their perspective (mindsight skill) when they are upset with you? Why or why not?
6. How long do you stay stuck when you encounter shame messages?
7. Even if the criticism does not sound accurate, what do you need when you feel ashamed? What do you need from people and from God?
8. Take a moment to remember an appreciation (or Immanuel) moment that brings you joy. Once you feel shalom pray and ask how Immanuel sees you. Notice what thoughts come to mind.
9. Find three people in your life who appear to handle shame in a way you appreciate. Ask them to tell you a time they felt like someone was not glad to be with them and how they responded.

Group: The Predator, Possum and Protector in Me

1. As each person shares their answers to the questions below, practice seeing them through Immanuel's eyes. Do not offer feedback.
   A. What predatory traits do you see in yourself that you would like to change? What role does fear play?
   B. What possum traits do you see in yourself that you would like to change? What role does fear play?
   C. In what ways are you a protector to your family, church, school and community? Give examples. What role does joy play? How can you strengthen your protector skills?
2. After each person finishes his or her answers to the questions above pray for the person and the specific needs that were expressed. Once the group completes the above steps, discuss how the group can grow joy to be better protectors.

References

Brown, A., Coursey, C. (2018). *Relational Skills In The Bible*. Carmel, IN:Deeper Walk International.

Coursey, C. (2021). *The Joy Switch*. Chicago, IL: Northfield Publishing.

Coursey, C., Warner, M. (2018). *The 4 Habits of Joy-Filled Marriages*. Chicago, IL: Northfield Publishing.

Coursey, C., Warner, M. (2021). *The 4 Habits of Raising Joy-Filled Kids*. Chicago, IL: Northfield Publishing.

Coursey, C. (2016). *Transforming Fellowship: 19 Brain Skills That Build Joyful Community*. Holland, MI: Coursey Creations, LLC.

deMause, L. (1999). *Childhood and cultural evolution*. The Journal of Psychohistory, 26(3).

Friesen, J. G., Wilder, E. J., Bierling, A. M., Koepcke, R., & Poole, M. (2004). *Living from the heart Jesus gave you*. Pasadena, CA: Shepherd's House.

Khouri, Ed. (2021). *Becoming a Face of Grace*. Illumify Media Global.

Khouri, Ed, (2021). *The Weight of Leadership: How Codependency and Misplaced Mercy Undermine Life and Ministry*. Illumify Media Global

Khouri, Ed. (2021) *Beyond Becoming: A Handbook for Small Groups*. Illumify Media Global.

Leaf, C. (2007). *Who switched off my brain?* Rivonia, South Africa: Switch On Your Brain.

Lehman, K. (2011). *Outsmarting Yourself*. Libertyville, IL: This Joy Books.

Lord, D. (2012). *Choosing joy*. Huntington, IN: Our Sunday Division.

Schore, A. N. (1994). *Affect regulation and the origin of the self*. Hillsdale, NY: Lawrence Erlbaum Associates.

Thomas, A. (2011). *Choosing joy*. New York, NY: Howard Books.

Warren, K. (2012). *Choose joy*. Grand Rapids, MI: Revell.

Warner, M., Wilder E. J., (2018), *The Solution of Choice*, Carmel, IN: Deeper Walk.

Warner, M., Wilder E. J., (2016), *Rare Leadership*. Chicago: IL, Moody.

Wilder, E. J. (2018), *The Pandora Problem*. Carmel, IN: Deeper Walk.

Wilder, E. J. (2020), *Renovated*, Colorado Springs CO: NavPress.

Wilder, E. J., Hendricks, M. (2020) *The Other Half of Church*, Chicago IL: Moody.

Wilder, E. J., Kang, A., Loppnow, S., Loppnow J. (2020), *Joyful Journey*, Los Angeles: CA, Presence and Practice.

Wilder, E. J., Coursey, C. (2010) *Share Immanuel*, Pasadena, CA: Shepherd's House.

Appendix A
Glossary

Attachment: Attachment is the foundational connectedness and emotional bond that develops between people. Attachment starts with a mother and child relationship and characterizes all lasting ties between people.

Attachment styles: There are two attachment styles, secure and insecure. A secure attachment is characterized by trust and autonomy. The mother's response time to her child is quick, predictable, and sensitive. Insecure attachment styles can be differentiated into three separate patterns of dysfunction that typically originate in the first attachment between a child and its primary caretaker (typically the mother), where the caretaker was unable to provide the basis of a secure attachment. The insecure styles are distracted, dismissive and disorganized. This insecurity in early attachment relationships develops, grows, and eventually interferes with a person's ability to regulate emotionally and adjust both socially and psychologically.

The distracted attachment pattern is the result of the inconsistent availability of the mother to care for the child. This inconsistency results in the child being anxious about and preoccupied with the times when the mother is actually available. The child keeps a watchful eye searching for times when mom will show up and take care of him/her. Each time the mother does respond, the child's hope is renewed. However, since the mother's response is inconsistent, the child's hopes are dashed more often than not. This intermittent response pattern keeps the child in a distracted state. In adults, this pattern is often referred to as a preoccupied attachment style.

The dismissive attachment pattern is the result of the complete disengagement of the mother. The mother is distant and consistently unavailable to the child. This unavailability results in the child cutting off from the mother and reciprocating the emotional distance. The child believes that his/her needs will never be met, which results in a dismissive pattern that serves as the ultimate defensive mechanism to protect oneself from further attachment pain. In children, this pattern is often referred to as avoidant attachment style.

The disorganized attachment pattern is the result of the mother's extreme response to the child's needs. The mother is erratic and frightening to the child. The child's reaction is often characterized by anger, depression, and passivity.

Attachment pain: Attachment pain is the result of separation from or the loss of someone to whom we are attached. Divorce, death, separation and abandonment are some sources of attachment pain. Lonely, homesick, rejected and heartbroken are forms of attachment pain. Attachment pain can also be the result of non-secure attachment. When experienced early in life, prior to twelve years of age, attachment pain can cause the brain to be rewired in ways that keep us from conscious awareness of attachment pain. While the pain continues to have a powerful effect on our lives, we may truthfully be unaware of its existence. Attachment pain is the main force behind BEEPS attachments and intensifies the effects of all unpleasant emotions and experiences.

BEEPS: Behaviors, Events, Experiences, People and Substances (BEEPS) that we use to help ease attachment pain, handle negative emotions, increase pleasure or decrease pain in the place of genuine relationships, joy and shalom.

Benevolent predator: This dominant predator is the "leader of the pack" who, it is hoped, will be a predator to outsiders, threats or potential prey but protective to the group (tribe, pack, gang, country, troops or corporation). However, when insiders become powerful they often are seen as threats and attacked or eliminated. Particularly attractive or vulnerable insiders are often preyed upon by these leaders. The vast majority of political, financial, military, sporting, union, corporate, social and religious leaders fit the benevolent predator profile. "Revolutionaries and liberators" frequently start as benevolent predators only to lose most of their benevolence once there is no external threat. Internal "threats" become the target and their own people become the prey while the rhetoric blames some external enemy.

Bonds: Also known as attachments, are the relational "glue" that holds identities and relationships together. There are two emotions upon which bonds form — fear and joy. There are two significantly different brain structures that help us maintain and use bonds — a two-way bond structure that is rapid and partially unconscious, and a three-way bond that is slower and mostly conscious. Bonds are very specific attachments that do not allow substitutions to other people and become loaded with significance and meaning.

Three-way bonds: This function of the prefrontal cortex allows us to be aware of what is going on in our mind plus the minds of two external people. By means of this three-way bond, I can watch a father and daughter play and be aware of what they are each feeling and, to some extent, thinking and intending to do. While there are many functions to a three-way bond, one of the principle ones for this book is the ability to participate in the joy shared by other people. Three-way bonds are the basis for the formation of joyful groups, spiritual families and stable identities.

Two-way bonds: A joy-based linkage that is possible only between us and one other person at a time that produces synchronized mental states that progress more rapidly than conscious thought. These bonds have profound effects on our sense of identity and reality and are used to transfer the gentle protector skills and form intimate emotional attachments. These bonds are specific to those two people alone and endure for life.

Fear bonds: A leading sign of abnormal development is relating to life and others out of fear. Fear is primarily the motivation to keep bad things from happening i.e., we study so we won't get a bad grade, we go home so Mom won't get mad, we dress so we won't be embarrassed, we don't eat things so we won't gain weight, we exercise so we don't get fat, we hurry to work so we don't get fired and we hide what we bought so dad won't yell. These are all fear bonds and are quite common but all signs of a defective development of our identities, motivation and brains.

Joy bonds: This desirable form of human motivation and attachment results from two people who are glad to be together. Not all joy bonds are beneficial as in the desire to be together between two people who are each married to someone else. However, joy is the basis for all strong bonds and stable relationships. Being together is always of great value so joy bonds allow us to share both sorrows and joys.

Capacity: The neurological limit for being able to act like our relational self is a physical limitation on our ability to handle emotions and stress. Capacity is developed by training in joy, shalom and returning to joy that is practiced with other people in a relational way. Exceeding our capacity results in a loss of synchronization in the brain so that our experience is no longer processed correctly leading to the possibility of trauma and blocking the processing of traumatic memories. Our capacity can be increased by alternating strong joy and shalom experiences in our relationships.

Cloud: The "cloud" that blocks the growth of joy is a metaphor based on "cloud computing" and stands for the myriad of one-way messages, attention-captivating activities through machines, unnaturally intense emotions, flavors, sounds and sensations that now occupy most of the time that human interaction occupied a century ago. The cloud is replacing face-to-face interactions that are needed neurologically to grow and propagate joy between people in neighborhoods, homes, schools and churches.

Comforting: Comforting is a function of a secure bond that has been internalized by the three-way bond structure in the prefrontal cortex. Comforting is done after validation or it does not work well. Validation agrees with the person about just how big the emotion feels. Comforting shows the person how much of life is still left outside the emotional experience. Without validation first, attempts at comfort come across as minimizing.

Community: The group of people with which we share a group identity.

Davidic Dance: Refers to a unique style of group dancing often seen in Messianic Christian congregations that is an effective way for growing joy levels, building a group identity, training the brain, exercising and more. This activity is based on the reference to King David who danced before the Lord with the ark of the covenant in 2 Samuel 6:14. Styles and preferences differ depending on the capabilities and goals of a group.

Downstream: Our way of describing if we have people who receive life from us. We are each downstream from others and need people downstream from us as well.

Gentle protector skills: The nineteen relational brain skills trained by the Life Model Exercises restore the gentle protector skill set that is eroded and damaged by A and B trauma. When the gentle protector skills are damaged or missing, predator patterns are left behind to dominate our relationships.

Grace: The essential quality of being special without which all people shrivel and fail to thrive. In Greek the word for grace is the third declension of the word for joy. All true joy springs from the sense of being special to someone and grace provides a quality of being special no one can give to themselves.

Hopeful daughters: This major indicator of whether a human culture will progress or regress was introduced in 1999 by Lloyd deMause in Childhood and Cultural Evolution, The Journal of Psychohistory, Vol. 26,

Number 3, Winter 1999. Under The "Hopeful Daughter" on page 651 deMause states, "those [cultural traits] that affect the daughter's psyche represent the main narrow bottleneck through which all other cultural traits must pass," which he then supports with historical examples.

Identity: A complex and often confusing set of attachments and characteristics that define who we are. Identity is particularly difficult for humans because it is slowly established over time and always subject to changes from normal growth (now I am a mother), achievements (I am a driver) and accidents (I am a widower). Humans have aspects of themselves that are almost unchangeable (I am a girl), aspects that are currently being changed, aspects that are yet to be achieved (I am a great-grandfather) and aspects that are simply incorrect (I am worthless). By our adult years, the protection of our identity becomes more important than life itself. Let us consider some additional aspects of identity:

Group identity: While not well recognized in the Western world where independence is highly valued, we become part of a people as infants who are learning to relate and speak. During our young adult years, we form a peer group identity that is further identified with our styles, values and lifestyle. During young adult life, the brain is rewired so that the survival of our group becomes more important than our individual survival. We are also wired to think and feel many things in common with our group identity without being conscious of where this influence arises.

Joyful identity: While "joyful" is not an identity per se, identities will be motivated largely by either joy or fear. Most people's actions are predicted more accurately by what they fear than by what they say is important. Fear produces a low-joy environment. A joyful identity is one that is powered by joy and a relational style of interacting with other people. A joyful identity will retain resilience, creativity, productivity and endurance more effectively than a fearful identity.

Individual identity: We live with a mixture of true, untrue and unknown aspects of who we really are. What we know about ourselves becomes our individual identity. All people have aspects of themselves that they do not like, and most of those are areas they consider to be weaknesses. The attitude they and their community have towards weaknesses will largely determine how much shalom and joy they will experience. God alone fully knows our identity but God also uses Kingdom people to help establish our true selves.

"Superman" identity: The "uber" man or superman identity has been popular with people since Cain killed Abel. This false identity is particularly important to this book because the superman is the king of predators and avoids weakness of all kinds if possible. The superman does not suffer well and seeks an existence where pain is avoided and generally falls to others who are weaker. Spiritual versions of the superman feature a preoccupation with power and the accumulation of power talk cloaked in language about the "Power of God," prayers for "more power" and descriptions of every spiritual event as "that was powerful." The spiritual superman or woman, for all their spiritual talk and power represent the opposite of the Kingdom of God. "Many will say to Me in that day, 'Lord Lord, have we not prophesied in Your name, cast out demons in Your name, and done many wonders in Your name? Matthew 7:22-23 (NKJV).

Interactive presence of God: Interactive moments and memories with God involve those times when we are aware of both God and ourselves. Contrast this with many religious experiences where people are aware of what they consider God and are not aware of themselves. Interactive moments with God involve unexpected thoughts, pictures, ideas, words and awareness that change us. During interactive moments, we are not trying to imagine what God would say, do or be like. When carried to completion, genuine interaction results in a relational sense of understanding, shalom and love from God. A moment of interactive presence is not to be confused with knowing God is there, believing in God, loving God, study of scripture or prayer, although these may be part of the moment.

Immanuel approach: This term (also called the Immanuel process) was created by Charlotte and Karl Lehman, M.D. to describe a counseling prayer method designed to resolve many forms of emotional distress linked to incompletely processed experiences. Key to the Immanuel process are the beliefs that 1) God is always with us, 2) God actively interacts with people about their lives, 3) connecting with God should come before focusing on an upsetting experience and 4) that full processing of an experience requires both the upset and the relationship with God to be active in the mind at the same time. More can be discovered in the many DVDs and websites by the Lehmans, kclehman. com, immanuelapproach.com and outsmartingyourself.org. The book *Outsmarting Yourself* by Dr. Lehman is an excellent resource on the Immanuel process approach.

Immanuel experience: The expansion of the Immanuel Approach outside of the therapeutic experience was carried on spontaneously by a variety of people who first went through the Immanuel approach in counseling. The Immanuel experience of being aware of God's interactive presence proved to be helpful in building joy, keeping shalom during the day, providing guidance, improving relationships as well as dealing with upsets. While first described in retrospect by Dr. Karl Lehman, the Immanuel experience was developed into a self-propagating format by Dr. Jim Wilder who added a story telling conclusion to the experience. Telling the Immanuel story improves our ability to incorporate the changes we experience and propagate the Immanuel lifestyle to others.

Immanuel lifestyle: This term was introduced by Chris Coursey as the Christian lifestyle that seeks to be continuously formed by an ongoing awareness of God's presence.

Iniquity: A deformity created by forming, growing or developing incorrectly. While there are physical deformities, the chief deformities are those of identity, leading to low joy for the person and those around him or her.

Islands of comfort: A common practice when strong people gather together to create a comfortable environment where they can rest, prosper and protect their interests. These islands of comfort help hide any weaknesses and keep threats away, but they also freeze the formation of Christian character, encourage growth of a pseudo-self and slowly replace joy with pseudo-joy.

Joy: Joy is the twinkle in someone's eyes, the smile from deep inside, the gladness that makes lovers run toward each other, the smile of a baby, the feeling of sheer delight that grows stronger as people who love each other lock eyes, what God feels when He makes His face shine over us and the leap in our hearts when we hear the voice of someone we have been missing for a long time. Joy is a relational experience that is amplified by right-hemisphere-to-right-hemisphere communication that is largely nonverbal except for voice tone. Joy is the life-giving feeling of mutual care.

Joy starter: We all share a deep desire to start joy around us by our very presence. The effects of trauma often make us run from our dream, but now we can start again. Everyone is a joy starter and with some training we can even keep joy going when the conditions are unfavorable. So start joy today!

Low joy environment: Here is the place where people remember you (if at all) by what you have done wrong, what you cannot do and by your weaknesses. There are many predatory interactions in a low joy environment. Low joy environments are places where the gentle protector brain skills are nearing extinction and the Immanuel presence of God is rarely noticed.

Low joy capacity: Our neurological capacity to regulate ourselves and behave as gentle protectors develops through practicing joy and therefore we call it our "joy capacity." This capacity to withstand life is both internal and external, based on the neurological capacity we have acquired and the joy in our relational network. We have joy in both our individual and group identities, but when our attachments are weak and our life has been anxious, our capacity will be low and we will be easily traumatized or reduced to the fear and predator/prey responses associated with low-joy.

Life Model: An idealized map for human development from conception to death developed at Shepherd's House Inc. in the 1990s (now Life Model Works) and the basis for many books and training programs. The Life Model is designed to be cross-cultural and based on scripture and the best science, but without requiring a Western education to understand and use the model. The model was developed to explain how our identities as groups and individuals are restored.

  Life Model Exercises: Real change in identity and maturity do not follow new information, but come from practicing relational skills with people who have them. We have spent decades developing exercises to improve the transferring and strengthening of skills.

   Skill acquisition exercises: Specific conditions are needed for learning a totally new skill. If you have never ice skated you cannot simply practice a triple lux. Likewise if you have never learned to match heart rate with someone and slow their heart down, you cannot just decide to do it. We need special learning exercises WITH someone who has the skill.

   Skill strengthening exercises: Once we have learned a skill, like how to hold, strum and make chords on a guitar, we can practice that skill and get better. Once we learn to swim we can get faster. We can often strengthen our skills with little teaching by practicing with our fellow learners or even alone. Repetitive exercises help us strengthen skills.

Idealized Model: The Life Model uses a form of model-building based on the ideal rather than statistical averages of how things already are. Although we built the Life Model from the ideals of the Bible and neuroscience, you don't need to have studied either one to use the model.

Life Model Resources: Descriptions of the resources developed under the Life Model are found on the lifemodelworks.org site contains links to many other organizations who are also using and developing Life Model resources.

Maturity: We use this word in two ways. The first meaning is as a map for growing a full identity. We are mature when we have all the pieces well developed. The second meaning measures our current development and says how we are doing for our stage of development. A mature apple blossom is mature for its stage but is clearly not a ripe apple. We can be very mature in one aspect of our identity and undeveloped in another.

Emotional maturity: How mature we are is always revealed during strong emotions, feelings or pain when our ability to maintain loving relationships is put to the test. Due to ignorance about how our brain actually works, many cultures have developed a view of maturity based on being strong or weak at withstanding feelings or pain. Unfortunately, this favors the development of predators. Emotional maturity is actually the ability to stay gentle and protective of weakness under increasing levels of emotional intensity, desire, distress and pain and still act like one's true self.

Spiritual maturity: Spiritual maturity is the ability to do everything required for emotional maturity and remain a gentle protector for people while also maintaining a clear relational connection with God. Spiritual maturity allows us to see ourselves and others as God sees us. This new identity expresses the full character of Christ in ways that no human maturity alone would expect, such as a true love for our enemies. Many people develop a false spiritual maturity by becoming rigid in their beliefs while unpleasant in their relationships.

Stages of maturity: Most human languages, including those of scripture, have terms that match the stages of neurological development across the life-span: 1) unborn, 2) infant, 3) child, 4) adult, 5) parent and 6) elder or grandparent. Most languages further modify these stages by adding the word "young" for those starting a stage and "full" for those completing a stage.

Misattunement: Misattunement is what happens when one person is not able to track or tune into (attune) another person's emotional state. When synchronized emotional interactions are missing, intimate relationships are painful and traumatic.

Multigenerational community: Sustainable joy requires at least three generations interacting in joyful ways. In this minimal configuration we have people who are more experienced as gentle protectors teaching a younger group that can practice with their peers and a third generation who is learning to live. Four generations are even better because this leaves the oldest group to make sure that everyone is growing a joyful identity. Joyful community uses our combined attention to amplify whatever is good, lovely, praiseworthy and honest – particularly for those who are weak.

Mutual mind state: The human brain, using functions that are largely synchronized through the cingulate cortex, is capable of entering into a shared state that is jointly controlled by another mind or brain. This kind of mind sharing is generally limited to people in a bonded relationship when they are face-to-face and open to emotional exchanges. A mutual mind state synchronizes brain activity and chemistry in a matter of seconds, and runs too rapidly to be controlled by conscious thought or choice. In a mutual mind state it is impossible to be sure what are "my" thoughts and feelings and what are "yours." Although mutual mind states are mutually produced, they are subjectively experienced as being controlled by the other person and are under the direction of the stronger brain. It is quite likely that God uses mutual mind states to communicate with people.

Peer group practice: Play and practice with peer groups insure that people of about the same level of power and skill are developing capacities together. When developing capacities together, the differences between the weak and the strong are minimized so there is less chance of harm from a lack of ability.

Perceive God: People often speak of "hearing God," "seeing" or even having God "lay something on their heart" as ways of trying to express the experience of perceiving God. For the vast majority of people there is a sense of God with no real words or pictures. In most cases, the interaction is like sharing a thought without being very certain if it is God's thought or our thought. However, the important feature is that something about this experience is new to us and not the way that we would think on our own. In addition, this new thought or point of view leads to shalom, a deeper joy and loving attachment with God.

Possum: Someone who thinks like a predator but does not want to act like a predator and lacks the skills to be a gentle protector. Avoiding attack becomes a possum's central preoccupation, motivation and even identity.

Predator: Someone who monitors weaknesses looking for a way to gain a personal advantage. All people have a predatory system inside their brain which develops with little to no training. Without training in relational skills and formation of secure bonds, everyone turns out predatory. Predator personality traits propagate easily and with little to no training.

Protector: A protector is one who helps others to maintain their relational identities under pressure. (Not to be confused with a benevolent predator who attacks enemies but not his or her own group.)

Pseudo-identity: Known in scripture as our "old self," this identity usually tries to be stronger than it really is and hide its weaknesses. This identity is also known by its ability to "self-justify," often using spiritual and religious language along with whatever is seen as powerful by culture.

Pseudo-joy: Any of a wide variety of substances, activities and even interactions with others that result in pleasure, but do not deepen a permanent joy-bond between people.

Pseudo-maturity: Mature behaviors that are based on fear or other motives. The tell-tale sign of pseudo-maturity is that the actions do not bring joy to the person doing them.

Pseudo-return to joy: This solution to problems does not help people act like their real self during problems but tries to make them happy so they will forget, forgive or get over what went wrong. Real return to joy involves wanting to be close to others so much we would gladly share their unpleasant feeling just to be with them. Pseudo-return to joy often leaves the other person feeling isolated or appeased rather than understood. Parents sometimes try to command this kind of "kiss and make up" solution.

Pseudo-shalom: People, particularly those with dismissive attachments, think that keeping the peace, avoiding problems or dismissing feelings as "no big deal" is shalom because there was no conflict or escalation of feelings. Quiet is not the same as shalom. Some tyrants keep a pseudo-shalom by punishing any opposition or expression of discontent, claiming peace when there is no peace.

Relational circuits: The brain systems involved with attachment, emotion, attention and mutual mind states include the capacity to understand and care for others, as well as ourselves, along with many other functions. Dr. Karl Lehman dubbed this system the brain's "relational circuits" when focusing on the way these brain regions must synchronize in order to process our experiences in a relational way. Dr. Lehman also developed the first simple test for impairment of the relational circuits. (Non-relational processing of experience is evidence of trauma and malfunctions of the brain.) The brain's relational circuits are often called "RCs" in the Life Model training. All three distinctive aspects of the Life Model (Multigenerational community, Immanuel lifestyle and relational skill training) do poorly if the relational circuits are not operating properly. Relational circuits can change their level of function quite quickly and, in some individuals, barely operate at all for most of their lives.

Relational skills: The skills we are calling "gentle protector" skills are the links between our identities, relationships and emotions. How we act (our identity) and interact with others to regulate, share and quiet our emotions determines how our relationships will flow. People who learn good skills will amplify joy and shalom with others. Those who lack relational skills will amplify distress and make problems "larger." The Life Model includes nineteen relational brain skills that form our identities and these can be studied in detail in Appendix B.

Relational skill training: Relational brain skills operate in a part of the brain that runs faster than conscious thought and so they cannot be carried out by plan, will or choice. Relational skills cannot be learned from reading, watching videos, computers or webcams, but only by face-to-face interactions with someone who already has the skills. Even in face-to-face interactions, our relational skills will only transfer if there is a joy-bond between the two brains that are training together. Skill training using strategic exercises is available using three-way bonds at the True Identity Track of *THRIVE Training* and two-way bonds at the three remaining tracks of *THRIVE Training*.

Returning to joy: Restoring our desire and ability to be with others during an unpleasant emotion is the focus of these gentle and protective brain skills. The ability to care about relationships must be learned independently for the six negative emotions of anger, fear, sadness, disgust, shame and hopelessness. The immediate result of "returning to joy" is a sense that we are not alone and we then begin to quiet the distress. During the process of quieting we are still distressed and obviously not "joyful" but it is much like the feeling of having fallen, so we cannot get up on our own and the relief of being found by someone who cares. We might even give them a small smile, but this is the return of joy during pain and does not look the same as joy by itself.

Rowing (spiritual): David Takle developed the image of "rowing" versus "sailing" in the *Forming* module to illustrate the difference between trying to change our own character (rowing) and seeking an interaction with God's Spirit that bonds us more firmly with God (sailing). Rowing exhausts us while sailing transforms our personality through the sheer joy and shalom God brings to the new and real "us."

Salvation: Being rescued from a dead and deadly state we could not get out of on our own, we then can form a new attachment of joy and shalom to the God who feeds us, gives us a new identity and makes us a source of joy to all who love God. Salvation begins immediately and it is a mistake to act as though salvation is only about what happens after we die.

Self-propagating recovery: Much like trauma needs no other training in order to be passed on to someone else, self-propagating recovery is the dream of the joy starting community. We seek to discover and deploy a way of healing that would contain in the experience all that is needed for the recipient to pass this gift on to others.

Sex trafficking: Exploitation of weakness in order to produce BEEPS for sale to sexual predators.

Shalom: When everything is harmonized and working together correctly, the right things are in the right place in the right amount so everything pleases God, we have reached shalom. In shalom all things work together for good for those who are synchronized with God.

Shame: Shame is not a single phenomena but actually refers to two different emotions, one that derives from thoughts and one that is a response to others who fail to respond to us with joy. For the most part, the shame that comes from thoughts is based on lies about our identities. The other response we call shame is the reaction that makes us want to hang our heads and hide when someone looks at us with displeasure. The shame based on beliefs is predominantly left-hemispheric and is made worse if anyone agrees with it. Right-hemispheric shame is made better when someone shares the feeling with us and shows us how to stay in relationship while in the feeling.

> **Healthy shame:** Healthy shame is based on the truth about our relationships and identity. Healthy shame does not force isolation but is rather an invitation back to be our better selves.

Toxic shame: Toxic shame is, by nature, isolating. One toxic characteristic comes from lies about our identity. Another toxic characteristic is that shame is used to obtain power, and the shame is continued until we comply. Shame is also toxic when there is no return to joy.

Sin: A malfunction of identity that causes us to fail to reach the potential God has for us. Chronic low-joy would be one sin of this sort as it is much lower than the life God wants us to lead. The failure to reach shalom is another example.

Spiritual maturity: Developing the full character of Christ in our dealings and relationships at all times and places. Our spiritual identity is the completeness of our humanity and not something separate from the life we live physically. Spiritual maturity therefore includes every conceivable aspect of maturity, and should not be artificially limited to how well we practice what is commonly understood as a religious life. What constitutes spiritual maturity is constantly expanding as we grow so that we become all that God means for us to be at this moment.

t-Zone: See Transformation Zone

Two-way bonds: See Bonds - two-way

Three-way bonds: See Bonds - three-way

THRIVE training: Strategic training events that include four interactive tracks, with each track focusing on a specific set of skills. Positive Identity at Track One strengthens joy and rest with capacity-building skill. Resilient Identity at Track Two follows Track One and focuses on recovery skills. Sharing Identity at Track Three brings solutions for pain, which are the five levels of pain the brain knows. Tracks One, Two and Three require preparation and training partners. Preparation for the training tracks includes reading materials with an online course. Each track includes 52-week skill guides to practice for a year.

True Identity, known as the Flex Track, relies on three-way bonds for exercises. Using three-way bonds makes the training less intense for participants. True Identity has no preparation requirements. Find more specific information in Appendix D.

Transformation Zone: The conditions necessary for identity change. Life-changing, maturity enhancing, joy spreading changes in character and community happen when three conditions are present at the same time:

1. The weak and strong are together and interacting
2. Tender responses to weakness are the rule
3. The interactive presence of God (Immanuel) maintains shalom

Transgression: This is the most willful and intentional of the ways to fail to be the person God created you to be. Transgression is the breaking of a law either by omission or commission. While we are deformed by iniquity and fail to reach the goal with sin, transgression violates God's standard and ordinances. Since God does not hold what we do not know against us, in practice a transgression is a violation to what we know God wants us to do.

Trauma: Trauma is damage caused by an impactful event that negatively alters our identity, integrity or function. While trauma has traditionally been defined by the size of an event needed to damage an average person, we define trauma as the damage done when the impact of an event exceeds a person's capacity at that moment. Two types of events can exceed our capacity; the first is depriving us of something we need and this always causes damage. The second type is events no one ever needs. These bad things that happen to us may or may not cause damage depending on our capacity at the time and resources immediately following the event.

> **Type A trauma:** The absence of necessary good things. Type A trauma is often referred to as "neglect" but the absence of the basic necessities in our lives produces traumatic effects of its own. Type A traumas include malnutrition, abandonment, insecure bonds and a lack of joy in the home.

> **Type B trauma:** Bad things that happen to us that exceed our capacity. Because we lack the necessary emotional and relational resources, a Type B trauma remains incompletely processed in a way that decreases who we are relationally and damages part of our identity.

> **What makes something a trauma?** The essence of trauma is that it either impairs the development of our relational identity or removes an aspect of our experience from our relational reality. Trauma means that some part of our experience is no longer being processed (or has not finished being processed) in a relational way. For this traumatized aspect of our experience we feel isolated from the loving care of others.

> **What resolves a trauma?** Trauma is resolved by raising our capacity as an individual or group so that we can process the traumatic experience in a relational way. In the case of Type A trauma this means that the missing necessary ingredient is now being provided.

Upstream: Our way of describing the people who give us life. We must each be a source of life to others or we will fail to thrive.

Validation: Validation is a function of a secure bond that has been internalized by the three-way bond structure in the prefrontal cortex. Validation agrees with the person about just how big the emotion feels. Validation ensures that the relationship with others remains intact even if an emotion appears to be very large. Validation also perceives small feelings accurately without making a "big deal" out of them.

Weakness: In Greek, the same word translated "weakness" means "illness." When Jesus healed the sick, He healed them of their weaknesses. Weakness can come from many causes such as young growth, injury, deterioration from use or neglect and aging. Weakness can affect the various aspects of being human, such as: physical, spiritual, mental or emotional. Weakness can also occur when abundance exceeds our capacity to sustain it, as when the disciples were fishing and an abundance of fish broke their nets.

Appendix B
Gentle Protector Skills

The Nineteen Relational Maturity Skills From
THRIVE

Skill One: Share Joy. Mutual amplification of joy through nonverbal facial expressions and voice tone that conveys, "We are glad to be together." This capacity allows us to bond and grow strong brains as well.

Technical description: Right-hemisphere-to-right-hemisphere communication of our most desired positive emotional state.

Skill Two: Soothe Myself, Simple Quiet. Quieting (shalom) after both joyful and upsetting emotions is the strongest predictor of life-long mental health. Lowering my own energy level so I can rest as I need to and on my own, makes me feel stable. This self-soothing capacity is the strongest predictor of good mental health for the lifetime.

Technical description: Release-on-demand of serotonin by the vegetative branch of parasympathetic nervous system to quiet both positive and distressing emotional states.

Skill Three: Form Bonds For Two, Synchronize Attachments. We can share a mutual state of mind that brings us closer and lets us move independently as well. We are both satisfied. The essence of a secure bond is the ability to synchronize our attachment centers so that we can move closer or farther apart at moments that satisfy us both. Synchronized attachment centers provide the basis for smooth transfer of brain skills and learned characteristics.

Technical description: Two-way bonds involve simultaneous activation of the attachment centers (Control Center level one) between two people. This activation helps create a state of mutual mind at the cingulate cortex level (Control Center level three) that can only be maintained by direct facial contact with one other person at a time.

Skill Four: Create Appreciation. High levels of the emotional state of appreciation closely match the healthy balanced state of the brain and nervous system. Creating a strong feeling of appreciation in yourself or others relieves unpleasant states and stress. Appreciation is very similar to the let down reflex that produces milk flow when nursing and the warm contented feeling that follows for mother and child.

Skill Five: Form Family Bonds, Bonds For Three. Family bonds allow us to feel joy when people we love have a good relationship with each other. We experience what they feel and understand how they see our relationships through our three-way bonds. Joy bonds between two adults form a couple style bond so community joy building requires bonds for three or more.

Technical description: The prefrontal cortex (Control Center level four) contains our capacity to maintain three points of view simultaneously.

Skill Six: Identify Heart Values From Suffering, The Main Pain and Characteristic of Hearts. Caring deeply can mean hurting deeply. Everyone has issues that particularly hurt or bother him or her and always have been the way he/she is likely to get hurt. Looking at these lifelong issues helps identify the core values for each person's unique identity. We hurt more the more deeply we care. Because of how much pain our deepest values have caused, most people see these characteristics as liabilities not treasures.

Skill Seven: Tell Synchronized Stories, Four-plus Storytelling. When our brain is well trained, our capacity is high and we are not triggered by the past, our whole brain works together. A simple test as well as a means to train the brain is telling stories in a way that requires all the brain to work together.

Technical description: The four levels of the right-hemispheric control center work together and allow the bonus (+) of having our words in the left hemisphere match our experience. When emotional and spiritual blockage is resolved our whole brain works in a synchronized way. By selecting stories we can test and train our brains to handle specific aspects of life and relationships.

Skill Eight: Identify Maturity Levels. We need to know our ideal maturity level so we know if our development is impaired. Knowing our general (baseline) maturity level tells us what the next developmental tasks will be. Knowing our immediate maturity level from moment to moment lets us know if we have just been triggered into reactivity by something that just happened or have encountered a "hole" in our development that needs remedial attention. Watching when our maturity level is slipping also tells us when emotional capacity has been drained in us or others.

Skill Nine: Take A Breather, Timing When To Disengage. Sustained closeness and trust requires us to stop and rest before people become overwhelmed and when they are tired. These short pauses to quiet and recharge take only seconds. Those who read the nonverbal cues and let others rest are rewarded with trust and love.

Technical description: All the brain-developing and relationship-building moments that create understanding and produce mutual-mind states require paired minds to stop a moment (pause) when the first of the two gets tired, near overwhelm or too intensely aroused.

Skill Ten: Tell Nonverbal Stories. When we want to strengthen relationships, resolve conflicts, bridge generations or cultures we get much farther with the nonverbal parts of our stories than with words.

Technical description: This workout for the nonverbal control center in the right hemisphere develops all the timing and expressive skills used to develop good emotional and relational capacity.

Skill Eleven: Return To Joy From The Big Six Feelings. Although we live most of our lives in joy and peace we need to learn how to stay in relationship and quiet our distress when things go wrong. When we take good care of our relationships even when we are upset the upset does not last long or drive people away. We quickly resolve our "not glad to be together" moments.

Technical description: The brain is wired to feel six unpleasant emotions. Fear, anger, sadness, disgust, shame and hopeless despair are each signals of something specific going wrong. We need to learn how to quiet each of these different circuits separately while maintaining our relationships. Training under these six emotional conditions covers the full range of our emotional distress.

Skill Twelve: Act Like Myself In The Big Six Feelings. Part of maintaining our relationships when we are upset is learning to act like the same person we were when we had joy to be together. A lack of training or bad examples causes us to damage or withdraw from the relationships we value when we get angry, afraid, sad, disgusted, ashamed or hopeless.

Skill Thirteen: See What God Sees, Godsight. Hope and direction come from seeing situations, ourselves and others the way they were meant to be instead of only seeing what went wrong. This spiritual vision guides our training and restoration. Even forgiveness flows from seeing people's purpose as more important than their malfunctions and makes us a restorative community instead of an accusing one. Through our hearts we see the spiritual vision God sees.

Skill Fourteen: Stop The Sark. False "Godsight" may seem true to us at the moment, but leads to: blame, accusation, condemnation, gossip, resentment, legalism, self-justification and self-righteousness. This Greek word (also rendered sarx) refers to seeing life from our personal view of who people are and how things should be. This conviction that I know or can determine the right thing to do or be is the opposite of Godsight in skill thirteen. For the sark, people become what they have done (the sum of their mistakes) or what we want them to become for us.

Skill Fifteen: Quiet Interactively. Facial cues, particularly of fear, help us to know when we are pushing others too hard. Sometimes we need and want to maintain a high-energy state without "going over the top," like knowing when to stop tickling so it stays fun. Fast recognition and response to facial cues means optimum interactions and energy.

Technical description: Using the ventromedial cortex that is part of level four together with the intelligent branch of the parasympathetic nervous system allows us to control the upper end of arousal states. Instead of taking us all the way to quiet/peace this type of quieting allows us to operate at high levels of energy and quiet just enough to avoid going into overwhelm. This system controls aggressive, sexual and predatory urges so we can avoid harmful behaviors.

Skill Sixteen: Recognize High And Low Energy Response, Sympathetic And Parasympathetic. Many characteristic responses to emotions and relationships are strongly shaped by our tendency toward high or low energy reactions. Recognizing who tends to respond with high energy (adrenalin based emotions) and who would rather withdraw helps us match minds with others and bring a more helpful variety to our own response tendencies.

Skill Seventeen: Identify Attachment Styles. How well we synchronize our attachments (skill three) early in life leave the most enduring pattern in our personality. These patterns change the way we experience reality. At one end we may give almost no importance to our feelings or relationships and at the other we may feel hurt almost constantly and think of nothing but feelings and people. We may also become afraid of the very people we need. All these factors distort our reality but feel real to us at the time. Knowing how to spot these distortions helps us compensate.

Skill Eighteen: Intervene Where The Brain Is Stuck, Five Distinctive Levels Of Brain Disharmony And Pain. By recognizing the characteristic pain at each of the brain's five levels we can pinpoint the trouble and find a solution if someone gets stuck. The type of pain gives us a good idea of the kind of solution we will need when someone is not "keeping it together," is "falling apart," or is "stuck" as we commonly call these losses of synchronization.

Technical description: There are five levels in the brain when we count the four in the right hemisphere control center and add the left hemisphere as the fifth. By knowing the characteristics of each we know when one level got stuck and what kind of interventions will help. For instance, explanations help level five but will not stop a level two terror like the fear of heights.

Skill Nineteen: Recover From Complex Emotions, Handle Combinations Of The Big Six Emotions. Once we can return to joy and act like ourselves with the six big negative feelings taken one at a time, we can begin to learn how to return to joy and act like ourselves when the six are combined in various combinations. Shame and anger combine to form humiliation. Fear and hopelessness (with almost any other feeling as well) form dread. These combination feelings can be very draining and difficult to quiet.

Appendix C
Maturity Stages

The Six Stages of Human Maturity On Earth
Essential Needs & Tasks For Maturity

THE UNBORN STAGE   Ideal Age: Conception > Birth

While acknowledging that this stage is crucial to the formation of bonds and a working body along with many learned patterns for voices, cries, food preferences, immune system functions and even a liberal transfer of DNA from the infant into the mother's body to provide stem cells, repair areas of damage in the mother's body, spend the rest of her life in her brain and other profound life-sharing changes, we will not include any list of tasks and needs for the development of the unborn child in this list.

THE INFANT STAGE   Ideal Age: Birth > Age 4

Infant Needs
Joy bonds with both parents that are strong, loving, caring, secure
Important needs are met without asking
Quiet together time
Help regulating distressing emotions
Be seen through the "eyes of heaven"
Receive and give life
Have others synchronize with him/her first

Infant Tasks
Receive with joy
Learn to synchronize with others
Organize self into a person through imitation
Learn to regulate emotions
Learn to return to joy from every emotion
Learn to be the same person over time
Learn self-care skills
Learn to rest

253

THE CHILD STAGE   Ideal Age: Ages 4 > 13

Child Needs
   Weaning
   Help to do what he does not feel like doing
   Help sorting feelings, imaginations and reality
   Feedback on guesses, attempts and failures
   Be taught the family history
   Be taught the history of God's family
   Be taught the "big picture" of life
   Be taught to do "worthy work" for mind and body

Child Tasks
   Take care of self (one is enough right now)
   Learn to ask for what he/she needs
   Learn self-expression
   Develop personal resources and talents
   Learn to make himself/herself understandable to others
   Learn to do hard things
   Learn what satisfies
   Tame the nucleus accumbens – our cravings
   See self through the "eyes of heaven"

THE ADULT STAGE   Ideal Age: Age 13 > first child

Adult Needs
   A rite of passage
   Time to bond with peers and form a group identity
   Inclusion by the same-sex community
   Observing the same sex using their power fairly
   Being given important tasks by his/her community
   Guidance for the personal imprint they will make on history
   Opportunities to share life in partnership

Adult Tasks
   Take care of two or more people at the same time
   Discover the main characteristics of his/her heart
   Proclaim and defend personal and community (group) identity

Bring self and others back to joy simultaneously
Develop a personal style that reflects his/her heart
Learn to protect others from himself/herself
Learn to diversify and blend roles
Life-giving sexuality
Mutual satisfaction in a relationship
Partnership
To see others through the "eyes of heaven"

THE PARENT STAGE   Ideal Age: From first child until youngest child becomes an adult at 13

Parent Needs
To give life
An encouraging partner
Guidance from elders
Peer review from other fathers or mothers
A secure and orderly environment

Parent Tasks
Giving without needing to receive in return
Building a home
Protecting his/her family
Serving his/her family
Enjoying his/her family
Helping his/her children reach maturity
Synchronizing with the needs of: children, spouse, family, work, & church
See his/her own children through the "eyes of heaven"

THE ELDER STAGE   Ideal Age: Youngest child is an adult

Elder Needs
A community to call his/her own
Recognition by his/her community
A proper place in the community structure
Have others trust them
Be valued and protected by their community

Elder Tasks

Hospitality
Giving life to those without families
Parent and mature his/her community
Build and maintain a community identity
Act like himself/herself in the midst of difficulty
Enjoy what God puts in each person in the community
(Seeing each of them through 'eyes of heaven')
Building trust of others through the elder's own transparency and spontaneity

NOTE: *Each stage builds on the previous stage: therefore each stage includes the needs and tasks of the previous stage. The 'ideal age' is the earliest age at which new tasks can be attempted. The end of that stage expects some degree of mastery. In no way does our maturity determine our value, but it does determine the level of responsibility we can handle.*

Appendix D
Joy Starting Resources

THRIVE Resources

Chris and Jen Coursey with THRIVEtoday

www.thrivetoday.org is the website for THRIVEtoday where Chris and Jen Coursey focus relational skill practice with a range of options, from the premier 5-day *THRIVE* Trainings to weekend events, online events, online courses, books and materials.

Relational Skill Resources

The Joy Switch: How Your Brain's Secret Circuit Affects Your Relationships…And How You Can Activate It
Introduces "Skill Zero" the Relational Circuit, aka the Master Switch in the 19 relational skills. *The Joy Switch* offers a number of exercises to practice staying in relational mode, our brain's "sweet spot" for growing joy and learning gentle protector skills.

Transforming Fellowship: 19 Brain Skills That Build Joyful Community
Overview of the 19 relational skills with introductory exercises.

Relational Skills In The Bible: A Bible Study Focused On Relationships
Amy Brown and Chris Coursey created this small group resource as a useful way for groups to practice the 19 relational skills and develop the transformation zone in their communities.

Basic THRIVE Skills: Mastering Joy and Rest exercise guide
Chris and Jen Coursey wrote this 52-week workbook to follow Track One of the *THRIVE Training* to continue the momentum gained from the 5-day *THRIVE Training*. This resource focuses on mastering capacity-building skills.

Intermediate THRIVE Skills: Mastering Returning to Joy exercise guide.
Chris and Jen Coursey wrote this 52-week workbook to follow Track Two of the *THRIVE Training* to continue the momentum gained from the 5-day *THRIVE Training*. This resource focuses on mastering recovery skills.

Advanced THRIVE Skills: Mastering Applied Strategy exercise guide.

Chris and Jen Coursey wrote this 52-week workbook to follow Track Three of the *THRIVE Training* to continue the momentum gained from the 5-day *THRIVE Training*. This resource focuses on mastering solutions for pain skills.

Skill Blogs

Chris and Jen along with guest authors write "Skill Blogs" on using relational skills on the Blog section of the thrivetoday.org website.

Home Resources Marriage

The 4 Habits of Joy-Filled Marriages: How 15 Minutes A Day Will Help You Stay In Love

Chris Coursey and Dr. Marcus Warner created this introductory resource for couples to practice relational skills and shrink the joy gap in their marriage.

4 Habits of Joy-Filled Marriages small group curriculum.

Here is a series of video curriculum to apply the *4 Habits of Joy-Filled Marriages* book with teaching, practice and interaction.

30 Days of Joy For Busy Married Couples

Chris and Jen say the month they practiced this book was the best month in their marriage. *30 Days of Joy* offers 30 exercises for couples to practice relational skills and start some joy.

Thriving Marriage Date Nights online events

Chris and Jen walk couples through teaching and exercises from the weekend Thriving Marriage weekend events.

Home Resources Parenting

The 4 Habits of Raising Joy-Filled Kids: A Simple Model for Developing Your Child's Maturity – at Every Stage

Chris Coursey and Dr. Marcus Warner created this resource for parents to raise mature children who are resilient and joyful.

Parenting blog

Jen Coursey and friends write a weekly parenting blog for mothers at thrivingmamas.org so mothers thrive instead of survive.

Ed Khouri Resources

Equipping Hearts for the Harvest
www.equippinghearts.com

Joy, the Brain, and Recovery

I'm Wired for Relationships, and I Want My Brain Back DVD.
This 5.5 hour-long training on the brain, addiction, and trauma was recorded at the Thrive Share Immanuel Addictions and Recovery Workshop. It includes teaching as well as live exercises, including a Share Immanuel group exercise.

Restarting Workbooks and DVDs
Part of the *Connexus*™ program, *Restarting* is designed to help jump-start recovery from addictions, trauma, painful relationships, and difficult life situations. This 12-week series is part of the *Connexus*™ program.

Belonging Workbooks and DVDs
Co-authored with Jim Wilder, *Belonging* is a 12-week follow-up series to help grow a healthy community where the weak and strong can be together and interacting. It includes training to monitor and restore relational circuits, learn the process of validation and comfort, discover how to monitor attachment pain, cravings, and BEEPS, and respond before they get out of control. You'll also find information and exercises to help you know when you need a break and how to avoid overwhelming others.

Grace-Based Approaches to Personal and Community Transformation.
These books can be used together by anyone wanting to develop a small group ministry and train leaders to facilitate them. They are also stand-alone books that help readers or small groups learn to receive and experience God's grace – and share it with everyone around them. These materials are specially designed for churches that don't want to grow ministry based on brain science or the importance of "joy."

Becoming A Face of Grace: Navigating Lasting Relationships with God and Others.

Grace, understood in its fullest, relational context, is the basis for the strongest attachments with God and others. This book, which includes individual journaling activities or small group sharing, explains why grace is the foundation for life, attachments that produce joy and grow strong, grace-filled identities. The book also describes what happens when grace is missing and how fear leads to the development of addictions. Discover how you can grow in grace so that you reflect it to everyone around you.

Beyond Becoming: A Handbook for Small Groups

Going beyond the basics in *Becoming a Face of Grace*, this book describes the essential grace-based principles that make small groups dynamic and includes detailed instructions with examples of activities that help group members grow stronger grace-based attachments with God and others. It contains stories from group members that describe how each activity impacted them. The book also explains how group leaders' creativity can be unleashed to facilitate groups without buying new workbooks or study materials every 3-4 months! This book will be available in late 2021 or early 2022.

The Weight of Leadership: How Codependency and Misplaced Mercy Undermine Life and Ministry

If you ever wondered why codependency and other addictions are so common in life, ministry, and leadership, this is the book for you. Building on the concepts of grace and fear found in *Becoming a Face of Grace*, this book takes a Biblical look at codependency as a fear-based behavior and explains why it's so easy for well-meaning leaders to "rescue" others. The book explores the sharp contrast between leadership guided by grace v. fear and describes grace-based leadership's essential characteristics. This book will be available in the second half of 2021.

Shelia Sutton Resources

Website: sheliasutton.com

High School English Teacher

I use the principles we write about in *Joy Starts Here* to facilitate joy and belonging in my classroom.

Certified EMDR Therapist

I am certified in EMDR and use it regularly in my private practice. EMDR stands for Eye Movement Desensitization and Reprocessing. EMDR therapy is an extensively researched, effective psychotherapy method proven to help people recover from trauma and other distressing life experiences, including PTSD, anxiety, depression, and panic disorders.

I work with attachment-focused EMDR trauma therapy which allows us to explore past traumatic experiences and challenge coping skills that no longer serve you. Through resourcing, I help you find a safe, peaceful place you can connect to in times of pain or distress. Rather than eliminating or forgetting about a traumatic memory, I assist you in shifting the focus and reframing your experience so that it no longer impacts your life in the present.

Certified Daring Way™ Facilitator

I am certified in Brené Brown's research on courage, vulnerability, shame, and empathy. As a Certified Daring Way™ Facilitator, I work across diverse populations and focus the therapeutic work on courage building, shame resilience, and uncovering the power of vulnerability.

Trauma Research Foundation's Certificate Program in Traumatic Stress

I'm in the process of completing this 32-week post-graduate level certificate program. The program covers fundamental issues necessary to become an expert clinician treating adults and children who suffer from traumatic stress.

As a Licensed Marriage and Family Therapist, I am only allowed to treat residents in the state of California.

Jim Wilder Resources

Jim Wilder works for Life Model Works

Vision: Everyone who encounters the church is transformed into the image of Christ

Mission: To equip existing networks to create identity transformation into the likeness of Christ in church and culture

The Life Model combines the Bible and brain science to grow a fearless people who love like Jesus. The Life Model Works guides the development and application of full-brained practices that transform.

Full heart, Whole brain

LifeModelWorks.org is the place to look for resources that start and build joy. Discover what others are doing to start joy and make it spread.

Selected books by Wilder

Friesen, J. G., Wilder, E. J., Bierling, A. M., Koepcke, R., & Poole, M. (2004). *Living from the heart Jesus gave you*. Pasadena, CA: Shepherd's House.

> This foundational book for the Life Model explains the five elements needed to thrive, basic maturity and living a life that is not controled by fear. A group study guide is included.

Warner, M., Wilder E. J., (2018), *The Solution of Choice*, Carmel, IN: Deeper Walk.

> Dr. Marcus Warner joins Jim to discribe four good ideas from the Enlightenment that do not match how the brain works. After entering Christian thinking, these ideas have disabled the Western church. Restarting our growth means avoiding these four traps.

Warner, M., Wilder E. J., (2016), *Rare Leadership*. Chicago: IL, Moody.

> Dr. Marcus Warner joins Jim to reveal four habits that create a rare leader. Applying the Bible and brain science to creating a joyful people gives new eyes into what God sees and expectes from us.

Wilder, E. J. (2018), *The Pandora Problem*. Carmel, IN: Deeper Walk.

> Joyful communties attract and grow narcissists if nothing is done to safeguard the group. The first sign that something is wrong is the sense,

"If I say anything it will only make it worse." The solution is not getting rid of the problem person or even screening out leaders more carefull. The solution lies in changing the members of the group into protectors. This is not something that can be done by gathering ideas - the change comes from learning new practices as a community. The book includes exercises. For a more complete guide to exercises see the *COMPANION GUIDE to The Pandora Problem* by Barbara Moon available through Deeper Walk International at deeperwalkinternational.org.

Wilder, E. J. (2020), *Renovated, God, Dallas Willard and Chruches that Transform,* Colorado Springs CO: NavPress.

How does neuroscience match with Christian beliefs and practices in ways that lead to real sustainable transformation? Jim and Dallas Willard exchange ideas that explain how we develop the spiritual and emotional maturity to live like Jesus. What emerges is how our attachment to God transforms us beyond what our beliefs alone can accomplish.

Wilder, E. J., Hendricks, M. (2020) *The Other Half of Church,* Chicago IL: Moody.

Michel Hendricks makes Jim's theories both understandable and useful for building a full hearted and whole brained church. The first of the four "soil ingredients" needed for the church is joy. The authors go on to develop the other three ingredients needed for joy to grow a harvest of sustainable Christian character and maturity.

Wilder, E. J., Kang, A., Loppnow, S., Loppnow J. (2020), *Joyful Journey,* Los Angeles: CA, Presence and Practice.

Joy and peace are sustained by thinking with God as we go through our day. The authors teach and explain a simple way to learn how to think with God.

Wilder, E. J., Coursey, C. (2010) *Share Immanuel,* Pasadena, CA: Shepherd's House.

This small booklet teaches a simple method to help others think with God and find peace - even when they are not yet Christians.